Living with The Black Death

Living with The Black Death

University Press of Southern Denmark 2009

© The Authors and University Press of Southern Denmark 2009
Typographical layout by Elsebeth Jensen, DTP-Funktionen,
University of Southern Denmark
Printed by Narayana Press, Gylling, Denmark
Cover design by Donald Jensen, UniSats
ISBN 978-87-7674-389-5

Proceedings of the 28th symposium organized by the Centre for Medieval Studies,
University of Southern Denmark, Odense
University of Southern Denmark Studies in History and Social Sciences vol. 377

Printed with support from:
Ingeniør N.M. Knudsens Fond
The Danish Research Council for the Humanities

Cover illustrations:
St. Roch, Stubbekøbing church, 1477-1500 (front)
Photo: Nationalmuseet

Plague epitaph, Rønne church, Bornholm, ca. 1654 (back)
Photo: Bornholms Museum

The articles in this book have been peer reviewed.

University Press of Southern Denmark
Campusvej 55
DK-5230 Odense M
Phone: +45 6615 7999
Fax: +45 6615 8126
Press@forlag.sdu.dk
www.universitypress.dk

Distribution in the United States and Canada:
International Specialized Book Services
5804 NE Hassalo Street
Portland, OR 97213-3644 USA
www.isbs.com

Distribution in the United Kingdom:
Gazelle
White Cross Mills
Hightown
Lancaster
LA1 4 XS
U.K.
www.gazellebooks.co.uk

Contents

Preface 7

Peter Christensen:
Appearance and Disappearance of the Plague:
Still a Puzzle? 11

Ole Georg Moseng:
Climate, Ecology and Plague:
The Second and the Third Pandemic Reconsidered 23

Manfred Vasold:
The Diffusion of The Black Death 1348-1350
in Central Europe 47

Janken Myrdal:
The Black Death in the North: 1349-1350 63

Lars Bisgaard:
Danish Plague Patterns, 1360-1500 85

Lise Gerda Knudsen:
The Course of a Mid-17th Century Plague Epidemic
in Denmark 113

Robert Braid:
Behavioural Economics,
the Black Death and the Labor Market 135

Heinrich Dormeier:
Saints as Protectors against Plague:
Problems of Definition and
Economic and Social Implications 161

Ebbe Nyborg:
The Black Death as Reflected
in Scandinavian Art and Architecture 187

Leif Søndergaard:
Imagining Plague: The Black Death in Medieval Mentalities 207

Preface

During a long period The Black Death in the years 1347-50 and later outbreaks were called the bubonic plague and attributed to fleas and transmission from rats to human beings. In recent years researchers have questioned this explanation. The way that the plague spread pointed towards another probable solution: the plague was caused by an infectious disease, transferred from man to man. This new approach has led to a renewed interest not only in the epidemiological field but also concerned with possible origins, patterns of spreading, demographic consequences, countermeasures and comparisons with outbreaks of plague epidemics during later periods.

Most of the contributors to this volume tend towards the new explanation – for various reasons. Among them is Peter Christensen who includes widespread international evidence in his introductory article in this volume and discusses the various points of view in medieval source material. He asks the question why the plague disappeared in the beginning of the 18th century and points to the countermeasures taken from the late 16th century onwards.

Samuel Cohn has argued thoroughly for the infectious disease theory in his standard work on *The Black Death Transformed* (2002) and Janken Myrdal, Lise Gerda Knudsen and others provide new material from Scandinavia to support this theory. On the other hand Ole Georg Moseng calls for circumspection. He tends to modify that the Black Death was due to fleas from rats, partly relying on Ole Jørgen Benedictows basic book *The Black Death 1346-53. The Complete History* (2004). He discusses various types of fleas and their possibilities to survive and spread what he takes to be an early and now unknown variant of a bubonic plague.

In his article on the the first pandemic in Scandinavia 1349-50 Janken Myrdal refers to new as well as traditional sources, including wills and testaments, historical chronicles and annals, donations, tombstones, letters and other sources. This research strategy he labels "source pluralism", finding it indispensable in areas with scarce and rudimentary sources left over in general. Lars Bisgaard undertakes a thorough study of surviving endowments and testaments in an attempt to date subsequent epidemics in Denmark after the first and severe blow in 1349-1350. One of the results is that outbreaks up to around 1450 follow those of Lübeck, hereafter they correspond more neatly to outbreaks in the Neatherlands. Lise Gerda Knudsen investigates into the richer material left over from a mid 17th century plague epidemic on the Eastern Danish islands. It is the earliest epidemic that is covered by parish registers, which give the opportunity of estimating a more exact mortality rate. The study also sheds an interesting light on the differences between plague raging in cities such as Copenhagen and in the countryside.

Manfred Vasold in his article argues that The Black Death spread faster than a bubonic plague would have done and that it attacked not only men but also animals (dogs and cats, donkeys, sheep and pigs). However, his main point is to stress that several cities and large areas in Germany and Central Europe were unaffected in the 1348-1350 epidemic.

The Black Death had a tremendous demographic impact on the population and the social relations all over Europe. Robert Braid revises the effects on the labour market and the relations between land lords and tenants or agricultural labourers. He criticizes the monocausal economic explanation and argues that we need to include several aspects, including mental factors, and to focus not only on *homo economicus* but rather on *homo sapiens*, man in general.

The apocalyptic vision about the imminent Last Judgment was reinforced in the years after The Black Death. The personal and social identity was questioned, and people might react in various ways. Heinrich Dormeier deals with the plague saints, first of all the classical plague saint St. Roch. In his case studies on Nürnberg and Lübeck Dormeier investigates into the introduction of the St. Roch cult in German speaking areas. Neither the church nor her religious orders had the initiating role, he argues, of much larger relevance were the confraternities and particular influental members of the laity.

Leif Søndergaard points to the fact that most studies focus on epidemiological, demographic and economic consequences of The Black Death and later plague epidemics. He examines literary sources in order to get access to the varying mentalities, ideas, explanations and reactions on the plague in various parts of medieval societies. Ebbe Nyborg investigates the traces that the plague and the general crisis left in paintings, sculptures and architecture. New motifs emerged in the decades following the devastating epidemics during the late 14th century, among them the *memento mori*, the *dance macabre*, the riding death and the wheel of fortune.

Most of the articles stem from papers given on a symposium in Odense in November 2004. They have been revised, enlarged and updated since then. Three articles (Myrdal, Knudsen and Søndergaard) have been added. Samuel Cohn who was the key note speaker at the conference has published extensively on the subject so he refers to his books and articles elsewhere on The Black Death.

This publication was made possible thanks to grants from *The Danish Research Council for the Humanities* and *Ingeniør N.M. Knudsens Fond*.

We would also like to extend our gratitude to Tom Pettitt for providing linguistic revision during the editing process. All errors are, however, ours.

Odense, Summer 2008.

Lars Bisgaard   Leif Søndergaard

ANNO 1602
DØDE AF SNEB
SOGEN 209 ME
NESKER AF PEST APS

In the year 1602 209 people from Snejbjerg parish died of the plague. APS.

This inscription on the wall of Snejbjerg Church in Jutland was put up in remembrance of the plague, which is recorded to have ravaged a number of parishes in the western part of Jutland in the beginning of the 17th century. The initials APS probably marks the stonecutter or churchwarden. Similar inscriptions from 1602-03 are found in the nearby churches in Skjern and Stauning.

The round projection on the church wall, also in Snejbjerg, was interpreted locally as a boil, among other things.

Photos: Herning Lokalhistoriske Arkiv, Mogens Kragsig Jensen

Appearance and Disappearance of the Plague: Still a Puzzle?

By Peter Christensen, Copenhagen

Between 1347 and 1352 an unknown and deadly disease, only much later known as the Black Death, swept across Europe leaving an estimated 30-50 % of the population dead. Contemporaries held various views as to what was the final, ultimate cause of this disaster. Many, probably most, thought it was God's punishment for the sins of humankind, others thought it was basically a natural phenomenon caused by a fateful constellation of the heavenly bodies. This was the authoritative explanation offered by the University of Paris and adopted by many learned persons such as the celebrated surgeon Guy de Chauliac who himself had barely survived the pestilence in Avignon.[1]

Whatever people thought were the ultimate causes, practically all contemporary sources agree that the pestilence had come from somewhere in the East. "It began in the Orient," noted Guy de Chauliac briefly in his medical textbook, *La Grande Chirurgie*.[2] According to the Carmelite friar and chronicler Jean de Venette in Paris "this plague, it is said, began among the unbelievers."[3] In Tournai the abbot Gilles li Muisis had

---

1. A.M. Campbell, *The Black Death and Men of Learning* (New York, 1931); Guy de Chauliac, *La Grande Chirvgie, Composée en l'An 1363*, (Ed.) E. Nicaise (Paris, 1890), p. 168.
2. Guy de Chauliac, ibid.
3. R.A. Newhall & tr. J. Birdsall (eds.), *The Chronicle of Jean de Venette* (New York, 1953), p. 48.

heard "persistent report of a mortality which had begun in the East, and spread throughout India and all Christian and pagan countries."[4] Others provided more details. Louis Sanctus of Beringen, another eye-witness in Avignon, had learned that:

> "terrible events and unheard of calamities had afflicted the whole of a province in eastern India for three days. On the first day it rained frogs, snakes, lizards, scorpions and many other similar poisonous animals. On the second day thunder was heard, and thunderbolts and lightning flashes mixed with hailstones of incredible size fell to earth, killing almost all the people, from the greatest to the least. On the third day fire, accompanied by stinking smoke, descended from heaven and consumed all the remaining men and animals, and burnt all the cities and settlements in the region. The entire province was infected by these calamities, and it is surmised that the whole coast and all the neighbouring countries caught the infection from it, by means of the stinking breath of the wind which blew southwards from the region affected by plague; and always, day by day, more people died."[5]

In Aleppo the learned ibn al-Wardi, who would die of the disease, believed that the pestilence had originated in the "land of darkness", usually understood to mean Northern Asia, and from there had spread to China, India and the land of the Uzbeks.[6] A generation later, Henry Knighton, the Leicester canon, knew for a fact that the pestilence had begun in India and then spread among the Saracens, Jews and Christians.[7]

---

4. R. Horrox (tr. & ed.), *The Black Death* (Manchester, 1994), p. 49.
5. Horrox 1994, pp. 41-45.
6. Ibn al-Wardi, *Risala al-naba' an al-waba'*, tr.M.W. Dols in D.K. Kouymjian (ed.), *Near Eastern Numismatics, Iconography, Epigraphy and History. Studies in Honor of George C. Miles* (Beirut, 1974), pp. 443-455; cf. A. von Kremer, "Ueber die Grossen Seuchen des Orients nach Arabischen Quellen," *Sitzungsberichte der Kaiserlichen Akademie der Wissenschaften, Philologisch-Historische Klasse* 96/1, 1880,Wien, p. 136 note 1 for the localization of "the Land of Darkness." A severe epidemic (*wabâ-é âzim*) had ravaged Tabriz in 1346-47, but whether this was in fact the Black Death is not clear, cf. Abu Bakr al-Qutbi al-Ahri, *Tarikh-é Shaykh Uways*, (ed.) J.B. van Loon (S'Gravenhage, 1954), p. 173.
7. Horrox 1994, p. 78.

It is of course unlikely that Louis Sanctus, Henry Knighton or even ibn al-Wardi had any real information about developments in "eastern India." References to "India" and "China" should not be taken any more literally than the report of rains of frogs and lizards. They are obviously stereotypes, another way of saying far-away and little-known regions where prodigies and natural disasters were likely to happen.

It seems fairly certain – and here again most contemporary sources agree – that in the better-known world of the Mediterranean, Constantinople and the remnants of the Byzantine Empire were infected first and that the plague spread from there to Italy. The two contemporary Byzantine accounts of the plague, however, do not make extravagant claims as to the origins of the plague. According to Nikephoras Gregoras the plague had begun "with the Scythians by the Maiotis and the mouth of the Tanais" in the spring of 1347,[8] i.e. in the regions north of the Black Sea. John Cantacuzenos, emperor at the time when the plague arrived in Constantinople, noted that it had started "first from the Hyperborean Scythians."[9]

Yet by the 18th century (if not before) the plague's origins in the far and mysterious East had become a generally accepted fact, China or Central Asia, however, replacing "Easternmost India" as the homeland of the disease because European scholars had gained access to Chinese sources that told of natural disasters and epidemics in the 1330s which of course seemed to fit nicely with the chronology of the Black Death. The seminal work appears to have been Joseph Deguignes' *Histoire générale des Huns, des Turcs, des Mongols et des autres Tartares occidentaux* (Paris 1756-58).[10] Deguignes' source for the plague's origins in far *Kathay* (i.e. China) was not his Chinese or Muslim histories, but another French historian, de Mézeray. In his *Abregé chronologie de l'histoire de France* (Paris 1667-68) de Mézeray, however, just paraphrased some of the Medieval accounts mentioned above.[11]

---

8. Nikephoras Gregoras, *Historia Rhomaïke* (XVI.5), J.L. van Dieten (tr. & ed.): *Rhomäische Geschichte*. Vierter Teil. Bibliothek der Griechischen Literatur 39 (Stuttgart, 1994), pp. 175-176.
9. C.S. Bartsocas, "Two Fourteenth Century Greek Descriptions of the Black Death," *Journal of the History of Medicine* 21, 1966, pp. 394-400.
10. J. Norris, "East or West? The Geographic Origin of the Black Death," *Bulletin of the History of Medicine* 51, 1977.
11. I am indebted to my former student cand.mag. Rasmus Rosengaard for this information.

Thanks to Deguignes the Chinese (or Central Asian) origins of the plague became a historical fact and made its way into the authoritative medical histories of the 19th and early 20th centuries such as Haeser's *Lehrbuch der Geschichte der Medicin und der epidemischen Krankheiten* (Jena 1853-82), Hecker's *Die grossen Volkskrankheiten des Mittelalters* (Berlin 1865) and Sticker's *Abhandlungen aus der Seuchengeschichte und Seuchenlehre* (Giessen 1908-10).

Later, the Central Asian theory seemed to receive extra support. In the 1880s Russian archaeologists had investigated a Nestorian cemetery in the Issyk Kul region. Some forty of the 330 headstones dated from 1338-39 and three (!) of them told of a "pestilence." The archaeologists took this to be evidence of the Black Death, and this was widely accepted even by distinguished scholars such as Robert Pollitzer in the 1950s.[12]

Meanwhile, modern bubonic plague had appeared in China. In 1894, it was identified with historical plague. This lent further support to the Chinese and Central Asian origins of the Black Death, as did the discoveries of the British plague commission in India that bubonic plague existed with wild rodents of which there are many in Central Asia. So a combination of unreliable sources and the retrospective diagnosis based on a variety of more or less reliable sources combined to draw a picture of a zoonose that resided among rodents in the depths of Central Asia and then sometimes – for reasons unknown – took to wandering along the Silk Road, infecting humans.[13]

In the general enthusiasm over having apparently solved the riddle of the plague historians and biologists also identified the epidemics of the early Middle Ages – usually known as "Justinian's Plague" – and the many visitations mentioned in the Bible as bubonic plague. While there are certain similarities between "Justinian's Plague" and the Black Death, none of them resemble modern bubonic plague. The most obvious difference being the mortality – bubonic plagues cause few deaths. But the retrospective diagnosis was nevertheless generally accepted and has confused the study of historical plague. Only recently has it been questioned.

---

12. D. Chwolsen, "Syrisch-Nestorianische Grabinschriften aus Semirjetschie," *Mémoires l'Académie Imperiales des Sciences de St,-Pétersbourg*, VIIe Série, Tome XXXVII, n° 8, 1890; R. Pollitzer, *Plague* (Geneva, 1954), pp. 13-14.
13. E.g. W. H. McNeill *Plagues and Peoples* (Oxford, 1977). McNeill's suggestion that the *Pax Mongolica* paved the way for the travels of *yersinia pestis* does not make much chronological sense. By the 1330s political conditions in Central Asia were quite unsettled.

Thirty years ago John Norris made a critical examination of the sources for the far eastern origins of the plague and concluded for good reasons that they were highly unreliable. He also showed how the internationally acclaimed plague expert, Wu Lien-teh, had manipulated the Chinese sources to make them fit the chronology of the Black Death. He pointed out that the Issyk Kul headstones did not say "plague" and that, furthermore, the unsettled political conditions of Central Asia in the 1330s would have made the spreading of the plague along the Silk Road unlikely.[14] Yet his conclusions were widely disregarded or even dismissed without argument.[15] The reason seems to be that Norris, never questioning the retrospective diagnosis, had suggested an alternative and equally improbable theory of the geographical origins of the plague based on the difference in the glycerine-fermenting abilities of various strains of modern *Yersinia pestis*.[16] Thus, even in quite recent works the headstones of Issyk Kul figure as proof of the plague's Central Asian origins,[17] and the history of the plague remains obscured by myths and ill-founded assumptions, the retrospective diagnosis being perhaps the most confusing

The origins of the plague remain unknown to us simply because extant sources are insufficient. The disease was first recorded as ravaging the Black Sea region and from there it spread to the Middle East and across the Mediterranean to Europe. Whether it actually originated in the Black Sea region or somewhere else we don't know. Neither do we know why it showed up when it did. Various attempts to make the appearance of the plague a consequence of an alleged "late Medieval agrarian crisis" and the great European famine can safely be dismissed. They make neither chronological nor biological sense and seem to be primarily an attempt to salvage structural, orderly history. And why would the plague ravage Syria and Egypt where there had been no structural "agrarian crisis"?

None of this makes the plague particularly enigmatic, however. Diseases have come and often disappeared again for more or less complex reasons, reasons that we are not always able to discern, because we lack informa-

---

14. Norris 1977, pp. 5, 13.
15. E.g. M. W. Dols, "The Second Plague Pandemic and its Recurrences in the Middle East, 1347-1894," *Journal of the Economic and Social History of the Orient* 22, 1979, p. 170, note 17.
16. Norris 1977, pp. 19-24.
17. E.g. W. Naphy & A. W. Spicer, *The Black Death* (Stroud, 2001), p. 31; J. Myrdal, *Digerdöden, pestvågor och ödeläggelse. Et perspektiv på senmedeltidens Sverige* (Stockholm, 2003), p. 17.

tion. To mention just one example, we don't know why another mysterious and deadly disease – the *sudor anglicus*, the English Sweat – appeared in the late 15th century. After five outbreaks in England and one on the continent (1529) it disappeared again. Just as mysteriously as the plague. But the English Sweat has never drawn attention to the same degree for the simple reason that – though lethal – it had no demographic impact comparable to that of the plague.

The plague circulated in Europe for more than 300 years. According to some historians the plague changed during this time, breaking out at increasingly longer intervals and becoming primarily an urban phenomenon.[18] Though not central to this paper I would like to point out that in a broader comparative perspective this "development" is just another unsubstantiated plague myth. Denmark for instance suffered no less than 11 major outbreaks between 1550s and 1650s, all of them ravaging rural as well as urban areas with equal ferocity.[19]

Then, in the mid-17th century the plague disappeared, almost as suddenly as it had appeared three centuries earlier. The last major outbreak in Denmark was in 1653-57 and in Western Europe in 1665-67.[20] There were some later localized outbreaks, e.g. in Marseille and Southern France 1720-22. We shall return to this in the following.

Finding an explanation for the disappearance of the plague has been confused by the retrospective diagnosis. During the plague cycle European authorities had gradually set up defences against the disease involving quarantining of travellers, isolation of the sick and their belongings etc – countermeasures based on the assumption that the disease was contagious, i.e. that is was somehow transferred from person to person. Though no state ever set up a system of defences that would compare with that of the North Italian cities, Venice above all, attempts to contain the plague became part of the general centralizing process, state-wide

---

18. E.g. P. Slack, *The Impact of Plague in Tudor and Stuart England* (London, 1985), pp. 9-17; J.-N. Biraben, *Les hommes et la peste en France et dans les pays européens et méditerranéans*, I-II, (Paris, 1975-76), vol. I, p. 118.
19. P. Christensen, "In These Perilous Times": Plague and Plague Policies in Early Modern Denmark," *Medical History*, 47/4 2003, pp. 413-450.
20. L. Knudsen, *Pesten grasserer! En undersøgelse af pesten i Danmark i 1650'erne* (Landbohistorisk selskab, 2005). A severe, but localized epidemic in Southern Jutland in the winter 1659-60 may have been plague brought by Polish troops, but this needs further research.

regulations replacing the local measures set up by city councils. North of the Alps England (1578) and Denmark (1625) were the first to issue state-wide regulations.[21]

In the 1800s, with the plague gone, contagion theory and the efficiency of quarantine were increasingly challenged. It has been argued uncharitably that this was largely due to commercial interests as quarantine provided an obstacle to free trade, and certainly anti-contagionists could point out that quarantine had done little or nothing to prevent yellow fever and cholera from spreading.[22]

Of course, with the discoveries of Koch and Pasteur and the rise of modern microbiology contagion theory was to some extent vindicated, as it was realized that infectious diseases were caused by microorganisms and could indeed be transmitted from person to person.

By then, however, British researchers working in India had found out that bubonic plague was a disease of rodents and was spread by fleas. Clearly a disease of this nature was unlikely to be stopped by quarantine and isolation of humans.

Nevertheless, when Biraben in the 1970s published his great work on the plague, which did much to revive the interest in the history of the disease, he cheerfully asserted that the credit for the disappearance of the disease must go to the quarantine and the whole array of precautionary measures. It was "une victoire des hommes."[23] He made the important observation that while plague had disappeared from Western Europe it continued to break out in the Ottoman Empire including large parts of South Eastern Europe, and unlike the Europeans the Ottomans for reasons we need not discuss here had never introduced any countermeasures. They only did so after the great epidemic in the 1830s and then the plague disappeared here as well.[24]

To make the quarantine explanation consistent with the retrospective diagnosis – which he never questioned – Biraben had to assume that the human flea was an important vector. This idea originated I believe with Georg Sticker who had had problems reconciling the retrospective diagnosis with the historical accounts which all insisted that plague was

---

21. Christensen 2003, pp. 431-439.
22. M. Harrison, *Disease and the Modern World* (Cambridge, 2004), pp. 97-105.
23. Biraben 1975-76, vol. II, p. 174.
24. For further information, see D. Panzac, *La Peste dans l'Empire Ottoman, 1700-1850* (Leuven, 1985).

contagious. However, even in 1913 British plague researchers in India had demonstrated that the human flea could not transmit bubonic plague.[25] Biraben's critics were quick to point out that quarantine and travel restrictions could not have been very successful in containing a disease spread by rats and fleas.[26]

In 1980 Andrew Appleby published a brief, critical survey of explanations advanced for the disappearing of the plague. So far, it remains one of the few attempts to discuss the issue seriously. He had of course to dismiss quarantine and the rest of the countermeasures. First, because such measures would have little or no impact upon a rodent disease spread by fleas. Second, because quarantine demonstrably had been ineffective. As proof he pointed to Venice which had suffered 25 outbreaks between 1403 – when the first lazaretto was established – and 1630.[27] And of course to Marseille in 1720. Having dismissed quarantine Appleby proceeded to review alternative explanations such as the spreading of the *Rattus norvegicus* at the expense of the "plague rat", *Rattus rattus*, the allegedly improved nutrional standards, changes in building practices (more bricks, fewer thatched roofs, thus less risk of contact between rats and humans) and the idea that people had developed resistance or immunity to the disease. For good reasons he found all of them unlikely. Instead he subscribed to the hypothesis that *rats* had acquired resistance or immunity to the plague. He had to admit, however, that he had no idea why only rats in Western Europe had done so, whereas Serbian, Anatolian (and Polish) rats had not, because, as Biraben had pointed out, the plague continued to ravage the Ottoman Empire until the 1830s. The disappearance of the plague, Appleby concluded, "is still an open question."[28]

---

25. Biraben 1976, vol. I, p. 13; L. F. Hirst, *The Conquest of Plague: A Study of the Evolution of Epidemiology* (Oxford, 1953), p. 237; G. Twigg, *The Black Death: A Biological Reappraisal* (London, 1984), pp. 19, 129, 144.
26. E.g. A.G. Carmichael, *Plague and the Poor in Renaissance Florence* (Cambridge, 1986), p. 3.
27. Appleby 1980, p. 168; E. Rodenwaldt, *Pest in Venedig, 1575-1577. Ein Beitrag zur Frage der Infektkette bei den Pestepidemien West-Europas*, Sitzungsbericht der Heidelberger Akademie der Wissenschaften, Mathematisch-Naturwissenschaftliche Klasse (Heidelberg, 1953), lists only 17 outbreaks in this period, p. 66 note 1.
28. Appleby 1980, p. 173. A slightly modified version of the rat resistance theory was advanced by D. Panzac, *Quarantaines et lazarets: L'Europe et la peste d'Orient* (Aix-en-Provence, 1986), pp. 115-116; see also Panzac 1985, pp. 512-513.

If we are to find a plausible answer to this question we must first of all definitively abandon the confusing and ill-founded retrospective diagnosis and accept what all contemporary accounts say: the plague (whatever its precise nature) was transmitted directly from person to person.[29] Historical plague was not modern bubonic plague and thus the quarantine and the rest of the countermeasures make good sense. This is not to say that the countermeasures were effective. It was one thing for the early modern European states to promulgate the various plague orders, quite another to implement them. Did European states in the 1600s and 1700s have the ability to enforce effectively quarantine and travel restrictions? From all over Europe we have evidence that ordinary people (not to mention smugglers) strongly disliked the countermeasures as these interfered with the daily effort to survive and therefore attempted to evade them. Even local town and city councils were often hesitant for economic reasons to enforce the orders, as they meant huge expenses and brought economic activity to a stand-still.[30]

Now let us return briefly to Venice. Appleby had not been entirely fair to the city. The elaborate plague defences administered by the famous *magistrato della sanità* were not fully developed until c. 1550.[31] Venice then suffered only 3 major outbreaks – 1555-57, 1575-77 (said to have been the worst since the Black Death) and 1630-31. So the precautionary measures did not work every time, but Venice did escape the great European epidemic of 1597-1604 and the Italian outbreak of 1656-57 which ravaged Naples, Rome and Genoa. In the same period (1550-1660) Denmark suffered at least 11 outbreaks, an indication that the Venetian quarantine measures did in fact have effect.[32]

Now we must reconsider the famous plague of Marseille in 1720-22 as

---

29. Christensen 2003; for a more detailed argument against the retrospective diagnosis see S.K. Cohn, *The Black Death Transformed. Disease and Culture in Early Renaissance Europe*, (London, 2002).
30. Cristensen 2003; C. Cipolla, *Cristofano and the Plague: a Study in the History of Public Health in the Age of Galileo* (London, 1973); G. Calvi, *Histories of a Plague Year. The Social and the Imaginary in Baroque Florence*. Tr. D. Biocca & B.T. Ragan (Berkeley-Los Angeles, 1989).
31. Rodenwaldt 1953, pp.12-15; E. Rodenwaldt, *Die Gesundtheitsgesetzgebung des Magistrato della sanità Venedigs, 1486-1500*, Sitzungsbericht der Heidelberger Akademie der Wissenschaften, Mathematisch-Naturwissenschaftliche Klasse (Heidelberg, 1956), pp. 18-19.
32. Christensen 2003.

it is frequently cited as proof that quarantine was ineffective, as we have just seen

As France's main sea port for trade with the plague-infested Levant, Marseille had quite elaborate defences, including a permanent board of health, something otherwise seen only in Northern Italy. The city had not been infected since the 1640s. In 1720 plague arrived on board a ship returning from Syria. It turned into a very severe epidemic – that left half of the inhabitants dead – because quarantine of the infected ship was shortened (for economic reasons) and because the city council (again for economic reasons) hesitated to admit that the disease spreading in the city was in fact plague.[33] Central authorities eventually succeeded in containing the outbreak as they had also done with the 1665-67 outbreak.[34]

The case of Marseille only proves that quarantine was ineffective when not administered properly. That the city was never infected again though it was in constant contact with plague-ridden North Africa and the Levant indicates that quarantine was in fact effective. Let me belabour the point by briefly turning to another late outbreak, that of Copenhagen in 1711.

Copenhagen, the capital and most important sea port of Denmark, had been free of the plague since the 1653-57 epidemic. Now, owing to the unsettled conditions during the Great Northern War, plague had spread from the Ottoman Empire into Eastern and Central Europe, reaching the Baltic coast areas in 1708. Danish authorities carefully watched the progress of the plague and took various precautionary measures such as restrictions on trade and travel. In spite of this plague reached Denmark. Those responsible seem to have been the town councillors of Elsinore, a sea port north of Copenhagen. The town had been infected in late 1710, probably from Sweden where the epidemic had reached major proportions, but for economic reasons the town council tried to hush things up and gave insufficient information to the central authorities. With the result that Copenhagen was infected in the following summer. An estimated 30 % of the population died in the epidemic. The authorities, however, managed to confine the outbreak to North Eastern Zealand and, like Marseille, Copenhagen was never infected again though it remained in

---

33. Ch. Carrière, et al., *Marseille ville morte. La peste de 1720*, (Marseille, 1968).
34. J. Revel, "Autour d'une épidémie ancienne: la peste de 1666-1760," *Revue d'histoire moderne et contemporaine* 17, 1970, pp. 954-983.

constant contact with the plague-infested regions across the Baltic (and eventually, in the 1700s, in the Mediterranean).[35]

It would be absurd to insist that quarantine and the rest of the precautionary measures adopted by the European states had to be 100 % effective to provide an explanation for the disappearance of the plague. Obviously, they were not invariably effective and other cases besides Copenhagen and Marseille could be mentioned, e.g. Messina 1743 and Moscow 1771-72. When quarantines failed the results could be very dramatic. So we hear about them. We do not hear about the many cases where quarantine worked. In the end, the combined public health efforts of the European states (some being more thorough than others, it is true) provide the most plausible explanation for the disappearance of the plague.

---

35. P. Christensen, "Copenhagen 1711: Danish Authorities facing the Plague" in S. Sheard & H. Power (eds.): *Body and City. Histories of Urban Public Health* (Aldershot, 2000), pp. 50-58.

Climate, Ecology and Plague: The Second and the Third Pandemic Reconsidered[1]

By Ole Georg Moseng, Oslo

To characterize plague as a modern disease appears less straightforward than we would want it to be, let alone historical plague epidemics. However comforting it may be to rely on traditional and often simplified concepts of plague, which generations of historians have passed on through numerous works, the complexity and versatility of this myth-embraced disease ought to evoke some concern.

Most attempts to shred light upon the late medieval and early modern epidemics in Europe will probably have to rest on basic conceptions of the dynamics of modern plague. That is a challenge medical historians will have to face, regardless of aims and points of departure. In that respect, the so called "third pandemic", which encompasses the world-wide distribution of plague from around 1890 up until today, has served both as a knowledge base and a laboratory.

Following the outbreaks in India in the 1890s, plague conquered – or re-conquered – five continents during the first decades of the 20th century. The disease is still present on three of them. Since 1954, yearly outbreaks have taken place in Brazil, Congo, Madagascar, Myanmar, Peru, USA and

---

1. The paper, now somewhat rewritten, summarized a number of conclusions from my recent monograph: O.G. Moseng, *Den flyktige pesten Vilkårene for epidemier i Norge i seinmiddelalderen og tidlig nytid*, Acta Humaniora nr. 265, (Oslo, 2006) (The Transient Plague: Conditions for Epidemics in Late Medieval and Early Modern Norway).

Vietnam. Health authorities are disturbed by an apparent increase in the number of plague cases over the last few decades.[2]

In order to effectively distribute itself to virtually every corner of the world, the plague pathogen must have had – and still has – the ability (if bacteria could in fact be attributed abilities of any kind) to adapt to a wide array of ecosystems, highly diverse climatic conditions and a multiplicity of biological factors.

A scrutiny of outbreaks in various parts of the world – where bacteriological examinations have confirmed beyond doubt that *Yersinia pestis* was the culprit – reveals a much differentiated picture of the epidemic. The etiologic and epidemic dissimilarities between the "classic" Indian epidemics and plague outbreaks almost everywhere else are particularly suggestive. The oriental rat flea *Xenopsylla cheopis* and the black rat *Rattus rattus* dominated completely during the outbreaks that took place in parts of India in the decades around 1900. There and then, the mortality was almost entirely caused by bubonic plague. In more or less the same period, pneumonic plague constituted the majority of cases in the large outbreaks in Manchuria in the 1910s and 1920s – which took place during the winter in temperatures down to minus 30 °C.[3] Hardly anywhere but India, do either *X. cheopis* or the black rat play important roles in the propagation of plague today. Madagascar represents one of the exceptions.[4] But even in this relatively restricted region, recent research has demonstrated the versatility of the disease.[5]

---

2. In 1999, WHO reported 2.603 cases (of which 212 were fatal). The corresponding numbers for 1980 were 513 (and 58). *Weekly Epidemiological Record*, World Health Organization, Geneva, 71, 22, (1996); *Weekly Epidemiological Record*, 75, 42, (2000); *Plague Manual: Epidemiology, Distribution, Surveillance and Control*, WHO, (Geneva 1999), p. 26.
3. Cf. Wu Lien-Teh, *A Treatise on Pneumonic Plague*, Publications of the League of Nations III, 13, (Geneva, 1926).
4. Cf. P. Boisier, L. Rahalison, M. Rasolomaharo et al., 'Epidemiologic Features of Four Successive Outbreaks of Bubonic Plague in Mahajanga, Madagascar', *Emerging Infectious Diseases* 8, 3, (2002), pp. 311-316.
5. J.-M. Duplantier, J. Catalan, A. Orth et al., 'Systematics of the black rat in Madagascar: consequences for the transmission and distribution of plague', *Biological Journal of the Linnean Society* 78, (2003); Boisier et al. 2002; S. Chanteau, L. Ratsifasoamanana, B. Rasoamanana et al., 'Plague, a Reemerging Disease in Madagascar', *Emerging Infectious Diseases*, Vol. 4, No. 1, (January-March 1998); A. Guiyoule, B. Rasoamanana, C. Buchreiser et al., 'Recent Emergence of New Variants of Yersinia pestis in Madagascar', *Journal of Clinical Microbiology*, (1997);

Today's plague researchers list more than 300 species of mammals and several dozens of flea species that have been associated with the dissemination and maintenance of plague in nature. The list of species on a global scale that have contributed to the spread of plague to man is much smaller, but still impressive.[6]

Not only is the plague bacterium an unusually flexible organism, which can adapt to a variety of enzootic reservoirs, insect vectors and ways of transmission. The many forms of plague in humans encompass clinical characteristics that are distinctly diverse. Moreover, symptoms as well as pathological expressions are often so ambiguous that diagnosis is complicated without bacteriological confirmation.

Even modern physicians are often confused by the elusive symptoms. In New Mexico, seven cases of plague were hospitalized and examined in the period 1966-1969. Only one of the patients was initially given the correct diagnosis. The diagnoses upon admission regarding the others were as diverse as *acute appendicitis* and *viral meningitis*.[7]

Roger Pollitzer, the WHO's expert on plague and author of one of the classic works in the field, *Plague* from 1954, was well aware of these problems. In 1960, he reminded his colleagues:

> Plague is a disease of so protean a character that it would be misleading to generalize the results of observations in one or a few areas, however suggestive they appear to be.[8]

M. Galimand, A. Guiyoule, G. Gerbaud et al., 'Multidrug Resistance in Yersinia pestis Mediated by a Transferable Plasmid', *The New England Journal of Medicine* 327, 10, (1997);. Cf. also G. Girard, Plague, *Annual Review of Microbiology* 9, (1955).

6. R. Pollitzer, *Plague*, WHO, (Geneva, 1954), pp. 623-641; R. Pollitzer, A Review of Recent Literature on Plague, *Bulletin of the World Health Organization* 23, (1960), pp. 837-400; R. Pollitzer and K. F. Meyer, 'The Ecology of Plague', in: J. M. May (ed.), *Studies in Disease Ecology*, Studies in Medical Geography, vol. 2, (New York, 1961), pp. 485-501; A. Macchiavello, 'Reservoirs and vectors of plague', *The Journal of Tropical Medicine and Hygiene* 57, 1-11, (1954), pp. 3-8, 65-69, 87-94, 116-121, 139-146, 158-171, 191-197, 220-224, 238-243, 275-279; A. B. Christie, 'Plague: Review of ecology', *Ecology of Disease* 1, 2-3, (1982); Plague Manual 1999, pp. 27-37; A. Ruiz, 'Plague in the Americas', *Emerging Infectious Diseases* Vol. 7, No 3, Supplement, (June 2001), pp. 539-540; Boisier et al. 2002.
7. W. P. Reed et al., 'Bubonic plague in the south western United States', *Medicine* 49, 6, (1970), pp. 465-486.
8. Pollitzer 1960, p. 361. Cf. Pollitzer 1954.

Like Proteus, the sea-god of Greek mythology, plague has the ability to appear in different skins, in different shapes and in different disguises.

THE MODEL OF PLAGUE BEHAVIOUR

In the 1990s, the archeo-zoologist Frédérique Audoin-Rouzeau and the entomologist Jean-Claude Beaucournu posed the same, relatively simple question: How could plague, an essentially tropical disease, be disseminated in medieval and early modern Europe?[9] It is certainly an even more difficult task to try and sort out what the conditions for the dissemination of plague would be like in Scandinavia – that is, in a climate fundamentally contrary to the core areas of modern plague.

In 1927, Leonard Hirst, one of the many researchers who worked in the wake of the second English plague research commission in India, summed up what he regarded as the key to the distribution of plague in the world:

> Broadly speaking, bubonic plague is confined to the belt of the earth's surface lying between latitudes 35° North and 35° South, which corresponds almost exactly to the zone in which X. cheopis can freely propagate.[10]

He referred to the oriental rat flea, which the commission found to be the only important insect vector in India at the beginning of the century. If Hirst were right, and the precondition that medieval plague would have behaved like modern plague is correct, then the combination of these two factors represents a serious obstacle to any attempts at analysing pre-modern plague in the light of recent medical and epidemiological research.

In the introduction to his controversial book *The Black Death Transformed*, the historian Samuel Cohn handled his fellow scholars roughly:

---

9. F. Audoin-Rouzeau, 'Le rat noir (Rattus rattus) et la peste dans l'occident antigue et médiéval', *Bulletin de la Société de Pathologie Exotique* 92, 5 bis, (1999); J.-C. Beaucournu, 'A propos du vecteur de la peste en Europe occidentale au cours de la deuxieme pandemie', *Bulletin de la Societé Française de Parasitologie* 13, 2, (1995) : 233-252 ; J.-C. Beaucournu, 'Diversité des puces vectrices en fonction des foyers pesteux', *Bulletin de la Société de Pathologie Exotique* 92, 5 bis, (1999)
10. L. F. Hirst, 'Rat-flea Surveys and their Use as a Guide to Plague Preventive Measures', *Transactions of the Royal Society of Tropical Medicine and Hygiene*, XXI, 2, (1927), p. 92.

> Without argument, historians and scientists have taken the epidemiology of the modern plague and imposed it on the past, ignoring, denying, even changing contemporary testimony, both narrative and quantitative, when it conflicts with notions on how modern bubonic plague should behave.[11]

He was of course entirely right. Very few scholars have bothered to pose essential questions about the nature of plague. But could the real sins of omission have been that historians to a large extent have taken for granted that plague has been a relatively stable phenomenon in time and space?

In 1985, the medical historian William Bynum warned against: "...the assumption that plague in fourteenth-century Europe should have behaved like plague in twentieth-century India".[12] The statement was worded in a review of the zoologist Graham Twigg's book *The Black Death: a Biological Reappraisal*, in which Twigg put forward the rather unfortunate hypothesis that the mortality crisis of late medieval Europe was caused by anthrax rather than plague. But Bynum's warning is definitely relevant also for more recent interpretations of the relations between modern and medieval plague.

The principal conclusions that were put forward by Susan Scott and Christopher Duncan in 2001, and by Cohn in 2002, were to a certain extent astonishingly unanimous – despite Cohn's refusal to point to any specific pathogenic organism as the causative agent of the Black Death. The crucial point in both cases was that modern and medieval plague would have to be two distinctly different diseases. In that respect, their views were in close accordance with Twigg's – and for that matter also an earlier critical voice, that of the zoologist John Shrewsbury, who they were all more or less in debt to.[13]

Their arguments were by and large founded on two crucial preconditions. Firstly, that rats were absent in Europe in the Late Middle Ages, or at least that rat populations were too scarce to have contributed to any

---

11. S. K. Cohn, Jr., *The Black Death Transformed*, (London, 2002), p. 2.
12. W.F. Bynum, review of G. Twigg, *The Black Death: a Biological Reappraisal*, (London, 1984), in: *Times Higher Education Supplement*, (5. April 1985).
13. S. Scott and C. J. Duncan, *Biology of Plagues: Evidence from Historical Populations*, (Cambridge, 2001); Cohn 2002; J. F. D. Shrewsbury, *A History of Bubonic Plague in the British Isles*, (Cambridge, 1970).

large-scale outbreak of plague. And secondly, that plague epidemics would have behaved as in India. Both appear questionable.

The former precondition appears to be inaccurate, a point that I will return to. The latter implies that the etiologic and epidemiologic characteristics of the outbreaks in India could serve as the prototypical plague, and, consequently, that deviations from the model justify grave concerns in terms of the nature of the disease. That would generally be a sound line of argument, at least within a modern context, given that the Indian experience actually represents plague proper.

It is, however, interesting to note that the most uncompromising defender of the view that medieval plague and modern plague were one and the same disease, the Norwegian historian Ole Jørgen Benedictow, at the same time has gone very far in generalizing the behaviour of plague on the basis of the Indian experience. In his monograph on the Black Death – with the somewhat unmodest subtitle *The Complete History* – from 2004, he developed further his viewpoints from the 1990s, and stated without reservations that every single plague epidemic that took place in Norway from the Black Death to 1654 was of the same type as the Indian outbreaks:

> Without exception, these epidemics of bubonic plague exhibited the characteristic features of bubonic plague as studied in India, China, Madagascar, Indonesia and Egypt in the first half of the twentieth century.[14]

Benedictow seems to have found a model for what plague should be like in the reports of the English commission that explored the conditions in India.

Paradoxically enough, so has Samuel Cohn. Pointing out the necessity of consulting the hundreds of pages that the commission published, mainly in *Journal of Hygiene* in the first decades of the 20th century, and impressed by their efforts, he wrote: "One objective of this book is to convince scholars that these pages are worth revisiting".[15]

The English plague research commission achieved truly impressive results: The recognition of the aetiology and epidemiology of plague, the

---

14. O. J. Benedictow, *The Black Death 1346-1353 The Complete History*, (Woodbridge, 2004), pp. 25, 157. Cf. O. J. Benedictow, *Plague in the Late Medieval Nordic Countries*, (Oslo, 1992), pp. 23, 160-171, 268.
15. Cohn 2002, p. 40.

relation between human plague and epizootics among rats, the discovery of the role of fleas, the physiology behind the blocking mechanism of certain flea species, the significance of temperature – all of which set doctors and health workers in the position of understanding the fundamentals of plague for the first time, and to put together measures to cope with it. It was a breakthrough with huge impact, also on plague research of recent years.[16]

But will it be fruitful to assume that we find *the* model for plague behaviour in India, a model that could be applicable for almost any other outbreak of the disease – regardless of widely different climatic, ecological and social conditions, and over a period of several hundred years?

On the presence of black rats in medieval Europe

A crucial precondition for outbreaks of plague in any form, whether we are speaking of bubonic or pneumonic or any other kind of clinical manifestations, is the presence of an epizootic – in most cases in a rodent population. That would be one of the few basic conditions that almost any plague researcher would agree on. In Europe, black rats represent the only species of rodents that are both susceptible to plague and able to pass the disease effectively on to human beings. Accordingly, the quest for plague should start with the quest for rats.

To substantiate any hypothesis regarding the presence of rats in medieval Europe, we will search in vain in contemporary chronicles – as a number of scholars have pointed out. But rather than the literary tradition, we should turn to interdisciplinary research, more precisely to the crossroads between biology, zoology and archaeology. Disciplines like paleo-biology and zoo-archaeology have been hiding in the shadows for some years, but recent research results have definitely shed light on the presence of rats in a European context.

Concerning the need for an interdisciplinary approach to the history of medicine, Frédérique Audoin-Rouzeau stated in 1999 the need for collaboration between several scholarly disciplines in order to reach a fruitful understanding of European plague: "... à la convergence nécessaire, cette fois, de cinq disciplines, l'histoire, la biologie, l'entomologie,

---

16. Cf. e.g. R. D. Perry and J. Fetherston, Yersinia pestis – Etiologic Agent of Plague, *Clinical Microbiology Review* 10, 1, (1997).

l'archézoologie et l'archéoentomologie.[17] Given that medicine is added to the list, this is most likely a very sound perspective.

One of the most important outcomes of an interdisciplinary approach so far came in 1994, when Audoin-Rouzeau and her colleague Jean-Denis Vigne published a comprehensive survey on studies of rats from antiquity to the early modern period.[18] On the basis of results from more then 200 archaeological excavations from large parts of Europe, they came to a number of highly interesting conclusions. The most fundamental one is that remains of rats have been found in several sites from antiquity, as far north as Britain, and that the black rat's colonization of Europe followed routes of trade and urbanisation. In that respect, negative results are as important as positive, in the sense that several of the excavations from antiquity and the early Middle Ages failed to produce any traces of rats.

The 11th century appears to have represented a turn of the tide, and by the 12th century black rats were widely distributed all over Europe. The absence of rats in the sites was no longer a prominent feature. Findings of rat skeletons increased significantly in the excavation sites dating from 11th to 15th centuries. Furthermore, the balance between non-commensal and commensal rats changed in the high middle ages. After that, black rats stood for the large majority of rodent discoveries.

Since 1994, more than 30 publications can be added to Audoin-Rouzeau and Vigne's list – which to a large extent contribute to the notion of the abundance of *Rattus rattus* in medieval Europe.[19] Claims that climatic conditions in northern Europe should have discouraged or precluded rat populations seem overstated. Rats propagate freely on the Hebrides as well as on the sub Antarctic Macquarie Island.[20]

Excavations with focus on rodents and small animals are few in the Nordic countries, but Anne Karin Hufthammer, the Norwegian archaeo-osteologist, is in the process of publishing results from a series of surveys made through several decades. From the unearthing of more than 500

---

17. Audoin-Rouzeau 1999, p. 426.
18. F. Audoin-Rouzeau and J.-D. Vigne, 'La colonisation de l'Europe par la Rat noir (Rattus rattus)', *Revue de Paléobiologie* 13, 1, (1994).
19. M. McCormick, 'Rats, Communications, and Plague: Toward an Ecological History', *Journal of Interdisciplinary History* XXXIV, 1, (2003), pp. 6-7.
20. McCormick 2003, p. 22.

skeletal remains from 16 different sites, she has been able to conclude that black rats were present in the major high medieval towns in Norway. The oldest discovery was from the 12th century in Bergen and rats were also found as far north as Trondheim, which is situated at the 64° northern parallel.[21]

Another interesting example in the Scandinavian context is Bengt Wigh's recent (2001) discoveries of black rats in five different strata from the Viking Ages in the ancient city of Birka near Stockholm, a work that as a matter of fact partly served as a confirmation of findings from as early as 1873.[22]

The rats seem to have been here. They had been here a while. But they also seem to have been here in numbers. In 2003, the American medieval historian Michael McCormick made a preliminary analysis of archaeological rat contexts, among c. 230 excavation reports, that permitted quantifying. The results were highly interesting. In 66 rat contexts in all, dating from the 9th to the 15th centuries, the average number of rats in each site was 9.1. In 13 sites the number of rats exceeded ten, and twelve of the most infested sites could be dated to the 13th century or later.[23] A relatively clear conclusion is that Europe was literally swarming with rats. No less important is the indication of an increase in rat density in the High Middle Ages.

In 2000 the English biologists Matt Keeling and Chris Gilligan analyzed fluctuations in rat metapopulations by ways of statistical models, and concluded that outbreaks of bubonic plague epidemics would require the presence of relatively small rat populations, and, furthermore, that the intervals between epidemics might be explained by cycles within the populations. A consequence of their analysis is that plague would not have to be imported. Cities of a fairly reasonable size could have acted like reservoirs of plague, and could have contributed to the local distribution of contagion.[24]

---

21. Personal communication. Cf. Moseng 2006, pp. 101-104.
22. B. Wigh, *Animal Husbandry in the Viking Age Town of Birka and its Hinterland*, doctoral dissertation, (Stockholm University, 2001).
23. McCormick 2003.
24. M. J. Keeling and C. A. Gilligan, 'Metapopulation dynamics of bubonic plague', *Nature* 407, (2000); M. J. Keeling and C. A. Gilligan, 'Bubonic plague: a metapopulation model of a zoonosis', *Proceedings of the Royal Society of London, Biological Sciences* 267, (2000).

THE FLEA VECTORS AND THEIR CLIMATE

So far the similarities between India and Europe across the decades seem intriguing: Populations of black rats could definitely have been acting as enzootic reservoirs in late medieval and early modern Europe.

However, a closer look at the second factor of the classic plague model – the insect vector – tends to complicate things a bit. I will approach this along two lines: considerations on climate and on the concept of vector efficiency.

Already the English commission in India noted that climate had a considerable effect on the propagation of plague. Temperatures over 30° C appeared to check the epidemics effectively. Thus the English workers were able to explain the observed seasonality – something which was an important feature in Europe as well. Flea physiology was the clue. It was the flea's ability to infect mammals that was affected by temperature, in terms of "blocking" the digestive system (which is an issue I will return to in more detail).[25]

In 1914, the British entomologist A.W. Bacot investigated also the lower temperature limits, concluding that 7 °C was fatal to the only important vector in India, the oriental rat flea *Xenopsylla cheopis*. Given that we consider indoor temperature as minimum requirements for the persistence of these fleas in medieval Europe, they could, under certain conditions, very well have survived.

But Bacot was obviously not satisfied, and his experiments at the other end of the flea's life cycle, the egg, resulted in the relatively firm conclusions that this species was unable to hatch in temperatures below 15°C. That would be a temperature limit which effectively rules out the oriental rat flea as a possible plague vector in Northern Europe.[26]

Bacot also concluded that other species could tolerate much lower temperatures than that. Among them were *Pulex irritans*, known under

---

25. *Journal of Hygiene* VIII, 2, (1908), pp. 266-301; R. St John Brooks, 'The Influence of Saturation Deficiency and of Temperature on the Course of Epidemic Plague', *Journal of Hygiene* XV, (1917); A. W. Bacot, and C. J. Martin, 'Observations on the Mechanism of the Transmission of Plague by Fleas', *Journal of Hygiene* XIII, Plague Supplement III, (1914).
26. A. W. Bacot, 'A study of the bionomics of the common rat fleas and other species associated with human habitations, with special reference to the influence of temperature and humidity at various periods of the life history of the insect', *Journal of Hygiene* XIII, (1914).

the misleading name "human flea", and the European rat flea, *Nosopsyllus fasciatus,* that hatched happily away down to 5°C. Bacot's results were largely confirmed by investigations performed in 1980 by the Russian entomologists V.A. Bibikova and I.F. Zhovtyi, who pointed out that the oriental rat flea was active between 20 and 40°C while its European relative had a range of temperature down to zero.[27]

In accordance with this, X. cheopis has never been found in Norway, and is apparently absent in Sweden, Denmark, Finland, Switzerland, Belgium, Luxembourg and the Netherlands as well.[28] Its distribution in Britain and France is extremely limited.[29] There are obvious problems connected with speculations on distribution of fleas in the Middle Ages based on modern maps. But the conclusion is somewhat strengthened by archaeo-entomological discoveries. French and British researchers have found no traces of *X. cheopis* in medieval sites, quite a few *N. fasciatus* and have concluded that *P. irritans* was abundant almost everywhere and at all times.[30]

---

27. V. A. Bibikova and I. F. Zhovtyi, Review of Certain Studies of Fleas in the USSR, 1967-1976, in: R. Traub and H. Starcke (eds.), *Fleas,* Proceedings of the International Conference on Fleas, Ashton Wold, Peterborough, UK 21-25 June 1977, (Rotterdam, 1980).
28. Reidar Mehl, The Norwegian Institute of Public Health, personal communication; K. Henriksen, *Siphonaptera,* The Zoology of Iceland III, 47, (1939); F. G. A. M. Smit, *Lopper,* Danmarks fauna 60, (København, 1954), pp. 30, 118; F. G. A. M. Smit, *Siphonaptera,* Insecta Helvetica1, (Lausanne, 1966); F. G. A. M. Smit, De vlooien (Siphonaptera) van de Benelux-landen, *Wetenschappelijke mededelingen van de Koninklijke Nederlanse Natuurhistorische Vereiniging* 72, (1967); F. G. A. M. Smit, 'A catalogue of the Siphonaptera of Finland with distribution maps of all Fennoscandian species', *Annales zoologici Fennici* 6, (1969); G. Brick-Lindroth and F. G. A. M. Smit, 'The Kemner Collection of Siphonaptera in the Entomological Museum, Lund, with a Check-List of the Fleas of Sweden', *Entomologica Scandinavica* 2, (1971), pp. 269-286.
29. F. G. A. M. Smit, 'The Recorded Distribution and Hosts of Siphonaptera in Britain', *Entomologist's Gazette* 8, (1957); R. S. George, Siphonaptera, in John Heath (ed.) *Provisional Atlas of the Insects of the British Isles* 4, (Huntingdon, 1974); J.-C. Beaucournu and H. Launay, *Les puces (Siphonaptera) de France et du Bassin méditerranéen occidental,* Faune de France 76, (Paris, 1990), pp. 80-82.
30. P. H. Yvinec, P. Ponel and J.-C. Beaucournu, 'Premiers rapports arcéoentomologiques de l'etude des Puces aspects historiques et anthroplogiques (Siphonaptera)', *Bulletin de la Société entomologique de France* 105, 4, (2000).

Vector efficiency

If the oriental rat flea, the plague vector "par excellence", could more or less be ruled out as a significant factor in Europe – and probably without reservations in Northern Europe – there are other flea species that are nearly as capable of transmitting plague from rodents to man, in terms of what is called *vector efficiency*. The expression has been defined as the product of three potentials: the *infection* potential, i.e. the percentage of fleas taking an infected blood meal that become infected, the *infective* potential, i.e. the percentage of infected fleas that become capable of transmitting, and the *transmission* potential, i.e. the observed ability to transmit prior to the flea's death.[31] Usually this concept is closely associated with the "blocking" of the digestive system in certain flea species.

Sucking blood from a plague infected animal results in the formation of a block of bacteria and blood which the flea regurgitates back to the blood stream of its host. The block contains huge numbers of bacteria – maybe several hundred times the amount that could be contaminating the proboscis of a flea by ways of other methods of transmission. This will represent an important distinction between flea species, in terms of the physiological capability to become blocked: Some species do block easily, others don't, and some do not block at all.

Experiments that were carried out by the Plague research commission in India made it clear that *X. cheopis* was the most effective in terms of blocking. But the researchers also assumed that other species were nearly as capable. The one that came closest was the European rat flea *N. fasciatus*. This was a species that, as much as its oriental cousin, would not hesitate to grab a meal from humans. These results were confirmed in the 1940s by Eskey and Haas, Wheeler and Douglas, and by Albert Burroughs.[32]

Eventually, there are several flea species that could be able to transmit plague effectively by way of blocking. These species were not abundant in India, and have tended to be forgotten. But in 1947, the American physician Albert Burroughs carried out a series of experiments, which indicated that "blocking" was not the only way by which fleas could transmit

---

31. C. M. Wheeler and J.R. Douglas, 'Sylvatic plague studies V, The determination of vector efficiency', *Journal of Infectious Diseases* 77, (1945).
32. C. R. Eskey and V. H. Haas, 'Plague in the western part of the United States', *Public Health Bulletin* 254, 1940; Wheeler and Douglas 1945; A. L. Burroughs, 'Sylvatic plague studies, The vector efficiency of nine species of fleas compared with Xenopsylla cheopis', *Journal of Hygiene* 45, (1947).

plague between mammals more or less efficiently.[33] Without being too technical, the crucial point is that blocking does not take place instantly, but within – on average – a fortnight. However, Burroughs found that when his rats were exposed to an attack by a relatively large number of fleas, the rodents died after 3 - 5 days.

Burroughs concluded that "... this brief time disallows transmission by blocked insects as the causal factor in the transference of organisms". And he considered this mode of transmission, which he called "mechanical", as a highly important alternative to the "biological" transmission by way of blocked fleas:

> Species of fleas which are feeble biological vectors of plague, or experimentally incapable of serving as such, may, nevertheless, be efficient mechanical vectors. ... During an epizootic of plague in a susceptible animal population, mechanical transmission is undoubtedly of paramount importance.[34]

Burroughs's experiments can, to a certain extent, be regarded as parallel to another investigation that took place in the 1940s. The French physicians and biologists Georges Blanc and Marcel Baltazard were sent from the Pasteur Institute to Morocco during a plague epidemic in 1940.[35] They collected fleas in the houses of the deceased, and performed two different types of experiments. The first was carried out by injecting guinea pigs with dissolutions of crushed, infected fleas – which by no means should be regarded as a very convincing experiment, as plague in nature is not spread by ways of hypodermic needles. But they also managed to infect guinea pigs solely by allowing large quantities of fleas to feed on them.

An interesting aspect of this experiment was that the large majority of fleas during the outbreak in Marrakech was not *X. cheopis*, as they would have expected, but the so-called human flea, *Pulex irritans*, which apparently swarmed in the homes of the plague victims. This is of particular

---

33. Burroughs 1947.
34. Burroughs 1947, p. 394.
35. G. Blanc and M. Baltazard, 'Recherches experimentales sur la peste', *Maroc-Médical, Journal de la Médecine et de la Pathologie Comparée, au Maroc* 217, (1941) (also printed in *Comptes redus des séances de l'Academie des Sciences* 213, 1941); G. Blanc and M. Baltazard, 'Recherches sur le mode de transmission naturelle de la peste bubonique et septicémique', *Archives de l'Institut Pasteur de Maroc* 111, 5, (1945), pp. 204-210, 228-271.

interest in comparison to Burroughs's work, because *P. irritans* in a number of experiments had turned out to be one of the flea species that hardly possessed the ability to become blocked at all.

In a series of articles, Blanc and Baltazard tended to overestimate the significance of their results grossly. In their opinion, the Moroccan plague represented a genuine plague *epidemic* (as opposed to the Indian epidemics that in their opinion basically were *epizootics* that also affected human beings).[36] Georges Girard, the head of the plague department of the Pasteur Institute in Paris at the time, warned against generalizing on the basis of individual cases. He nevertheless accepted Blanc and Baltazard's conclusions as valid – at least in Morocco.[37]

Another interesting aspect of the experiences from Morocco was that not only could rats transmit plague to humans. The opposite direction was an option as well. On the basis of this, and of his own experience from Madagascar, Girard put forward a concept of a circular course of plague transmission: man – flea – rat – flea – man, in addition to the classic, linear transmission route from India: rat – flea – man.

It goes without saying that the experiments that the two Frenchmen conducted in Morocco were highly problematic. But Burroughs's conclusions were apparently not. The bottom line seems to be that the modes of transmission in the case of plague, and the range of flea vectors that are able to transmit the disease, are more ambiguous than superficial reading of literature on historical plague, by and large, leads us to recognize.

THE NOTION OF VERSATILITY

As far as I have been able to confirm from extensive reading of medical literature on plague, the notion of ringing unanimity regarding the dominance of the Indian model seems deceptive. It's the very opposite. Quite a few of the leading experts have tended to agree that even though

---

36. Blanc and Baltazard 1941; G. Blanc and M. Baltazard, 'Quelques remarques a propos du mémoire de G. Girard sur les "ectoparasites humains dans l'épidémiologie de la peste', *Bulletin de la Société de Pathologie Exotique* XXXVI, 7-8, (1943); Blanc and Baltazard 1945; M. Baltazard, 'Déclin et déstin d'une maladie infectieuse: la Peste', *Bulletin of the World Health Organization* vol. 23, No. 2-3, (1960).
37. G. Girard, 'Les ectoparasites de l'homme dans l'épidémiologie de la peste', *Bulletin de la Société de Pathologie Exotique* XXXVI, (1943); Girard 1955, pp. 264-267. See also Girard's comments to Blanc og Baltazard 1943 in *Bulletin de la Société de Pathologie Exotique* XXXVI, 7-8, (1943), pp. 216-217.

the oriental rat flea must rightly be considered the vector par excellence that it has long been claimed to be, there are other ways of transmission that have to be taken into consideration.

Already Charles Martin, one of the pioneers behind the discovery of the blocking mechanism of *X. cheopis* in India in 1914, stated that *P. irritans* under certain conditions could transmit plague to man. In 1913, he spoke to the *Royal College of Physicians*:

> A variation of the plague bacillus in the direction of greater infectivity, with perhaps diminished toxicity leading to a higher degree of septicaemia in man, would permit of direct transmission by human fleas. Bubonic plague would then be independent of the rat, and spread directly from man to man. For several reasons it seems to me not improbable that this may have happened in the plagues of the middle ages.[38]

His collegue, A. W. Bacot, was of the same opinion. In 1919 he was inclined to think that the human flea was underrated as a plague vector, and maintained in 1924 that: "My opinion is that this species is highly underestimated as a possible factor".[39]

Investigations on plague in the highlands of Ecuador around 1930, led C. R. Eskey, one of the leading plague researcher of his time, to believe:

> By the process of elimination, one is compelled to believe that P. irritans is the chief transmitting agent in the causation of plague in the localities of Ecuador where no X. cheopis is found.[40]

At an altitude of 600-700 meters in Peru, Atilio Macchiavello observed the total absence of *X. cheopis* under an outbreak of plague in 1946.[41] Ricardo

---

38. C. J. Martin, *Brit. med. J.* 1, (1913), pp. 59 ff (citation in: L. F. Hirst, *The Conquest of Plague*, (Oxford, 1953), p. 238.
39. A.W. Bacot, *J. R. sanit. Inst.* 40, 1919, pp. 53 ff (citation in Hirst 1953, p. 238); A. W. Bacot, *Bull. Off. Int. Hyg. Publ.* 16, (1924) (citation in Girard 1943, p. 16). *Mon avis est qu'on a plutôt négligé cette espéce comme facteur possible* (my translation to English of Girard's translation to French).
40. C.R. Eskey, *Publ. Hlth. Rep., Wash.* 45, (1930) (citation in: Hirst 1953, p. 238).
41. A. Macchiavello, 'A Focus of Sylvatic Plague on the Peruvian-Ecuadorian Frontier', *Science* 104, 2710, 1946.

Jorge, who was in charge of the international plague research commission during the plague epidemic in Porto in 1899, in 1933 gave voice to the idea that *P. irritans* was the cause of epidemics in medieval and early modern times, and denied that the oriental rat flea ever was numerous in Europe.[42] That was an opinion supported by the president of the *Royal Society of Tropical Medicine and Hygiene*, William P. Mac Arthur.[43]

Leonard Hirst, the author of *The Conquest of Plague* from 1953, was decidedly critical of Blanc and Baltazard and the notion that the human fleas played any role of importance in the transmission of plague: "If accepted, it would stultify the work of the Plague Research Commission and the main parasitological thesis of this book".[44] But he nevertheless admitted:

> This is an important addition to our knowledge which justifies the belief that human fleas may play a significant part in the interhuman spread of plague when their density is very high and the blood in human cases contains many plague bacilli. ... Let it be admitted that human fleas present en masse are capable of carrying plague between human beings in homes where a man has died acutely of plague of rat origin.[45]

Less ambiguously, Robert Pollitzer established in 1954:

> It is conceivable that, in areas like Morocco, where P. irritans occurs abundantly, it might play an important role in the transmission of plague, the high incidence of this species compensating for what it lacks in vector capacity.[46]

Thus, he more or less rephrased Girard's statement in his comments on Blanc and Baltazard: "La notion de densité du parasitisme doit être complétée par celle de la qualité ...".[47] Even though the conclusions from

---

42. R. Jorge, *Bull. Off. int. Hyg. publ.* 25, (1933): 425 ff (citation in: Hirst 1953, p. 239).
43. W. P. Mac Arthur, 'Habituation of Pulex irritans to animal host', *Transactions of the Royal Society of Tropical Medicine and Hygiene* XXXIX, 4, (1946).
44. Hirst 1953, p. 239.
45. Hirst 1953, p. 241.
46. Pollitzer 1954, p. 380.
47. Girard 1943, p. 38.

Morocco represented a clear contrast to his own experience from other parts of the world, as well as Girard's, Pollitzer maintained that mechanical transmission of plague was something that had to be taken seriously:

> However, as confirmed by the recent work of Blanc and Baltazard,[...] and by Burroughs,[...] no doubt can exist that a transmission of plague may be effected through mass attacks of fleas with contaminated proboscises.[48]

Moreover, Pollitzer gave his readers a word of warning: "... one should beware of being dogmatic when dealing with a problem, for the solution of which one has to depend on surmise rather than on factual data".[49] That seems to be a word of wisdom which both plague researchers and historians will do well remind each other of from time to time.

In a comprehensive article from 1958 on plague in the USA, Leo Kartman and Frank Prince, also among the leading experts in the field, expressed the view that blocking was not the only mechanism connected to transmission of plague, although firmly established in the history of the disease, "... the phenomenon of mass transmission must be mentioned as another mechanism that has received insufficient attention".[50] They concluded:

> Obviously, the phenomenon of mass transmission must be taken into account in the ecology of wild-rodent plague. [...] Future work is faced with the problem of integrating the concept of mass transmission with current hypotheses regarding the mechanisms involved in sylvatic plague.[51]

In the introduction to an extensive article on the ecology of plague from 1961, Pollitzer and his co-author Karl F. Meyer, one of the prominent authorities of post-war plague research, summed up four main modes of transmission of plague to humans: from mammal to man through the bite

---

48. Pollitzer 1954, p. 350.
49. Pollitzer 1954, p. 373.
50. L. Kartman, F. M. Prince, S. F. Quan and H. E. Stark, 'New Knowledge on the Ecology of Sylvatic Plague', *Annals of the New York Academy of Sciences* 70, 3, (1958), p. 691.
51. Kartman, Prince et al. 1958, p. 692.

of a flea, directly from mammals, interhuman – and a fourth mode that could occur when human parasites were sufficiently numerous to allow transmission from man to man without rats as necessary intermediate hosts. Pollitzer and Meyer stated that the background for the disease's apparent flexibility, was that "... the ecology of plague, which figures conspicuously among the infectious organisms, is of a complex character.".[52] They recognized two main forms of transmission: by way of blocked fleas, and "mechanically" with the flea's plague infected proboscis.

More recently, the internationally acknowledged experts on plague, J.D. Poland and A.M. Barnes, regarded *X. chepois* as "... the classic vector against which all other flea species are compared". But they also pointed out that:

> The intensive research efforts focused on X. cheopis (the oriental rat flea) – although there is some risk of overgeneralization – provide insight into the multiple and complex interactions among flea vectors, hosts, pathogens, the environment, and victims that is necessary for the maintenance, epizootic amplification, and transmission of plague to man.[53]

And, furthermore: "Under certain situations, human flea (Pulex irritans) transmission has been suspected and reasonably well proved."[54]

Perspectives like these were essential also for the epidemiologist A. B. Christie, who in 1982 referred to 343 mammals and over 30 species of fleas that were susceptible to plague and pointed out that a great many environmental and ecologic factors would have to coincide for a transmission of infection to take place. Christie made use of the term "landscape ecology", and underlined that whether fleas were blocked or not, frequently was less important than their quantity.[55]

Robert Perry and Jaqueline Fetherston at the University of Kentucky have published numerous articles on *Yersinia pestis*, and approached problems associated with the modes of transmission to man in a com-

---

52. Pollitzer and Meyer 1961, p. 433.
53. J. D. Poland and A. M. Barnes, Plague, in H. Stoenner, W. Kaplan and M. Torten (eds.), Bacterial, Rickettsial, and Mycotic Diseases, section A, volume 1, in J. H. Steele (ed.) *CRC Handbook Series in Zoonoses*, (Boca Raton, 1979), p. 537.
54. Poland and Barnes 1979, p. 538.
55. Christie 1982.

prehensive overview in 1997; probably one of the most frequently cited articles on plague over the last few decades. After having characterized *X. cheopis* as one of the most effective plague vectors in terms of vector efficiency, they also asserted:

> While these experimental determinations have proven useful, poor vectors cannot be dismissed as unimportant in the ecology of plague. Some of these fleas are capable of transmitting the disease in nature or en masse in the laboratory.[56]

Regarding the role of the human flea, they wrote:

> The role of P. irritans (erroneously called the human flea despite its wide host range) in sustaining epidemics is controversial. While a majority opinion is that this flea is rarely involved in human-to-human transmission, others assign it an essential role in human epidemics.[57]

This is a crucial statement: By pointing out this ambiguity, Perry and Fetherston at the same time accentuated the versatility of the disease and drew attention to a complex set of problems that has puzzled plague researchers in more than 100 years.

Problems related to the vectors of transmission are still issues of interest. Recent research seems to have strengthened the hypothesis that mechanical transmission from non-blocked fleas must be considered an actual option. David Engelthaler, Joseph Hinnebusch and their group at the Centers for Disease Control and Prevention in USA, were in 2000 able to bring forward results that unambiguously demonstrated that fleas could cause an infection in animals with a minimal quantity of bacteria in their intestinal tracts. "This was too early for a block to have developed, suggesting that mechanical transmission may have occurred", they concluded.[58] As late as 2006, a research group which included Kenneth L. Gage firmly concluded that the efficient transmission by unblocked fleas described in their study

---

56. Perry and Fetherston 1997, p. 53.
57. Perry and Fetherston 1997, p. 55.
58. D. B. Engelthaler, J. Hinnebusch, C. M. Rittner and K. L. Gage, 'Quantitative competitive PCR as a Technique for Exploring Flea-Yersinia pestis Dynamics', *American Journal of Tropical Medicine and Hygiene* 62, 5, (2000), p. 558.

calls for a paradigm shift in concepts of how Y. pestis is transmitted, "... including, perhaps, the Black Death".[59]

This enquiry into the transmission mechanisms of plague and how the question has been dealt with in the last century, should not serve the purpose of enforcing a firm belief that the plague of the Middle Ages was of a certain character. My intention has rather been to point out that there are several possibilities of how plague could have behaved and, accordingly, that one of the critical pitfalls may be to assume that the Indian plague represents the genuine plague. Likewise: We know nothing about how the presumed differences in the transmission of plague could have altered the epidemiological patterns – if they are significant or recognizable at all. Still, it would be fruitful to pose the question. When Jean-Claude Beaucournu considered the conditions for the dissemination of plague in Europe, he assumed that the human flea was the most likely candidate. Frédérique Audoin-Rouzeau on her side suggested that the European rat flea represented an option.[60] Paradoxically enough, they could both have been right.

Some concluding remarks on epistemology

The history of medicine has been described as the double face of Janus, but it could be appropriate to choose Medusa's hair as a symbolic representation of plague. Attempts to translate concepts of diseases from the past and to try to fit them into modern classifications represent one of the common pitfalls of medical history. To perform diagnosis across long periods of time can easily turn into an anachronistic straitjacket.

Historical diseases have appeared, and they have disappeared. Most of them have left very vague clues, like the "English Sweat", or none at all. But some have left traces with so close resemblance to modern classifications that the task of identifying them as such is tempting. The so-called "Norwegian radesyge" first appeared in the mid-18th century. It was characterized both as leprosy, syphilis and scorbut by contemporary physicians, but was also considered a specific epidemic with features that

---

59. R. J. Eisen, S. W. Bearden, A. P. Wilder et al., 'Early-phase transmission of Yersinia pestis by unblocked fleas as a mechanism explaining rapidly spreading plague epizootics', *Proceedings of the National Academy of Sciences of the United States of America* 103, (2006), p. 42.
60. Beaucournu 1995; Audoin-Rouzeau 1999.

distinguished it from other known diseases and that required specific cures.[61] The disease vanished after 1850, or, more precisely: it was the classification that vanished. The "radesyge" can be seen as a disease that arrived with the new ways of medical thinking during the scientific revolution, and which also disappeared as a result of a later phase in the same process, as conceptions of diseases underwent changes.

In our own time, diseases come and go as well, because they no longer fit into present classifications, or because the classifications change. Classifications of diseases should be regarded as unstable manifestations in coherent – but changing – systems of knowledge. Regardless of points of view, it is important to have in mind that the descriptions of diseases by doctors and chroniclers of the past reflect conceptions of diseases rather than the diseases themselves.

Gabriele de' Mussis and Giovanni Boccaccio represent the most famous descriptions of plague from the 14th century. In de Mussis' words: "... the Tartars died as soon as the signs of disease appeared on their bodies: swellings in the armpit or groin caused by coagulating humours, followed by a putrid fever". Boccaccio's narrative tells more or less the same story:

> ... its earliest symptom, in men and women alike, was the appearance of certain swellings in the groin or armpit, some of which were egg-shaped whilst others were roughly the size of the common apple.[62]

The two texts appear surprisingly parallel, and they could effortlessly be linked up to early modern accounts as well as clinical descriptions of plague from modern textbooks in medicine. A medical report from 17th century Rome described plague this way:

> Onset is marked with very high temperature, very severe headache, bilious vomiting, sleepiness, occasional diarrhea, and cloudy, dark urine. If the above-mentioned signs did not appear on the first day, they did not fail to appear on the 2nd. [...] In many patients buboes and carbuncles appeared with the first attack of tempera-

---

61. O.G. Moseng, *Ansvaret for undersåttenes helse 1603-1850*, (Oslo 2003), pp. 244-264.
62. R. Horrox, *The Black Death*, (Manchester and New York, 1994), pp. 17, 27.

> ture. [...] In other patients buboes and carbuncles appeared on the 2nd, 3rd or 4th day ...

Modern medical textbooks give accounts like this:

> Temperature then rises rapidly [...]. Vomiting, thirst, unsteady gait, generalized pains, mental dullness and headache are the most frequent symptoms. [...] Buboes (enlarged, painful, tender lymph nodes) usually appear between the 2nd and the 5th days, and may suppurate.[63]

The Italian historian Carlo Cipolla underlined that early modern doctors were frequently uncertain of symptoms and classifications. Their diagnoses were ambiguous and contradictory and they often expressed indecisiveness.[64] They had to rely solely on external signs in order to make a diagnosis, as opposed to the modern doctor who has both the laboratory and the bacteriologic paradigm at hand. In 1992, the British historian Andrew Cunningham pointed out that the total dominance of laboratory medicine in the wake of the bacteriologic revolution has had a vast impact also upon our interpretation of diseases of the past:

> ... leading us to read them as if they were laboratory diseases; hence the coming of the laboratory has led to the past of medicine being rewritten to accord with the laboratory model of disease, and it has thereby been misunderstood.[65]

The pioneers of plague research in India in the 1890s worked in the golden age of bacteriology. To them, the need for affirmative definitions of diseases was imperative. But for a historian to approach historical diseases with the same firm grip can easily lead to hasty conclusions. In this context, there are two worlds colliding in the attempts to establish a connection between modern plague and the plagues of the past. The con-

---

63. C. M. Cipolla, *Fighting the Plague in Seventeenth Century Italy*, (Madison, 1981), pp. 90-91.
64. Cipolla 1981, pp. 91-96.
65. A. Cunningham, 'Transforming plague. The laboratory and the identity of infectious disease', in A. Cunningham and P. Williams, *The laboratory revolution in medicine*, (Cambridge, 1992), p. 209.

trasts between concepts of plague on either side of Pasteur and Koch are probably much more noteworthy than the contrasts between the Middle Ages and, let's say, 1830. It will nevertheless be necessary to interpret the accounts of epidemics and diseases from early modern times and earlier, rather than to translate them, if the object is to relate the Black Death to the plague as it appeared in India.

Quite a few of the leading scholars in the field of medicine seem to have accepted that plague is a highly versatile disease in time and space, which is an insight that hardly any historian has given serious consideration. Although the modern experience seems to be important for the study of late medieval and early modern outbreaks of plague, the assumption that plague in 14th century Europe should have behaved like plague in India in the 20th century could easily be misleading. The presence of black rats in Europe – a decisive condition for the dissemination of plague pandemics – appears no longer to be questionable. On the other hand, the oriental rat flea, the *vector par excellence* in India and elsewhere, was probably never there. But other flea species may have been nearly as capable, and the mechanisms of transmitting plague to humans are far from limited to those emphasized by the English plague research commission.

I do not feel comfortable with the role of an energetic defender of the "traditionalist" view – even though this in the main could describe my present position, with a few, not unimportant, modifications. The "revisionist" approach definitely has much to commend it (if the use of a somewhat disrespectful phrase can be excused), by accentuating the apparent differences between present outbreaks of plague and the epidemics of the past, and not the least by pointing out the failure to consider thoroughly to what extent knowledge of modern plague is decisive for understanding plagues of the past. That is a question which historians and other scholars gravely have neglected.

I do not consider it very fruitful to look upon this discourse as an insurmountable gap. I have wanted to stay away from any debate on whether the medieval plague and the modern plague could have been the same disease. But if someone should ask (which certainly not would be irrelevant, in the light of my statements) the crucial question if "plague" was plague; then my answer would have to be two-fold: "Yes, it could very well have been the same disease." But then again: "No, it was not – if the precondition is that "plague" is what took place in India."

The Diffusion of The Black Death 1348-1350 in Central Europe

By Manfred Vasold, Rohrdorf

In the middle of the 14th century a deadly epidemic was ravaging Italy, and during the following years it spread out very quickly over many parts of Europe. In fact it diffused so fast, that anybody who studied the plague in other parts of the world would doubt whether this medieval epidemic – also known as the Black Death – really was plague. Bubonic plague, which hit western India in 1896, did not spread so fast, although by this time India as the first nation in Asia had modern means of transportation like the railway. During this epidemic in Europe in the 14th century, mortality rose very high, much higher than in India around 1900, and again one would doubt whether the epidemic around 1348 really was plague in its bubonic or pulmonary form. Modern historiography claims that in some countries, especially in Italy, England and parts of Mediterranean Spain the epidemic in the middle of the 14th century devoured one third of the population or perhaps even more.[1]

---

1. A good summary is presented by Ole J. Benedictow, *The Black Death 1346-1353. The Complete History*, (Woodbridge, 2004), pp. 380-384. Cf. Josiah Cox Russell, 'Population in Europe 500-1500', in: Carlo M. Cipolla (ed.), *The Fontana Economic History of Europe. Vol. 1: The Middle Ages*, (London, 1972), pp. 55 f. Cf. Josiah Cox Russell, 'Effects of Pestilence and Plague, 1315-1385', in *Comparative Studies in Society and History* 8, (1965/66), pp. 464-473; M. M. Postan, *The Medieval Economy & Society*, (Harmondsworth, 1972), pp. 41f.; Paul Slack, *The Impact of Plague in Tudor and Stuart England*, (Boston, 1985), p. 15.

Was it really plague – and only plague – which was devastating Italy? According to the contemporary chronicler Marchionne di Coppo Stefani, "dogs and cats, cows, donkey and sheep" died, even pigs, as Giovanni Boccaccio reports[2] – but these animals are not susceptible to plague, as modern biological research has shown. Rats on the other hand are very much susceptible to plague – but nobody in Italy in 1347 reports about dead rats. In India and Africa, around 1900, as also in other parts of the world, where plague was raging, the rodents died before humans began to die: so why not in Italy? Some knowledgeable medical historians and bacteriologists (e. g., Robert Koch) claim that plague only commences among humans after it has run its deadly course among the rats. As far as we know "not a single Western chronicler notes the occurrence of an epizootic, the massive mortalities of rats, which ought to have preceded and accompanied the human plague", the American historian David Herlihy writes. And that is only one part of the puzzle. "How could the disease have spread so quickly and so powerfully, over land as well as water? Humans cannot infect humans [with bubonic plague] and the grey rat is alledgedly a homebody that will not migrate spontaneously. The mechanisms by which bubonic plague diffuses in a human population are singularly cumbersome".[3] Bubonic plague is transmitted by fleas, normally by the rat-flea (*Xenopsylla cheopis*), and that insect needs certain ecological circumstances, especially warm temperatures and high degrees of humidity, which it does normally not find in Central Europe.

But did the plague really spread out so quickly? Before we decide about the nature of that epidemic we should ascertain a few facts about the diffusion of the epidemic north of the Alps.

The Epidemic on its Way into Northern Europe

The epidemic, which started in Italy, spread out into western and soon into northern and central Europe. The Norwegian historian Ole Jørgen Benedictow, who does not evince any doubt that this evil really was plague,

---

2. Klaus Bergdolt (ed.), *Die Pest 1348 in Italien. Fünfzig zeitgenössische Quellen*, (Heidelberg, 1989), p. 42. Vide p. 34, 66, where the death of other vertebrates is mentioned.
3. David Herlihy, *The Black Death and the Transformation of the West*, (Cambridge/London, 1997), pp. 26 f.

states that "the Black Death probably landed in Norway before it invaded southern Germany roughly 1,500 km to the south".[4]

The Alps, between Italy and Central Europe, should have acted as a powerful barrier which slowed down both traffic and the transmission of those pathogens. The disease spread much more quickly by ship than on land. It might have reached some cities east and west of the Alps, Vienna in the east and Basel in the west, as early as spring 1349.[5] It is supposed to have climbed up into the Carnithian Alps quite high and fast, and killed a surprising number of people up there.[6]

When did this epidemic reach Bavarian or German territories? We do not really know. The territories immediately north of the Alps, the Southern parts of Bavaria, seem to have been spared this first epidemic, the Black Death.[7] Very little is really known about that. The chronicles usually refer only to the cities, although it is hard to believe that an epidemic like the plague struck only the cities and not the countryside. The great majority of the German people lived in the countryside, but very little research has been done on this.

---

4. Benedictow 2004 (n 1), p. 153.
5. Cf. Roman Sandgruber, *Ökonomie und Politik. Österreichische Wirtschaftsgeschichte vom Mittelalter bis zur Gegenwart*, (Wien, 1995), p. 49; Alois Niederstätter, *Die Herrschaft Österreich. Fürst und Land im Spätmittelalter (Österreichische Geschichte 1278-1411)*, (Wien, 2001) tries to give a more differentiated judgement, but then he hesitates to draw the consequences. "Latest research assumes [!] that generally speaking on the average one third of the population died due to the epidemic, but with great regional differences" (p. 15).
6. Herbert Klein,'Das große Sterben von 1348/49 und seine Auswirkung auf die Besiedlung der Ostalpen', *Mitteilungen der Gesellschaft für Salzburger Landeskunde* 100, (1960), pp. 118 f., concludes, that "it can only have been the plague which caused such great changes." Cf. Walther Fresacher, 'Die Pest in Kärnten im 14. Jahrhundert', *Carinthia*, I,153, (1963), pp. 350 f.; and Amalie Fößel, 'Der Schwarze Tod in Franken 1348-1350', *Mitteilungen des Vereins für Geschichte der Stadt Nürnberg* 74, (1987), pp. 7 ff. n 19. Cf. Dieter J. Weiß, 'Des Reiches Krone – Nürnberg im Spätmittelalter', in Helmut Neuhaus (ed.), *Nürnberg im Europa der Frühen Neuzeit, in: Nürnberg – Europäische Stadt in Mittelalter und Neuzeit. (Nürnberger Forschungen 29)*, (Nürnberg, 2000), pp. 24 f.; Alfred Dopsch (ed.), *Geschichte Salzburgs. Stadt und Land.*,vol. I/1, (Salzburg, 1983), pp. 475 f.
7. Karl Lechner, *Das große Sterben in Deutschland, in den Jahren 1348 bis 1351 und die folgenden Pestepidemien bis zum Schlusse des 14. Jahrhunderts*, (Innsbruck, 1884), p. 39.

Since plague is an infectious disease – some even claim that it is highly contagious[8] – it is not necessary to take account of all cities of that region; it should suffice to refer to the bigger cities along main roads or thoroughfares, since these places should have been endangered quite early. The epidemic should have reached Germany from the south, so one might assume that the Bavarian cities were touched earlier than others. Let us have a look at them, going from east to west.

Passau: Passau was, in the late Middle Ages, a city of medium size, situated on a navigable river, the Danube. The sources for this city are, for these early times, not particularly good, since many archives were destroyed when the city burned down many decades later. The remaining collections do not give a reliable reference to the plague or mass-burials in the years 1348 or 1349; and the latest city history of Passau does not even mention the Black Death.[9]

Ratisbon (Regensburg): Ratisbon was, in the middle of the 14th century, an important commercial town, situated just like Passau on the Danube, a bit further upstream, further to the west. The latest city history of Ratisbon does not explicitly mention an epidemic around 1350.[10] "The sources do not mention an outbreak of plague or cases of plague between 1348 and 1350. Reliable accounts of an epidemic can be found in the years 1357, 1371, 1375 and 1380."[11]

Munich: In the middle of the 14th century Munich was not yet the capital of Bavaria, but it was the most important economic centre of Upper Bavaria, an important city of commerce and artisan production, as a commercial place not quite as important as Ratisbon or Augsburg.[12] The

---

8. Klaus Bergdolt 1989(n2), Einleitung, p. 16, refers to the "agggressive contagiosity" of plague. Vide Franz Pruner, *Ist die Pest denn wirklich ein ansteckendes Uebel*, (München, 1839). Pruner was a German doctor, who treated many cases of plague in Egypt in the 1830'ies, he doubted that bubonic plague was easily transmittable.
9. Letter of Prof. Dr. Hartinger, 10 Nov. 2001, to the author. Cf. Egon Boshof/Walter Hartinger/Maximilian Lanzinner et. al. (eds.)., *Geschichte der Stadt Passau*, (Regensburg, 1999), p. 207.
10. Peter Schmid (ed.), *Geschichte der Stadt Regensburg*, 2 vols., (Regensburg, 2000).
11. Dr. A. Dirmeier, director of the Hospital Archives of Ratisbon, in a letter to the author (22 Dec. 2000).
12. Manfred Döbereiner, 'Münchens Weg zur relativen Selbständigkeit 1294 bis 1365', in Richard Bauer (ed.), *Geschichte der Stadt München*, (München, 1992), pp. 75-85, esp. p. 83.

"Mattseer Annalen" mentions a "crudelissima pestilencia", which supposedly hit Munich and some other cities (Braunau am Inn, Landshut) at that time; but there is no convincing proof of mass-burials in Munich in those years. The latest city histories usually make no reference to an epidemic.[13] Especially: "No far-reaching consequences of the very first plague-wave can be seen in Upper Bavaria. It was only the later epidemics, of 1356, 1380 and 1396, which cause a momentous demographic decline."[14]

Ingolstadt: For the city of Ingolstadt there is no indication of an outbreak of plague in the years 1348/49 or immediately thereafter.[15] It cannot be shown that a great epidemic occurred at that town or that very many people in Ingolstadt died. "Epidemics like plague" occurred here during the Middle Ages, "but in the more reliable sources they can only be proven after the foundation of the university, after 1472".[16]

Augsburg: Augsburg was an important Imperial City in the later Middles Ages: it was an important trading place even in those early times, with a great amount of traffic, more populous and more important than Munich. Augsburg was situated on the most-frequented trade routes: There was an important thoroughfare running through Augsburg, connecting Italy and Innsbruck with Augsburg and Nuremberg, and further north with Lower Germany; another road connected Augsburg with the area north of Lake Constance and with Ratisbon, another one ran from Strasbourg via Ulm to Munich.[17] Augsburg constituted an important connection between Italy and northern Germany. The latest voluminous city history does not

---

13. Cf. Franz Solleder, *München im Mittelalter* (München, 1938), pp. 391, 537; Helmuth Solleder, *Chronik der Stadt München. Herzogs- und Bürgerstadt: Die Jahre 1157-1505*, (München, 1995), p. 132: Solleder assumes that the plague ravaged Munich in 1349 and that it caused great demographiy losses; but he solely relies on the Mattseer Annalen. Cf. *Urkundliche Chronik von München und allen umliegenden Orten, von der ältesten bis zur neuesten Zeit*, by Dr. Joseph Heinrich Wolf, vol. II, (München, 1854), p. 248.
14. Christine Rädlinger, 'Finanzielle Probleme und Verfassungskämpfe 1365 bis 1403', in Bauer 1992 (n 12), 98. Vide also H. Rubner, 'Die Landwirtschaft der Münchner Ebene und ihre Notlage im 14. Jahrhundert', *Vierteljahrschrift für Sozial- und Wirtschaftsgeschichte* 51, (1964), pp. 442 f.
15. Siegfried Hofmann, *Geschichte Ingolstadts*, (Ingolstadt, 2000), p. 182.
16. Ibid., pp. 648 f.
17. Volker Schmidtchen, 'Technik im Übergang vom Mittelalter zur Neuzeit zwischen 1350 und 1600', in Karl Heinz Ludwig / V. Schmidtchen (eds.), *Propyläen Technikgeschichte, vol. 2: Metalle und Macht 1000 bis 1600*, (Berlin, 1997), p. 499 and map pp. 500/501.

mention the Black Death.[18] "Consequences of an epidemic"cannot be shown and the number of inhabitants supposedly even rose in this period. "Reliable accounts of a plague-wave at A. do not exist before 1380."[19]

Nuremberg: The Imperial City of Nuremberg in the late Middle Ages was, similar to Augsburg, one of the most populous and important commercial places in Germany. Emperor Charles IV decreed in the Golden Bull (Nuremberg, January 1356), that every newly elected emperor had to hold his first Imperial Diet in this town. Situated at the very heart of the German Empire, "like a spider in its web"(Hector Amman), Nuremberg had important commercial connections in all directions. There was a pogrom against the local Jews in December 1349, yet there is no hint of an epidemic. This was not unusual: quite often the Jews were killed in medieval Europe before the plague arrived. The written sources of the Nuremberg Archives are plentiful, but again there is no indication of a great epidemic or of mass-burials; the plague first showed up at Nuremberg in the year 1359.[20] And the same seems to be true for its immediate surroundings.[21]

Würzburg: Around the year 1350 Würzburg was a medium-sized town, situated on the Main River, a navigable river. The most recent research about Würzburg comes to the conclusion that Würzburg was not devastated by the Black Death.[22] And the same seems to be true of the mountainous area to the north of Würzburg, the Rhoen.[23]

Ulm: The Imperial City of Ulm was a middle-sized town, situated on the Danube and on an important road between Italy and Central Germany. There are no chronicles from the 14th century. "There is as of today no

---

18. Gunther Gottlieb et. al. (eds.), *Geschichte der Stadt Augsburg. 2000 Jahre von der Römerzeit bis zur Gegenwart*, (Stuttgart, ²1985).
19. Claudia Kalesse, Art. 'Pest' in Günther Grünsteudel/Günter Hägele/Rudolf Frankenberger (eds)., *Augsburger Stadtlexikon*, (Stuttgart, ²1998), p. 706; Kalesse, *Bürger in Augsburg. Studien über Bürgerrecht, Neubürger und Bürgen anhand des Augsburger Bürgerbuchs I (1288-1497)* (Abh. zur Geschichte der Stadt Augsburg 37), (Augsburg, 2002), pp. 205 f.
20. Fößel 1987 (n 6), esp. pp. 14 f; Cf. Weiß 2000 (n 6), pp. 24 f.
21. Helmut Mahr, 'Die Pest in Zirndorf', *Fürther Heimatblätter* 47, (1997), pp. 3-21.
22. Stuart Jenks, *The Black Death and Würzburg: Michael de Leone's Reaction in Context*, Diss. phil. Yale U. 1976, (Michigan, 1984), p. 29. Cf. Helmut Martin, 'Die Pest im spätmittelalterlichen Würzburg', *Mainfränkisches Jahrbuch für Geschichte und Kunst* 46, (1994), pp. 24 ff.
23. Karl-Heinz Lübben, *Beiträge zur Kenntnis der Rhön in medizinischer Hinsicht*, (Weimar, 1881), p. 54.

reliable evidence about the plague years 1348/50 at Ulm. [...] As far as we know, it should not be a simple task, to find solid evidence" for an epidemic in Ulm in the years 1348/49, the archivist says. [24] However, the fact that in 1377 Ulm started building a huge cathedral, the Ulmer Munster, should make us careful about a substantial demographic decline.[25]

Rothenburg ob der Tauber: Rothenburg was an Imperial City, much smaller than Nuremberg or Augsburg, situated on a thoroughfare between the Rhine and Bohemia. There are no symptoms of a great epidemic in the middle of the 14th century; the Black Death most probably did not touch Rothenburg.[26]

Kempten and Memmingen: These cities are not far apart from each other and are both situated along a thoroughfare between Italy and Northern Germany. Around 1350 Kempten was a city of medium size. The latest history of that city does not contain any allusion to the Black Death, nor are there any consequences like mass-burials to be seen.[27] And the same is true of Memmingen.[28]

Freiburg im Breisgau: On the right hand side of the Rhine, not far away from that river lies Freiburg, an important thoroughfare passes by on the left hand side of the Rhine. The latest history of Freiburg claims: "We cannot give an immediate account of the events, but we do know of a terrible side-effect [!] of the plague: Even before the first wave of the epidemic reached Freiburg, there was – as it happened in so many places in Europe – a well-organised pogrom against the Jews, who were too will-

---

24. Prof. Dr. Specker in a letter (8 May 2002) to the author.
25. Gottfried Geiger, *Die Reichsstadt Ulm vor der Reformation. Städtisches und kirchliches Leben am Ausgang des Mittelalters* (Forschungen zur Geschichte der Stadt Ulm 11), (Ulm, 1971), p.76.
26. Ludwig Schnurrer, 'Die Pest in Rothenburg im ausgehenden Mittelalter', *Die Linde*, March 1987, (Rothenburg, 1987), pp. 21-24.
27. Volker Dotterweich et. al. (eds.), *Geschichte der Stadt Kempten*, (Kempten, 1989). "Our sources do not say anything about a plague epidemic around 1348/50. There are only very few written documents and they do not mention the plague. We cannot say when the plague ravaged Kempten for the first time." Letter to the author, by Birgit Kata, City Archiv Kempten, 27 March 2002.
28. Rudolf Kießling, 'Memmingen im Spätmittelalter', in Joachim Jahn (ed.), *Die Geschichte der Stadt Memmingen. Von den Anfängen bis zum Ende der Reichsstadt*, (Stuttgart, 1997), p. 167: "As far as the consequences of that great plague, whose first wave between 1348 and 1349 ravaged almost the entire central Europa and decimated the population by roughly one third [!], and successive waves in the following decades there are no reliable accounts for Memmingen".

ingly taken to be guilty for the epidemic [...]. The plague epidemic of 1348/49 was perhaps not the most devastating, under no circumstances was it the last one of this kind at Freiburg."[29]

Speyer: The city of Speyer is situated on an important thoroughfare between Basel and Mainz. The latest city history says: "In summer [1349] there was a general feeling of being threatened prevailing which showed itself also in the pogroms against the Jews, an epidemic of plague was approaching – although we cannot register an immediate effect of that threat for Speyer."[30]

In the past many German historians gave the impression that the plague is a highly contagious disease which spreads extremely fast, just like small-pox or influenza. So they concluded that the Black Death in Europe must have shown up in all places, that it devastated all regions and cities.[31] But in reality many regions to the east of the Rhine were not affected for a long time. The kingdom of Bohemia was not touched by the plague for some time. "It was historiography which brought the plague to Bohemia, Silesia and Poland", the historian Robert Hoeniger wrote sarcastically in 1882. In Bohemia the plague occurred for the first time in 1357, and the "Annales Wratislawienses maiores" mention for the city of Wrotclaw (Breslau) for the first time in 1373 a "maxima pestilentia et karistia"[32]. Knowledgeable German physicians of the 19th century were

---

29. Ulrich P. Ecker, 'Bettelvolk, Aussätzige und Spitalpfründner. Armut und Krankheit als zentrales Aufgabenfeld der Stadtverwaltung., in *Geschichte der Stadt Freiburg im Breisgau. Vol. 1: Von den Anfängen bis zum "Neuen Stadtrecht" von 1520*, (Stuttgart, 1996), p. 480; Cf. *Handbuch der Geschichte Baden-Württembergs*, ed. Meinrad Schaab / Hansmartin Schwarzmaier, vol. I/2, (Stuttgart, 2000), p. 494.
30. Ernst Volmer, 'Von der Bischofsstadt zur Reichsstadt. Speyer im Hoch- und Spätmittelalter', in Wolfgang Eger (ed.), *Geschichte der Stadt Speyer*, vol. 1, (Stuttgart, ²1983), p. 330. For Heidelberg and the plague see Rosemarie Jansen / Hans Helmut Jansen, 'Die Pest in Heidelberg', in Wilhelm Doerr, Berlin u.a (eds.), *Semper Apertus: Sechshundert Jahre Ruprecht-Karls-Universität Heidelberg 1386-1986*, (1985), p. 371-398.
31. Hartmut Boockmann, *Stauferzeit und spätes Mittelalter. Deutschland 1125-1517 (Das Reich und die Deutschen, vol. 8.)*, (Berlin, 1987, 1994), p. 228. "Southern Germany was hit by a plague wave, which by the year 1351 hat gone through the whole of Germany, killing one third of the population."
32. Robert Hoeniger, *Der Schwarze Tod in Deutschland*, (Berlin, 1882), p. 31. Cf. Niederstätter 2001 (n 5): "Some regions were not touched by that first plague wave, e.g., the Imperial City of Nuremberg, parts of Flanders, Brabant and the Hennegau or landscapes in Central France, although nobody knows why."

not surprised by this finding. "High mountains and forests can hinder the plague in its diffusion [...]. According to old chronicles the plague was stopped more than once by the Thuringian Forest, when it tried to spread from Saxony through Thuringia into Franconia", wrote Jacob Henle, a teacher of Robert Koch.[33]

But we need assume that the epidemic by-passed only large parts of Bavaria, Bohemia and Silesia: we do know that also some bigger cities and regions in the north and west of the Holy Roman Empire – such important commercial regions as Brabant and the southern parts of the Netherlands[34] - and also parts of France[35] as we learned a couple of years ago, were not touched by the very first plague, the Black Death, and the same applies most probably to places like Treves (Trier)[36], Frankfort-on-the-Main[37], Göttingen[38], Düsseldorf[39] and Duisburg[40], perhaps also Berlin[41]. The Black Death (1349/50) probably did not ravage these towns.

Many German historians have often neglected or exaggerated the demographic losses of the plague in the 14th century. Heinrich Reincke estimated (1951) that Hamburg lost between one half and two thirds of its inhabitants and Bremen even more; in Lübeck a quarter of the aldermen

---

33. Jacob Henle, *Von den Miasmen und Kontagien* [1840.], (Leipzig, 1910), p. 64.
34. Georges Despy, 'La "Grande peste" noire de 1348" a-t-elle touché le roman pays de Brabent?', in *Centenaire du Séminarie d'histoire médiéval de l'université libre de Bruxelles 1876-1976*, (Bruxelles, 1977), pp. 195-217.
35. Cf. the map in Henri Dubois, 'La Dépression (XIVe et XVe siècles)', in Jacques Dupâquier (ed.), *Histoire de la Population Française. vol. 1: Des origines à la Renaissance*, (Paris, 1988), pp. 313-366, map 315.
36. Vide *2000 Jahre Trier. Vol. 2: Trier im Mittelalter*, (eds.) H. H. Anton/A. Haverkamp, (Trier, 1996), pp. 458 f., 509-511, does not explicitly say that the plague did come or did not come.
37. Konrad Bund, 'Frankfurt am Main im Spätmittelalter 1311-1519', in *Die Geschichte der Stadt in neun Beiträgen*, (ed.) Historischen Kommission (Veröff. der Frankfurter Historischen Kommission, vol. 17.), (Sigmaringen, 1991), pp. 53-149. There was obviously no demographic decline around 1350 (p. 53 f.); the first reference to "bubonic plague" is made for the year 1412 (p. 126).
38. Walter Kronshage, *Die Bevölkerung Göttingens. Ein demographischer Beitrag zur Sozial- und Wirtschaftsgeschichte vom 14. bis 17. Jahrhundert*, (Göttingen, 1960), pp. 27 f.
39. *Düsseldorf. Geschichte von den Ursprüngen bis ins 20. Jahrhundert*, vol. I, (ed.) Hugo Weidenhaupt, (Düsseldorf, 1988), p. 282.
40. Kurt Hofius, 'Die Pest am Niederrhein, insbesondere in Duisburg', *Duisburger Forschungen*, vol. 15, (1971), pp. 173-221.
41. *Geschichte Berlins*, (ed.) Wolfgang Ribbe, vol. 1, (München, 1987), p. 219.

supposedly died.[42] Recent investigations do not bear out these results: It seems that even the great commercial Hanseatic cities like Bremen and Hamburg were devastated rather late, and the demographic losses seem to have been rather low, too.[43] The social historian K. Schwarz warns against exaggerating the mortality of Bremen, since that Hanseatic city, he says, was able to widen its sphere of influence after 1350.[44] The historian H.-J. Wenner doubts that Hamburg was devastated by plague as early as 1349 – he takes 1350 as the earliest date for this event.[45] He claims that many statements about demographic losses were simply made up, invented.[46] The Hanseatic city of Lübeck on the Baltic Sea has a rich tradition of historical sources with many Last Wills from the middle of the 14th century; but one should bear in mind that half of those 124 testators survived.[47]

There is a more recent study about the plague in the modern German state (Land) of Schleswig-Holstein, which claims that a rise of mortality in that region cannot be given in any exact figures.[48]

The Black Death, it seems, spread out over Germany east of the Rhine quite slowly and it did not touch upon all cities and towns and regions. In this respect one might conclude that the epidemic showed the same kind of behaviour as it showed in the subtropic and tropic regions of India or Egypt in the 19th century.[49]

---

42. Heinrich Reincke, 'Bevölkerungsprobleme der Hansestädte', *Hansische Geschichtsblätter* 70, (1951), pp. 9 f.
43. Klaus Schwarz, *Die Pest in Bremen. Epidemien und freier Handel in einer deutschen Hafenstadt* (Veröffentlichungen aus dem Staatsarchiv der Freien Hansestadt Bremen, ed. Adolf E. Hofmeister, 60), (Bremen, 1996), esp. pp. 97-102. For Hamburg: H.-J. Wenner, *Handelskonjunkturen und Rentenmarkt am Beispiel der Stadt Hamburg um die Mitte des 14. Jahrhunderts* (Beiträge zur Geschichte der Stadt Hamburg 9), (Hamburg, 1972), esp. pp. 25, 94.
44. Schwarz 1996 (n 43), esp. pp. 97-102.
45. Wenner 1972 (n 43), pp. 25, 94.
46. Ibid., p. 134.
47. Cf. ibid., pp. 134-139.
48. Jürgen Hartwig Ibs, *Die Pest in Schleswig-Holstein von 1350 bis 1547/48. Eine sozialgeschichtliche Studie über eine wiederkehrende Katastrophe* (Kieler Werkstücke. Reihe An: Beiträge zur schleswig-holsteinischen und skandinavischen Geschichte, (ed.) Erich Hoffmann, 12), (Frankfurt/M. et al., 1994), pp. 87, 90 f.
49. Klaus Bergdolt, *Der Schwarze Tod in Europa. Die Große Pest und das Ende des Mittelalters*, (München, 1994), p. 30, mentions, referring to the foundation of the university of Prague in 1348, the "Pestjahr 1348". He continues: "It must be taken as a whim of history that this new metropolis [i.e., Prague] which was visited by

THE DEMOGRAPHIC LOSSES

In Italian cities the demographic losses were quite high, one third or even more, and the same seems to be true for England and the coastal regions of Spain. The losses might have been high in some places in Germany, too; but there is very little reliable data for that early period and very often it is no more than a mere conjecture to say that the plague ravaged the city and killed many people. Not infrequently German historians even allude to plague epidemics before 1348, and in talking about demographic decline, they usually include the famine in the second decade of the 14th century and an unidentified mass-motalitity around 1339/40, which it also took place in Italy.[50]

Many other sources than written accounts are left from the Middle Ages only, and they must also be taken into account. There were many literary sources in Italy, but not north of the Alps, where there are much fewer. But where great churches or other public buildings were constructed after 1350 or great enlargement of cities was undertaken, it seems doubtful, that very many people died. If one third or even more of a population dies all of a sudden, there should be more evidence other than a chronicle entry.

It is not unusual that historians or other people simply draw the conclusion that an epidemic ravaged a town or a region, because other regions were struck by an epidemic or because certain social phenomena occurred. The pogroms of 1349 or before are no proof of the plague; this is untenable. Quite often the local Jews were killed in Central Europe before the

---

people of all nations, was one of the few cities in central Europe, which was not ravaged by the plague of 1348/50."

50. Cf. the graphs in Lorenzo Del Panta, *Le epidemie nella storia demografica italiana (secoli XIV-XVIII)*, (Turin, 1980), pp. 108 f. "It [i. e., the plague] shows up for the first time in 1313, (coming up the Rhine and the Moselle) killing supposedly 16 000 people in Mayence. This might be an exaggerated number. Franz Dumont, 'Helfen und Heilen – Medizin und Fürsorge in Mittelalter und Neuzeit', in Ibid./ Ferdinand Scherf/Friedrich Schütz (eds.), *Mainz. Die Geschichte der Stadt*, (Mainz, 1998), p. 773; Friedrich-Wilhelm Henning, *Handbuch der Wirtschafts- und Sozialgeschichte Deutschlands, vol. 1: Deutsche Wirtschafts- und Sozialgeschichte im Mittelalter und in der frühen Neuzeit*, (Paderborn/München/Wien/Zürich, 1991), p. 394, states that there was more than only one plague epidemic before 1348 in Germany, and the same is true for Hermann Kellenbenz, 'Das Deutsche Reich', in Jan A. van Houtte (ed.), *Handbuch der Europäischen Wirtschafts- und Sozialgeschichte*, vol. 2, (Stuttgart, 1980), p. 509.

plague struck.[51] "Today it is generally believed that these events occurred in the following order: first the Black Death, then came the flagellants, and then the anti-Jewish pogroms", the historian R. Hoeniger wrote more than a hundred years ago[52], and this apparently "logical" chain of events can be found in German historiography up to the present. In reality the chronology happened the following way: First the Jews were murdered, then came the flagellants, and later on the epidemic. And the epidemic might have come the following year or even years later – in Nuremberg a great pogrom took place in December 1349; but the epidemic did not strike that town before 1359.[53] Pogroms are not reliable evidence of the plague; they might indicate a great fear, but no more.

How high were the demographic losses in Germany around 1350? It is hard to tell, since there were famines and plagues before 1348 which we cannot really quantify – shortly after 1310 and in 1339/40. Immediately after the modern plague had been identified in India and China, shortly after 1900, there were demographic estimates for Germany, which seem much more realistic than that "one third"[54], which is so often quoted. Germany "has been less devastated than other countries", the historian Johannes Nohl wrote; he assumes that the losses were higher in northern than in southern Germany, for the whole country he estimates the demographic losses – for the time of the Black Death around 1350 – at less than ten per cent.[55] That estimate could be realistic for the whole of Germany for the years 1349/52.[56]

---

51. František Graus, *Pest-Geissler-Judenmorde. Das 14. Jahrhundert als Krisenzeit*, (Göttingen, 1987), pp. 24 f.
52. Hoeniger 1882 (n 32), p. 106.
53. Fößel 1987 (n 6), pp. 9 ff.
54. E. g., Georg Sticker, *Die Pest*, 2 vols. (in 3 volumes), (Gießen, 1908/10). Sticker was a physician, he joined the group around G. Gaffky and R. Koch, which travelled to India in 1897/98 to do research about the plague; he was infected, but survived bubonic plague.
55. "Germany, whose demographic losses have been given with 1 244 434 in 1348, has been ravaged less than other countries", writes Johannes Nohl, *Der Schwarze Tod. Eine Chronik der Pest 1348 bis 1720*, (Potsdam, 1924), p. 40. The medical doctor and baceriologist Stefan Winkle, *Geißeln der Menschheit. Kulturgeschichte der Seuchen*, (Düsseldorf/Zürich, 1997), p. 448, takes this figure to be true, he writes that "alone in the year 1349" 1,24 million people in Germany fell victim to the plague.
56. It is esp. British historians who doubt that it was plague which ravaged parts of Europe around 1350, esp. Graham Twigg, *The Black Death. A Biological Reap-*

For the present time more exact estimates are not possible. If we try to quantify the losses by taking into account the decimated regions of Germany, we must not forget that the German population was in decline even before 1348 due to the famines in the second decade of the 14th century and an epidemic around 1340.[57] The desertions ("Wüstungen") of the late Middle Ages might give us an approximate account of the population decline, but not for an exact period of time. The desertions show that the population was shrinking, but we cannot be certain about a given year. The desertions were not very high in Southern Germany, between 10 and 20 percent, between the Danube and Main rivers even less, perhaps as low as ten percent.[58] And in Northern Bavaria the latest research has shown that new urban agglomerations were founded even shortly after 1350.[59]

The desertions were higher in other regions of Germany, but one must not exaggerate this fact. Even a "Flurwüstungsquotient" (desertion rates) of 50 per cent does not mean that one half of the population was all of a sudden gone; it simply means that one half of the land was deserted. People usually left the poorer, infertile soils, since it was not worth while

---

praisal, (London, 1984); Susan Scott/Christopher Duncan, *Biology of Plagues. Evidence from Historical Populations*, (Cambridge, 2001), pp. 354-362; and Samuel K. Cohn Jr., *The Black Death Transformed. Disease and Culture in Early Renaissance Europa*, (London, 2002), p. 1. Inside Germany Erich Woehlkens, *Pest und Ruhr im 16. und 17. Jahrhundert. Grundlagen einer statistisch-topographischen Beschreibung der großen Seuchen, insbesonders in der Stadt Uelzen* (Schriften des Niedersächsischen Heimatbundes, Neue Folge Bd. 26.), (Uelzen, 1954), took a similar position.

57. S. Lucas, 'The great European famine of 1315', *Speculum* 15, 1930, p. 343 f.; Ian Kershaw, 'The Great Famine and Agrarian Crisis in England 1315-1322', *Past & Present* 59, (1973), 3-50. – The Nuremberg Chronicle *Müllners Annalen. Part I: Von den Anfängen bis 1350* (Quellen zur Geschichte und Kultur der Stadt Nürnberg), (Nürnberg, 1972), p. 306, claims, that "one third of all mankind" ("der dritte Teil aller Menschen") perished in 1312, and there was another famine in 1315.

58. Boockmann 1987/94 (n 31), p. 233. Wilhelm Abel, *Agrarkrisen und Agrarkonjunktur. Eine Geschichte der Land- und Ernährungswirtschaft Mitteleuropas seit dem hohen Mittelalter*, (Hamburg/Berlin, 1978), p. 90, shows (graph 17) that the desertions between Daunbe and Maine River were only medium ("mittelmäßig"), i. e., 20-39 percent.

59. Wolfram Unger, 'Grundzüge der Städtebildung in Franken. Träger – Phasen – Räume', *Jahrbuch für fränkische Landesforschung* 59, (1999), esp. pp. 68-86.

to cultivate them any longer, as the prices for agricultural produce were in decline, too.⁶⁰ It is true that these prices in Germany show a strong decline after 1350 – but the prices of agricultural produce are dictated more by the weather than by a loss of demand.

Germany did have demographic losses in the early and later 14th century and the 15th century, and there were many epidemics in these later years. But it is hard to believe that the epidemic of 1349/50 could have killed one third of the German population.⁶¹ The medievalist Erich Meuthen (Cologne) estimates the German population for 1350 around 13 to 14 millions; it reached its nadir, he claims, around 1470, with 7 to 10 millions.⁶² This sounds credible, although – or because – it is not very precise. There was a population decline in the late Middle Ages, but we cannot say that it occurred in or immediately after 1350; it might have taken place in the following one hundred years or more. The German population began to grow again after 1470; it grew quite fast in the 16th century, before the epidemics during the Third Years' War, especially plague and typhus, cut it down again to 10 millions or a little more.

Conclusion

The Black Death, i.e. the first great epidemic in the middle of the fourteenth century, which in the next centuries was followed by several other blows, left many cities and areas in Germany and other parts of Central Europe unaffected as shown by recent archive research. Also historians may have paid to little attention to subsequent ravaging epidemics generally.

The bubonic plague which in particular hit China, India, but also Egypt in the nineteenth century, often ends fatally, but is in no way a

---

60. Cf. Wilhelm Roscher, *Ueber Kornhandel und Theuerungspolitik*, (Stuttgart/Tübingen, ³1852), pp. 3-5.
61. Karl Helleiner, 'Europas Bevölkerung im späten Mittelalter', *Mitteilungen des Instituts für österreichische Geschichte* 62, (1954), p. 257, takes demographic losses of one third (1348/50) for "nothing but sheer surmise". Similarly Ernst Schubert, *Einführung in die deutsche Geschichte im Spätmittelalter*, (Stuttgart, ²1998), p. 12.
62. Erich Meuthen, *Das 15. Jahrhundert*. (Oldenbourg Grundriß der Geschichte, vol. 9.), (München/Wien, 1980), pp. 3-5. The demographic development in many European countries reached a nadir only in the 15th century. Cf. Ole Jørgen Benedictow, *Plague in the Late Medieval Nordic Countries. Epidemiological Studies*, (Oslo, 1992), pp. 105 f.

contagious infectious desease. There is nothing astonishing about that because ectoparasites (such as flees) need a rather long transmission time. On the other hand, the Black Death seems to have spread very fast and caused the death of many people, when and where it appeared.

The German demographic losses are hard to estimate. The decline in population in the later Middle Ages was already a fact before 1348 and has largely to be ascribed to other factors. The loss in population as a consequence of the plague did not amount to one third, as is so often read, but was more likely considerably less. Furthermore, at least in Italy, where so many other vertebrates were affected by the epidemic, we have to deal with quite another type of infectious desease such as an outbreak of epidemic caused by a virus.

The Black Death in the North: 1349-1350

By Janken Myrdal, Uppsala

In countries with an abundance of sources, the dramatic years of the Black Death can be described with the help of elaborate chronicles or detailed tax-registers. Italy, France and England are the prime examples, and research on these countries has formed the foundation of broad outlines of the Black Death in Europe.[1]

In countries with a paucity of written data, the situation is different. Instead of concentrating on a few excellent sources, the scholar has to utilize all available data.

In this article, I try to reconstruct the Black Death 1349-50 in Scandinavia, mainly in Sweden, but also in Denmark and Norway (Finland has been left out). Perhaps one could argue that there is no need for investigations on such regions, as we can infer from better-known parts of Europe. Such a standpoint could lead to misinterpretations: for instance, it has been argued that Sweden did not suffer heavily from the Black Death.[2] In another article, I have written about the sequence of major identified

---

1. Recently published are: Samuel K. Cohn, *The Black Death transformed. Disease and Culture in Early Renaissance Europe*, (London, 2002); and Ole Jørgen Benedictow, *The Black Death 1346-53. The Complete History*, (Woodbridge, 2004). They agree on a high mortality, but are deeply divided concerning the nature of the disease, with Cohn arguing against "bubonic plague" as the disease.
2. E. Österberg, 'Methods, hypotheses and study areas', in *Desertion and land colonization in the Nordic countries c. 1300-1600*, (Stockholm, 1981), pp. 55-59.

epidemics in Sweden between 1350 and 1500 (1350, 1359-60, 1368-69, 1413, 1420-21, 1439-40, 1455, 1464-65, 1495).[3]

The research strategy can be labelled "source pluralism", the basic assumption being that a major course of events, such as the Black Death, left an imprint in different sources. None of them will answer the exact question I ask, but they will all give parts of the answer and, besides, reveal other aspects. The basic question in this article is: "when did the Black Death hit the North?" I also want to show that the normal pattern for this, as in all later outbreaks, was that the disease peaked in late summer and during the autumn. The level of mortality will also be touch upon.

I do not discuss the nature of the disease, as my sources have little to say about this. As I understand it, the disease was *either* some sort of plague, not exactly the disease called "bubonic plague" and explored in the early 20th century, *or* another disease with similarities to some sort of plague. For conventional reasons, I will use the label "plague" as the name of the disease. (Identifying the exact microbe that caused the disease will have to await new investigations by archaeologists and natural scientists working together.)

Mentioning the Great Mortality

Traditionally, this pandemic in the Nordic countries, 1349-50, has been described with the help of annals. From this period, we have no chronicles telling a story in a literary stile, though there are such chronicles about earlier periods and about the 15th century.

Most information in the annals is brief, but the Icelandic annals have two lengthy entries on the plague in Norway. A well-known story concerns a ship from England at the quayside in Bergen. Its cargo had already begun to be unloaded as the disease spread from the crew to the townspeople. Iceland itself was spared, due to the halt in ocean-going shipping in 1349-50.

---

3. J. Myrdal, 'The forgotten plague. The Black Death in Sweden', in (ed.) Pekka Hämäläinen, *When Disease makes History. Epidemics and great historical turning points*, (Helsinki, 2006). Here I also include other sources such as miracles, tax registers over individuals, etc. Both articles are based on a book about epidemics, desertion and change of agrarian production in the Late Middle Ages: J. Myrdal, *Digerdöden, pestvågor och ödeläggelse*, (Stockholm, 2003). On Denmark, see Erik Ulsig, 'Pest og befolkningsnedgang i Danmark i det 14. århundrede', *Historisk tidskrift* (Danish) 1991, pp. 21-43 and on Norway, Ole Jørgen Benedictow, *Svartedauden og senere pestepidemier i Norge*, (Oslo, 2002).

From Norway, no medieval annals have survived. Danish contemporary annals are few in number, while from Sweden they are more numerous although most are written some time after the Black Death.

I have presented the information in table 1, excluding annals and chronicles written down after the middle of the 15th century, and also those quoting other earlier annals. In the table, the region and the dating of the annals are given as well as the main information about the plague in addition to mentioning an enormous mortality rate, which they all do. Icelandic annals also describe the disease, and name important clergy who succumbed to itdisease. This information was written by Icelandic clerics who had close contacts with Norway, but they mainly report about Western Norway and seldom mention anything from Eastern Norway.

That the annals do not present the "truth" is a truism; what they describe are the rumours and memories related in the late 14th and early 15th centuries.

Table 1. Annals on the Black Death in Scandinavia

Region	Dating	Years of plague	Extra information
Icelandic			
Norway	1362-1393	1349	By ship from England to Bergen 2/3 died
Norway	late 13th	1349	many died in Bergen & W. Norway Ship could not sail to Iceland
Danish			
Zealand	late 14th	1348-49	
Scania	late 14th	1350	
Scania*	1420s	1350	1/3 died
Swedish			
?*	late 14th	1350	1/3 died
?	late 14th	1350	
?	late 14th	1350	cattle plague
Östergötl	early 15th	1350	prophesy by Holy Bridget
Gotland	1410s	1350	
Uppland*	ca 1420	1350	5/6 died
Östergötl	ca 1430	1350	
Östergötl	1446	1350	
Stockholm*	mid 15th	1350	cattle plague

Sources: Ulsig, 1991, p. 22; Myrdal, 2003, p. 25, 38-44; Benedictow, 2004, p. 154-55.

Annals marked with stars in the table have a chronogram, a poem where capital letters express the year: *Mors CeCat CeLos/ditans orbem spoilavit* = **MCCCL** (1350). Translated, this is: the blind death has enriched heaven (with souls) and destroyed the world.[4] The reason for a chronogram is to memorize the year, and it is somewhat easier to construct one about 1350, but in no way impossible to construct a chronogram about an uneven year such as 1349.

The Danish annals from Zealand have two different dates and both appear to be before the actual arrival of the disease in 1350. Misdating has been suggested, but the annals were written soon after the plague and they are held to be reliable. This information about the plague in the annal is from the end of the years 1348 and 1349, which is also in accordance with the prevailing pattern of the plague.[5] Annals from Eiersted in Southern Jutland, written late in the 15th century, relate that more than ¾ of the population died in The Great Mortality in 1350, which occurred before November 11th that year. However, the information from the 15th century in the Eiderstedt annals is not as reliable as that from the 14th century.[6]

From Norway, two medieval pieces of information have been preserved in copies from the 16th to the 18th century. Both are from inland Eastern Norway, and both talk about the autumn of 1350 as the time of the plague. Modern scholars have declared that this date is incorrect, but one should hesitate to talk about misdating just because facts do not fit into the preconceived pattern.[7] In a medieval register over Norwegian Archbishops, Arne Einarsson, who according to Icelandic annals died in the Black Death, is said to have succumbed in October 1349.[8]

Very few contemporaneous letters talk explicitly about the plague. A charter from the autumn of 1349, probably issued late in September in Western Sweden (Lödöse at the coast), is of importance. The king of Norway and Sweden, Magnus Eriksson, gave instructions about remedies to be undertaken before the Great Mortality, which was approaching (namely, gifts to be given to the churches). The letter also contains a

---

4. About this chronogram, Myrdal 2003, p. 42.
5. Ulsig 1991, p. 22, cf. Myrdal 2003, p. 25; Benedictow 2004, pp. 159-160.
6. Johannes Jasper, *Chronicon Eiderstadense vulgare oder die gemeine Eiderstedtische Chronik 1103-1547*, (St. Peter-Ording, 1977), pp. 26-27.
7. Benedictow 2002, pp. 58-59, 63, cf. Myrdal 2003, p. 22.
8. *Monumenta historica Norgeviæ. Latinske kildeskrifter*, (ed.) G. Storm (Kristiania, 1880), p. 190. In a will Arne is said to have been alive 10/17 1349, his own testament is from September.

description of the disease, and it says that half the population died, and that it was already in Norway and in Halland, on the west coast of what is today Southern Sweden. This gives some support to the Zealand annals about a plague in Southern Scandinavia as early as in 1349.[9]

The king also sent a letter to the pope in Avignon. This letter has not been preserved, but three answers from Clement VI, issued on March 14-15th 1351, have. Magnus Eriksson's letter was most probably sent in the second half of 1350. The king excuses his inability to crusade against Russia, and explains that the disease had emptied his country of able men.[10]

Another reference to the Black Death comes from Visby, a thriving Hanseatic town, situated in the middle of the Baltic on the island Gotland. In two letters to Rostock and Lübeck, the council of Visby wrote that they had arrested and in July, 1350, burnt at the stake some foreigners, who had poisoned the wells in the town and on the island with the aim of spreading the disease. This was a part of the pogroms in Europe, and the letters state that the foreigners were not Jews, but that they had admitted that they had acted on behalf of the Jews. As there were no Jews at all in the Nordic countries at this time, substitutes had to be found to organize a pogrom. An interesting fact is that the first cases of the disease, according to these letters, were reported in May, 1350, on northern Gotland.[11]

These two Visby letters, and the first preserved letters from the king, were all written before the plague broke out at full scale, and were thus dictated more by the fear of an approaching disease, than by an ongoing epidemic.

Other letters give uncertain hints. A few Swedish wills from late 1350 have extra sinister formulations about dark and hard times, besides the ordinary lamentations over the inevitability of death.[12] Ole Jørgen Benedictow points to a donation to St. Sebastian in February, 1349, as evidence of plague in Oslo in the autumn of 1348,[13] but this donation could just as

---

9. The text is preserved in a copy from the late 15th century: Michael Nordberg, *I kung Magnus tid*, (Stockholm, 1995), pp. 159-160; Myrdal 2003, pp. 86-87; Benedictow 2004, pp. 152, 160-161, slightly different dating and provenance: early September and inland Sweden instead of the seaport Lödöse.
10. Nordberg 1995, p. 161.
11. Jürgen Ibs, *Die Pest in Schleswig-Holstein von 1350 bis 1547/48*, (Frankfurt am Main, 1994), pp. 162-164.
12. Myrdal 2003, pp. 88-89.
13. Benedictow 2002, p. 53. Two letters from 1349 concern the St. Sebastian altar, from 2/20 and 10/3.

well have been made when rumours of the disease were heard. In Jutland, a letter from May, 1350, about the plundering of churches has been seen as an indication of disorder after the plague,[14] but this interpretation of the connection with the plague is highly dubious. Times were not peaceful even before the disease.

Immediately after the Great Mortality, letters mention decreasing rents and falling prices of land as well as a shortage of parish priests. Then, and for more than a hundred years, the dramatic years of the Black Death continued to be a reference point in a number of situations, for instance, in disputes over land, when old men could tell the judge that "this had been so-and-so since The Great Mortality".[15]

To summarize, the Black Death struck Western Norway in 1349, Eastern Norway in 1350?, central Denmark (Zealand, Halland) in 1348-49?, Southern Jutland in the autumn of 1350, Sweden in 1350, Gotland with early cases in May and mass-hysteria in July, 1350.

INDICATIONS OF MORTALITY

This group of sources concerns the dating of a person's death, as in the *register of deaths* and *tombstones*, or dating of a person's fear of death, as in *testaments* and many of the donations.

Registers of deaths were kept in monasteries and churches to keep track of donors, and especially their day of death so as to know when to say prayers for their souls. Most of the registers are from Denmark, from: Ribe in Southern Jutland, Roskilde on Zealand, Lund in Scania and a short death-register from Copenhagen on Zealand.

---

14. Kai Hørby, *Danmarkshistorie 5: Velstands krise og tusind baghold*, (Copenhagen, 1993), p. 209.
15. Examples from letters and accounts in Myrdal 2003, pp. 89-92, 100-102; Ole Jørgen Benedictow, *Plague in the Late Medieval Nordic Countries*, (Oslo, 1992), pp. 94-98, has used six letters, written years after the Black Death, where the "summer" or "autumn" of the plague are mentioned, to construct the exact spread through Norway in detailed maps. These maps are reproduced in Benedictow 2002, p. 51. The maps must be considered highly speculative, and actually not reliable. See review of Benedictow in Erik Ulsig, 'Plague in the Late Medieval Nordic Countries', *Historisk tidskrift* (Norwegian) 1994.

Table 2 Registers of deaths in Medieval Denmark

	Ribe	Roskilde	Lund	Copenhagen	Total
Per year					
1340-49	1.5	1.3	1.1	0.4	4.3
1347	0	0	0	0	0
1348	1	0	3	1	5
1349	2	2	4	1	9
1350	17	6	6	3	32
1351	0	1	1	1	3
1352	0	1	2	0	3

Source: Ulsig, 1991, p. 37 (Ribe, Roskilde); Myrdal, 2003, p. 59 (Lund), *Scriptores Rerum Danicarum* 8, Copenhagen, 1834, pp. 538-549 (Copenhagen), cf. Ulsig, 1991, p. 38.

For the whole period 1301-1390, Ribe has 122 entries, Roskilde 107, Lund 95 and Copenhagen 33 (a total average of 4.0 per year). Until 1340, the archdiocese Lund had more entries than Ribe and Roskilde, but fewer after 1340.[16] This table seems to give some support to claims of an early attack of the plague in 1348-49 in the centre of Denmark, around Lund. A problem with this interpretation is that 9 of the deaths in 1348-49 occur during the first half of the year, most of them in April-May, which is not according to the prevailing pattern of the plague. In 1350, the deaths in Lund occurred in January and in October-November (and one in May). Intensive trade through the Sound could have brought forerunners of the major outbreak of the disease to the region, but this is only conjecture.

In Ribe and Roskilde, we find the normal pattern of the plague, a marked concentration in late summer and early autumn, 1350: in Ribe with 3 in July, 6 in August, and one each in September, October and December; in Roskilde with 5 in October and in Copenhagen with one in August and one in September.

The Franciscan monastery in Visby, Gotland, kept two death-registers, one was a burial-register the other a register of donors. The burial register has regular entries from 1324 until 1350, but no exact dating. It covers four categories of persons buried: townspeople (194), monks at the

---

16. Ibs 1994, p. 87, argues that in 1350 in Ribe, the number should be 16 and not 17, cf. Ulsig 1991, p. 22.

monastery (84), parish priests (14) and other people in the countryside (30). The last-mentioned group was certainly wealthy peasants as there was no nobility on the island. From around 1340, an increasing number of townspeople were registered, and the average number of entries rose from around four to more than ten. (After 1350 the register seems to have become disarranged, and cannot be followed from year to year.)

Table 3 Burial register in Visby

Per year	Visby	Countryside	Total
1340-49	9.3	1.3	10.7
1348	6	2	8
1349	7	0	7
1350	142	11	153

Source: Myrdal, 2003, p. 57.

Both townspeople and monks had a higher mortality rate than parish priests and others in the countryside. In the town, the increase was 13-16 fold, and in the countryside 8-9 fold. The other register, of donors, starts in 1348 with 1 donor, and the next entries consist of 14 donors registered in 1350. Exact dates are given: 1 died in July, 9 in August, and 1 in September, October and November.[17]

From Norway only a few remnants of death-registers have been preserved, and in one of them the bishop of Stavanger's date of death is January 7th, and in an Icelandic annals the bishop, Guðþormr Pálsson, is said to have died during the Black Death 1349, but Norwegian historians instead often give 1/7, 1350 as his date of death.[18]

Wills and testaments have long been one of the main sources for the Black Death in Europe. A known source-critical problem is that wills could be drawn up even if the donor was not sick or dying. For instance the archbishop of Norway issued his last will in 9/23, 1349, when he declared himself to be in god health, and he died a month later.

In the Nordic countries, no specific lists of testaments were kept, and they have to be searched for among charters and letters. The last will as

---

17. Myrdal 2003, pp. 56-57, 145.
18. *Monumenta historica Norgeviæ*, p. 197, cf. Benedictow 2002, pp. 77-78.

a specific form of document was introduced in the Nordic countries in the 13th century, in the early 14th century, at least in Sweden, they tended to merge with donations due to legal conflicts over the right to donate landed property and later as an adaptation to the Swedish legal system. Only documents about more expensive donations, namely, landed property, have been preserved.[19]

For Sweden, I thus chose to count documents containing donations to religious institutions, with a number of delimitations to identify donors who gave out of fear of impending death and purgatory. Accordingly, I did not include donations given when a person was taken into a monastery (most of them women) or donations given by the king or queen (most often gifts for political reasons). Furthermore, I did not include donations given by people from abroad, as they did not indicate domestic mortality. Another category excluded is land transactions when the price is said to be adjusted to give advantages to the church for religious reasons. Finally, I had a group resembling last wills or testaments, presented in table 4a. Among these documents, I have separated those where the donor stated that he or she, although sane in mind, was sick in body, "corpore debilis". All today's regions in Sweden have been included, including, for instance, Scania (formerly Danish).[20]

Danish testaments up to 1450 have been published by Erslev, but with a more narrow demarcation than mine. Benedictow has counted donations to religious institutions, but his demarcations are not clearly stated.[21] Norwegian charters and letters are all published, and donations

---

19. Published in the series *Diplomatarium Suecanum*, (Stockholm, 1844- (until 1375)), *Diplomatarium Danicarum*, (Copenhagen, 1938- (until 1400), 1400-1410 published on the net: http://www.diplomatarium.danicum.dk). All Swedish documents on: http://www.ra.se/ra/diplomat.html. Literature about Sweden: Anna Wásko, *Frömmigkeit und Ritteridee im Lichte der schwedishen ritterlichen Testamente aus dem 14. Jahrhundert*, (Kraków, 1996); Myrdal 2003, pp. 118-130; on Denmark: Lars Bisgaard, *Tjenesteideal og fromhedsideal*, (Århus, 1988), Per Ingesman, 'Kanniketestamenter fra dansk senmiddelalder som social- og kulturhistorisk kilde', *Kirkehistoriske samlinger* 1987, pp. 203-232; Ole Bay, 'Donationer til kirken i dansk senmiddelalder', in Per Ingesman & J.V. Jensen (eds.), *Danmark i senmiddelalderen*, (Århus, 1994), pp. 317-341.
20. Myrdal 2003, pp. 134-139, nine different criteria. Also in Myrdal 2003, pp. 126-132, 251-254, there I also give statistics for all known "testaments", 1405, in Sweden 1250-1400. This, however, also includes later confirmations, and is thus a more blunt indication of mortality per year.
21. K. Erslev, *Testamenter fra Danmarks Middelalder indtil 1450*, (Copenhagen, 1901);

have been counted for this article with the same method as for the Swedish donations.²²

In the table below, different measures are presented: testaments and letters with donations to religious institutions for Denmark; letters with donations and of them those made by sick donors for Sweden. There is a certain amount of overlapping since documents from Scania are registered among both Danish and Swedish testaments and letters of donation.²³ Norway is presented in a separate table, as the plague struck earlier.

Table 4a. Letters and charters indicating mortality

	Denmark Testaments	donations	Sweden donations	sick donors
Per year				
1340-49	0.5	6.4	7.3	1.1
1348	0	7	6	0
1349	0	13	10	0
1350	4	31	34	6
1351	2	-	14	3
1352	1	-	7	2

Source: Erslev. 1901. pp. 81-110; Benedictow 2004 p. 160; Myrdal 2003. p 139, for this article 1340 has also been included, source: *Diplomatarium Suecanum*.

Benedictow 2004, pp. 165-167; Bay 1994, p. 318, presented a table showing donations to religious institutions, but unfortunately not for single years, the period 1340-49 had 14 and 1350-59 had 29.

22. *Diplomatarium Norvegicum*, (Kristiania/Oslo, 1849-1975), and: http://www.dokpro.uio.no/dipl_norv/diplom_felt.html.

23. Benedictow 2004, pp. 174-176 also has a presentation of a similar investigation for Sweden. Benedictow, excluding Scania, arrived at an average of 7.1 for the years 1341-49, and for single years: 5 in 1348, 7 in 1349 and 28 in 1350. The results are close to my investigation, but statistics based on medieval sources tend to give different results for different scholars, as reflection over every single document is involved in the counting. I note that as early as in 1999, I presented the investigation of donations to religious institutions in 1341-70 as a sign of morality in Janken Myrdal, *Jordbruket under feodalismen*, (Stockholm, 1999), p. 116.

Table 4b Letters and charters indicating mortality, Norway

	Donations	sick donors
Per year		
1339-1348	0.7	0.3
1347	0	0
1348	2	0
1349	10	4
1350	0	0
1351	0	0

Source: *Diplomatarium Novegicum*

The increase in the number of letters of donation in Sweden in 1349 does not correspond to an increase of the number of sick donors, and the increase as early as in 1349 is probably due to the rumours and fear of the approaching disease. An obvious parallel is the king's letter from September, 1349. The Danish increase in the number of donations in 1349 could have the same cause, and we cannot say anything about an early outbreak in Denmark on the basis of these documents.

The most reliable sign of disease is sick donors: from Norway 2 in August, one in October and one in November 1349;[24] From Sweden in 1350 4 in September, one in October and one in November.[25] Letters of donation are from roughly the same periods.

---

24. Of the Norwegian letters of donation 9 are from the second half of the year: 1 in January, 4 in September, 2 in October, 2 in November, 1 in December 1349. Benedictow 1992, pp. 50, 280-281; Benedictow 2002, pp. 64-65, 75, 78 presents five testaments from 1339-1348 (one of them a donation from the king, not included in table 4b), and from 1349 9 testaments, 8 of them from September to November. Grethe Authen Blom, *Norge i union på 1300-tallet*, (Oslo, 1992), p. 559 has included a register not presented in *Diplomatarium Norvegicum* and she has 14 donations to religious institutions from 1349, of them 1 from the spring, 10 from September until the end of the year and 3 undated. She does not give numbers about the foregoing years.
25. Swedish letters of donation are concentrated to the second half of the year: 4 in August, 5 in September, 3 in October, 5 in November and 2 in December, Myrdal 2003, p. 150; Benedictow 2004, p. 176, has a similar table, but he has included several endowments in connection with women's entry into nunneries, definitely not sick or dying. On the other hand, he has overlooked documents published in a complementary volume of *Diplomatarium Suecanum*.

Geographical provenance is important for identifying the spread of the disease. In Norway letters normally state where they where issued, and most of them are from towns along the coast, from Trondheim in the North to Oslo in the southeast, the earliest from Bergen 9/19.[26]

In Sweden most of the letters do not state the place where they were issued. I have tried to identify the manor or farm where the donor lived, but there is still uncertainty as to the exact place where he or she issued the document. We can only get a rough idea of where the disease struck. In Sweden, the epidemic afflicted the whole country, from Scania and Småland in the south to Uppland, from September to November.[27] In Denmark, Jutland seems to have been hit at about the same period.[28]

Tombstones as a source for mortality and epidemics have not been widely used in Europe, perhaps because most other countries have better sources. However, tombstones have certain advantages: they give the date for the time of the death, and they give a clue about provenance, even if the dead body could have been transported over some distance. I have

Table 5. Tombstones from Medieval Sweden

Per year	Mainland	Gotland	Total
1340-49	1.9	2.1	4,0
1348	2	3	5
1349	2	0	2
1350	5	14	19

Source: Myrdal, 2003, p. 60-64.

---

26. Bergen 3 in September (2 sick); Trondheim 1 in September and 1 in October (sick); Oslo 1 in October; Tönsberg 2 in November (1 sick), cf. Benedictow 2002, pp. 65, 74-75, 351.
27. Myrdal 2003, pp. 150-51. Among the sick: Småland, 2 in September; Uppland, 1 in September, 1 in November; Södermanland, 1 in September; Scania, 1 in October. The principal regions for all letters of donation during the peak of the epidemic were: 3 in Scania in September-October; 4 in Småland in August-September; 4 in eastern-central Sweden, that is, Uppland, Södermanland and Västmanland, in September-November; other regions are only represented by 1-2 cases.
28. Benedictow identifies provenance with the help of the landed property donated, and Benedictow 2004, p. 167 gives 3 cases for Jutland in August-October.

only studied this source for Sweden, not including Scania. Many of the tombstones are from Gotland in the Baltic, and this island is a "museum" of the High Middle Ages. From the Late Middle Ages, trade passed by Visby as it went directly across the Baltic, and the town was left with its monuments and memories.

All of the five tombstones on the mainland with the date 1350 are from the cathedral in Uppsala, and they date from August to November. One of them is that of a parish priest in Västmanland, the region immediately west of Uppland, who, three days before he died, drew up a testament in which he declared himself to be "mente et corpore sanus". Death struck fast. Of the tombstones from Gotland in 1350, four have no precise dating, while 8 are from August and 3 from September. Nine of the tombstones on Gotland are from Visby. (An interesting fact is that the number of tombstones made after the Black Death decreased, as did many other investments in sculpture, paintings and building in the Swedish churches.)

To summarize these indications, the epidemic struck Western Norway from September, 1349 to December 1349/January, 1350 (death-register, donations: none of them from late 1350); Southern Jutland in July-August, 1350 (death-register, donations); central Denmark (Zealand) from August to October, 1350 (death-registers); Scania perhaps already in late 1349, but certainly in October-November, 1350 (death-register, sick donor); Gotland from July to November, 1350 with a peak in August-September (death-register, tombstones); Eastern Central Sweden (Uppland, Södermanland, Västmanland) from August to November (sick donors, tombstones), and Småland in the South of Medieval Sweden from August to September (sick donors and donations).

INDIRECT SOURCES

The next group, indirect sources, give an approximate time for the epidemic, either as a result of disruptions of vital functions in society such as *tax registers* and *the total number of charters and letters*, or by narrowing down the time period for the death of a person, e.g. by using *prosopography*.

No *tax registers* of households in towns, villages or smaller regions have been preserved from the time of the Black Death; instead, Scandinavia has accounts of *Peter's Pence* for five dioceses in Norway and six in Sweden. This was a fee paid to the papacy, which originated in England in Anglo-Saxon times, and spread to countries in Northern and Eastern Europe during the High Middle Ages.[29] In principle, every household in Norway and Sweden had to pay every year, and there has been much discussion of the question of whether this source can be used to estimate the total population. Tax evasion, local regulations, outstanding debts paid later, currency of low value (a common complaint after the Black Death), etc. make such estimates unreliable. Instead, we have to restrict the discussion to changes in payment and their general causes.

The value of Peter's Pence, in "marks" is presented in two diagrams. The "mark" is a coinage of roughly the same value in the Nordic countries, but with regional differences. Registration started in the 1320s, and in the 1330s, the amount paid increased, probably not only because of the growth of the population but also due to more efficient collection of the fee. Often, payment was given for several years in a row and such cases, the average per year has been registered in diagrams. Uppsala and Nidaros/Trondheim were the archdioceses. Gotland is a specific problem, as it belonged to the Linköping diocese, but only paid for a shorter period, and not after 1350. In northernmost Sweden, under the archdiocese of Uppsala, the Peter's Pence was not paid at all.

Diagram 1. Peter's Pence in Swedish dioceses. Upps=Uppsala, Linköp = Linköping, Gotl = Gotland, Sträng = Strängnäs, Väster = Västerås. Source: Myrdal 2003, pp. 36-37.

---

29. *Dictionary of the Middle Ages*, vol. 1-13, (New York, 1982-1989), s.v. "Peter's Pence"; *Lexikon des Mittelalters*, (Stuttgart, 1999), s.v. "Peterspfennig".

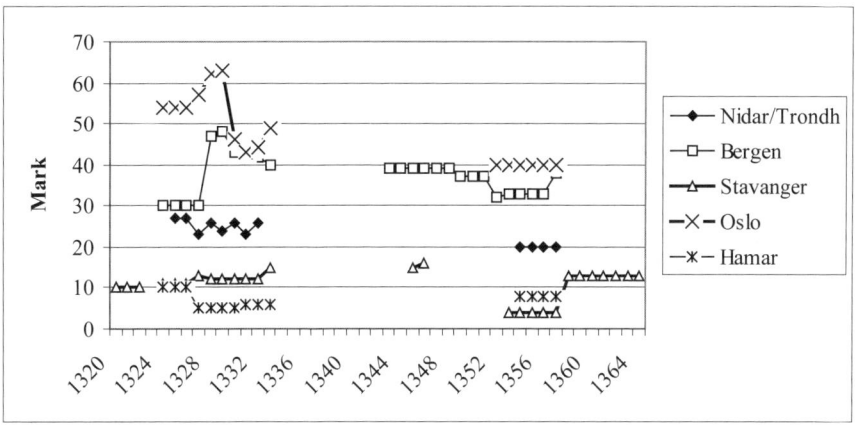

Diagram 2. Peter's Pence in Norwegian dioceses. Nidar/Trondh = Nidaros/Trondheim.
Source: Asgaut Steinnes, Roma-skatt og folketal, *Historisk tidskrift* (Norwegian) 1940-42, p. 167.

The sudden decrease after 1350 is evident in the Swedish dioceses. Norway is more problematic as the decisive 1330s and 1340s to a large extent are lacking. We cannot identify a general decrease in payment after 1349 in Norway even if there is a falling trend from the 1320s to the 1350s.

If we turn to the next source, Norway seems to have been harder hit. That the *number of charters and letters* decreased in Norway after the Black Death has been known for a long time, but it was Grethe Authen Blom who researched the phenomenon. She only counted documents issued in the country. All letters from Avignon or from other foreign countries were excluded (but not, of course, letters from Sweden, as this country was in a personal union together with Norway under King Magnus Eriksson).

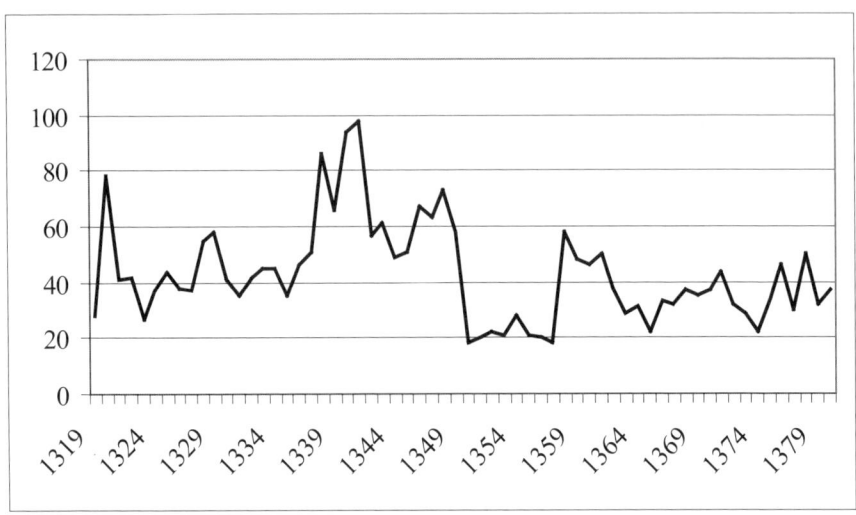

Diagram 3. Charters and letters, Norway.
Source: Blom, 1992, pp. 10-11, table and diagram up to 1349, p. 558, diagram for the period from 1350 and later.

The curve starts with a slight increase over time, and in 1348 over 70 documents have been preserved. Up until July, 1349, everything seemed to function as usual, 30 letters being issued during this first half of the year. In August, 1349 not a single preserved letter was issued, and during the rest of the year only 13 (dated) letters were issued, nearly all of them testaments (the total number of letters from 1349 being 50). The decrease continued in the next year with a total 18 letters from 1350 (though none of them donations) after which a slow recovery started, with a new drop after the epidemic in 1359-60.

Blom's conclusion is that the administration, both clerical and royal, was partly paralysed in the years after the Black Death. She also investigated the geographical distribution of the documents, and the decrease was far from evenly spread over Norway. In Trondheim and Bergen as well as in the countryside surrounding these towns, the decrease of the average number of letters per year from the decades before the Black Death to the decades after was spectacular. Among letters where provenance can be identified, Bergen's share fell from 400 during the first period to 70 during the second, and Trondheim's share fell from 75 to 20. In southern Norway, in Oslo and around the Oslo fjord, the number of charters and letters remained fairly constant during the whole period (after a dip the years around the plague).³⁰ It seems as if the weight of the country tipped southwards.

Interestingly, the decrease continued in 1350, which could have been caused by an ongoing epidemic for two consecutive years. I have looked at letters from Jämtland, a province on the border between Norway and Sweden in the North, and found a similar continuing decrease through 1349 and 1350,³¹ as in Northern and Western Norway.

Estimating the total number of Swedish and Danish charters and letters I have not done such detailed research as Blom did, but instead worked with the total number of published or registered documents in the Swedish and Danish *Diplomatarium*. There is some overlapping as Scania and surrounding provinces are registered in both the Danish and the Swedish collections of documents (actually Scania was a part of Sweden during the decades before the Black Death, even if it normally belonged to Denmark during the Middle ages.)

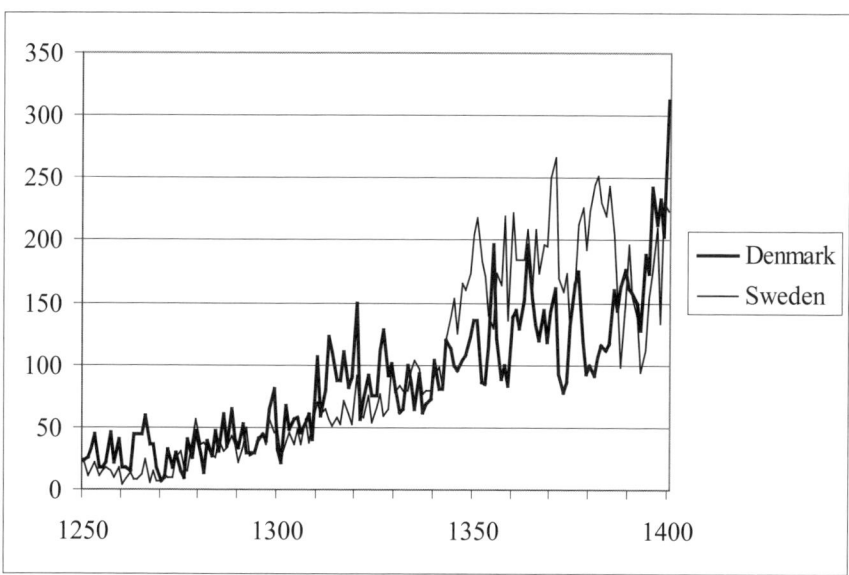

Diagram 4. Charters and letters, Sweden and Denmark.
Sources: For the Sweden table: Myrdal, 2003, pp. 251-256, for Denmark: *Diplomatarium Danicarum*

---

30. Blom 1992, pp. 26-27, 566-567.
31. Myrdal 2003, pp. 114-116.

The two curves follow each other remarkably well. Denmark, the more developed country, took the lead until the early 14th century. Then Sweden took over as a result of a new national law issued around 1347, where two regulations came to be of importance: one was the regulation that all land transactions had to be confirmed in written documents; the other was that documents should preferably be in Swedish and not in Latin. The number of letters and charters written in Swedish increased dramatically, and in a few decades the total dominance of Latin was replaced by the dominance of Swedish. At the same time, charters and letters were used in a more diversified way. However, in the late 14th century Denmark caught up again as regards the number of letters.

In the years after the Black Death, there was no a significant decrease in the number of written documents in either Sweden or Denmark, and, in fact, some types of documents even became more common: testaments as well as litigation concerning landholding during the troubled years after the epidemic. The question is: why was there no breakdown of the administration in Denmark and Sweden as was apparently the case in Northern and Western Norway?

Prosopography is a method, not a source. By tracking individual life stories, one can get an idea of during which period a person passed away, and several life stories makes it possible to roughly identify periods when more people died. Two different kinds of indications can be used. One is the last time the person was engaged in some dated activity, such as signing a charter. The other, especially concerning clerics, is to identify when the person was replaced and not transferred to another position.

It is in the nature of things that this method on the first hand registers the upper class in the medieval society, and it proves that the upper strata generally fared better then poor people. England, where the source situation is much better than in the Nordic countries, has a clear difference: Among the general population, mortality could reach 40-50%, while among the higher nobility and bishops mortality stayed at 15-25%.[32]

I have only carried out preliminary studies and much remains to be done. The first step is to find a well-defined group among the upper strata of society. At the top of the clergy hierarchy we find the bishops, and of the eight bishops in Sweden (including Scania and Finland) all survived the Black Death. For two dioceses, Strängnäs and Västerås, I have followed

---

32. Benedictow 2004, p. 264, 343, further examples and discussion about social differences in mortality Cohn 2003, pp. 50, 127, 204-205.

the canons, and about three quarters of them survived through the years around 1350. The most powerful members of the high nobility belonged to the King's council. There were 15 of them and 12 survived the plague, while two of those who passed away were quite old and could have died of other diseases. The royal family is a less well-defined group, but few of them died (only two half-brothers of the King).[33] It seems that the upper class in Sweden survived rather well during the crisis.

Peter's Pence gives some idea of general mortality, especially in Sweden with continuous data from 1320s to 1350s. The decrease was 40-45% after 1350 (from a total of 221 to 129 marks), and even if this cannot be translated into population figures, it proves that general mortality was higher than prosopography shows for the upper strata of society.

This low mortality among the upper class (in Sweden) also implies that in countries where only a few rich persons draw up their final wills writing, as in most of Scandinavia, the increase in donations to religious institutions cannot be used as an indication of general mortality.

In Norway the situation seems to have been different. Of the five Norwegian bishops only one (in Oslo) survived the plague according to the Icelandic annals. The prosopographic method gives the more precise picture. During the years 1346-1348 no bishops died, in late 1349 4 died, in 1350 2, and in late 1351 one, thereafter it was not until 1355 before any of the bishops in Norway died.[34] The two who died 1350 are from inland and southern Norway, which gives some support to Norwegian annals talking about The Great Mortality in inland Norway in 1350. Of 12 canons in Trondheim, just one survived the plague according to the Icelandic annals, and using prosopography none can be proved to have been alive after the plague.[35] It seems that the top clergy in Norway was hard hit, but more investigations are needed before we can draw any further conclusions.

Summarizing these sources, it seems as if Norway was ravaged by the catastrophe through 1349 and 1350, and it could have started in August (no letters preserved). Apparently, the administration of the country

---

33. Myrdal 2003, pp. 93-97.
34. Oluf Kolsrud, *Den norske Kirkes erkebiskoper og biskoper indtil reformationen*, (*Diplomatarium Norvegicum* 17B), (Kristiania, 1913), pp. 207, 224, 235, 243-44, 254. Death dates for Norwegian bishops: *Trondheim*: -October 1349 (after 10/17)/-8/14 1370/; *Bergen*: -1349/-3/14 1369/; *Stavanger*: -1/7 1350/-1350/-10/7 1355/; *Oslo*: after 8/23 1351, before November/ -1358-59/; *Hamar*: -1349/-1350/-1363/.
35. Benedictow 2002, pp. 61-82; Blom 1992, p. 550.

was shattered and it was only in the south that it could be reconstructed. Could one reason be that the upper strata of society were harder hit than in neighbouring Sweden?

Conclusion

Western Norway was hit in 1349. The earliest documentary evidence is from Bergen, and perhaps the Icelandic annals were mainly right: it came from England, and it spread all along the coast during the autumn of 1349. We have no detailed information about eastern Norway, but probably the whole country was ravaged during 1349, and parts of it also during the following year.

The Black Death had reached northern Germany at the end of the summer of 1350.[36] From there, it spread to southern Jutland, and probably also to the harbours along the Baltic west coast in July-August, 1350, and from them to the interior of Sweden. This was a pattern found in many later epidemics in the region.[37] Evidence from Småland could indicate that the Great Mortality also spread along inland routes in Southern Sweden. The centre of Denmark, around the Sound, is still a problem. Did forerunners of the epidemic strike as early as in 1349? In Scania, in 1350, it seems to have peaked rather late, in October-November.

There are other pieces of the picture, such as a decrease in building activity in Northern Sweden, proved by dendrochronology, which shows that the Black Death ravaged also these parts of the country even if no written documents can prove it.[38] And still much remains to be done, especially in research on life stories in order to investigate differences in upper-class mortality between Norway and Sweden.

The total loss of population in the North was probably at the same level as in the rest of Europe. Migration started, from poorer regions to richer, from smaller farms to larger farms: much of Norway lost population and the plains in Denmark and Sweden gained relatively speaking.

---

36. Ibs 1994, pp. 79-89.
37. Edward Eckert, *The Structure of Plagues and Pestilences in Early Modern Europe: Central Europe 1560-1640*, (Basel, 1996), pp. 76-77.
38. Myrdal 2003, p. 214.

Map 1. Towns and provinces mentioned in the text.

Map 2. Dioceses in Sweden and Norway.

Danish Plague Patterns, 1360-1500

By Lars Bisgaard, Odense

"There is something rotten in the State of Denmark", goes a well-known phrase. This seems an almost prophetic statement about the Danish archives, in which very few documents from the Middle Ages, and not nearly as many as in most western European countries, have been preserved. Whether the reason for this is to be found in an absolutist monarchy's centralisation of institutions around Copenhagen, where war, fires and other incidents led to widespread loss of documents, or whether the administrative structure of the Danish medieval period relied upon oral agreements for longer than other places, need not detain us. It can merely be noted that the two explanations are by no means mutually exclusive.

Our point of departure should be the fact that, with regard to Denmark, sources illustrating the extent and consequences of the Black Death are few and far between. There are so few, in fact, that for a long time any discussion of the plague's significance could be dismissed by simply casting doubt on whether the epidemic even reached Denmark in the mid-fourteenth century. Here it has been of great significance that the plague has been reassessed on an international level, and is now seen as an indispensable factor behind the great changes that materialised in European societies in the fourteenth and fifteenth centuries. In a strictly Danish context, Ulsig's article on the plague from 1991 is pivotal:[1] Using

---

1. Erik Ulsig, 'Pest og befolkningsnedgang i Danmark i det 14. Århundrede',

studies of surviving obituaries from Ribe and other Cathedral towns, he argues that the plague did come to Denmark, and is thereby a decisive factor in the decrease in population. In Danish plague research, the plague's first impact in the years 1349 to 1350 has by far overshadowed the recurrent bouts of the plague which, as we know from domestic and foreign sources, appeared in the following centuries. The sparse remarks in sources regarding the plague in the fifteenth century have never been compiled, and the epidemic in Copenhagen in 1553-54 is the first to have made its mark in literature.[2] The focus of the present article is to pinpoint possible Danish epidemics in the period of time between 1360 and 1500. The epidemic in 1349-1350 is deliberately excluded, since it is already thoroughly described.[3] There are several reasons for dating these later epidemics as precisely as possible. First of all, it is of course crucial to clarify whether such plague epidemics ever hit Denmark. Secondly, dating them would mean that we can take a fresh look at other material. Finally, assessing the significance of later plague epidemics in relation to the first one is evidently relevant.

DEEDS OF GIFT AND PLAGUE EPIDEMICS

In 1988, Samuel S. Cohn's extensive book on testaments from Siena through almost 600 years from 1205 to the year 1800[4] was published. Here he argues that isolated incidents could lead to significant changes in the gift giving pattern of a given age. For Cohn, the Black Death was such a single factor. It didn't make a lasting mental impact the first time, but it did so after Siena was struck by the plague around 1360-63, the

---

      Historisk Tidsskrift, (1991), pp. 21-43. ("Plague and decrease in population in Denmark in the fourteenth century")

2. 'Tre breve fra Peder Godske angaaende Pesten i Kjøbenhavn 1553', meddelt af N. Jacobsen, ('Three letters from Peder Godske regarding the plague in Copenhagen in 1553'), *Danske Samlinger*, vol. 3, (1867-68), pp. 69-83. F. Skrubbeltrang, *Det danske landbosamfund 1500-1800*, (*Danish Rural Society*), (Copenhagen, 1978), pp. 61-63 provides an overview of the plague epidemics for the sixteenth and seventeenth centuries.
3. Latest dealt with in Ole J. Benedictow, *The Black Death 1346-1353. The Complete History*, (Woodbridge, 2004), pp. 159-169.
4. Samuel K. Cohn, *Death and Property in Siena, 1205-1800. Strategies for the Afterlife*, (Baltimore and London, 1988), for the following see esp., pp. 2-5 and Part 1.

argument being that while a single occurrence of some terrible disease may be interpreted as a whim of nature, there is surely a reason behind two succeeding epidemics. People always took precautions. In this sense the book was a contribution challenging the *Annales School* and its use and interpretation of serial documents. The notion of *la longue durée* predates the investigation, Cohn claims, and is not something an investigation into serial documents would in itself necessarily lead to.

However, it is not on this point alone that the book achieved its significance, but rather for its new line of thought within plague research. It showed quite clearly that donations to the church could be studied and used as sources regarding the precautions the common man took in relation to the plague. The very number of testaments from a given year could thereby be interpreted as an indication of whether society had been struck by unusual occurrences such as an epidemic. At the same time, the book pointed out that not only material conditions changed after the plague: so did their way of looking upon the world. Many new investigations have since seen the light of day. In this context, it is particularly interesting to point out that in areas such as Scandinavia, where there are, generally speaking, few remaining records, the source material through which to study the plague was suddenly greatly increased. It was demonstrated that there were other means than just mapping out the number of derelict farms.

Janken Myrdal has recently described this development as a step towards a pluralistic approach to the plague and has argued that the more the signs found in different source groups concur, the more certainly may we determine whether or not a plague epidemic has struck a given area.[5] By means of this method, he has investigated how the plague hit Sweden and Finland from the first severe blow until about 1500. Jürgen Ibs has done the same for the area of Schleswig-Holstein, inspired by the research carried out in Norway by Ole J. Benedictow and others.[6]

For a Danish survey, this means investigations are to be coordinated with substantiated statements regarding times in which we may be confident there has been plague in regions bordering the kingdom of Denmark.

---

5. Janken Myrdal, 'The Forgotten Plague: The Black Death in Sweden', in Pekka Hämäläinen (ed.), *When Disease Makes History*, (Helsinki, 2006), p. 144. Cf. J. Myrdal, *Digerdöden, pestvågor och ödeläggelse*, Stockholm 2003.
6. Jürgen H. Ibs, *Die Pest in Schleswig-Holstein von 1350 bis 1547/48*, (Frankfurt am Main, 1994).

Therefore, by articulating the available material concerning Danish donations, establishing an overview of the distributions given over time, we may be able to compare this material with that of neighbouring regions. If there are concurrent culminations for certain years, this would be an indication that Denmark has been struck by the plague in those years. We would furthermore be able to assess how it was distributed within the country in order to obtain an indication as to whether the plague struck on a national, or merely a local scale.

The challenge for such an investigation in Scandinavia, however, is that we do not have surviving documents which may be seen as serial. The closest we get are the number of privately bought masses for the soul (endowments) from the later Middle Ages. In the following, along with the much fewer testaments, these will be our main source.

Deeds of Gift and Statistics

It is no easy task to find and separate the Danish deeds of gift from 1360 to 1500 from the source material as a whole. Most of the letters concern endowments for perpetual masses. Such masses can vary in frequency, from daily readings to annual remembrances of donators. The reasons behind the perpetual masses were also varied. They may have been established in gratitude for some joyous occurrence, they may have been part of a long-term family strategy with the choice of specific convents or churches, they may have been an attempt to avert evil, both in this world and in the beyond, etc. Declarations of intent regarding the endowment are also to be found, and are in such cases often concurrent with the enrolment of the benefactor as a lay brother/lay sister in a convent specifying how they are to be provided for. Perpetual masses were, in other words, not only established in connection with deaths, although their essence was the promise of an advantage in the afterlife. Seen in connection with the plague, this means that they would often be established when the rumour of plague spread, or after deaths have occurred where the bereft wish to help the deceased in the afterlife. Therefore a certain chronological spread in and around the time of a plague epidemic is to be expected. These various forms of masses for the soul are all included in the following tables.

Testaments are special deeds of gift. While the endowments can be regarded as one gift, concerning the donor's relationship to one specific ecclesiastical institution, the testament is characterised by the very opposite. It typically contains many gifts to heterogeneous institutions. In this sense, it may be claimed that the testament expresses the attitude of the giver in its entirety concerning churches, convents and other pious institutions such as hospitals and fraternities. Be that as it may, for this investigation testaments will be regarded as one gift and one gift only, because it is the overall number of deeds of gift per year that is to be estimated.

For both testaments and perpetual masses, it is the case that throughout the period they were part of one's general preparations for death, and were not exclusively connected to the actual time of death. Chantries may be included in testaments, not least the older ones. But over time, it became more usual to issue separate documents for masses for the soul, as a result of which their mention in the testaments slipped into the background.[7] There are but few preserved testaments in Denmark. The reason is hard to determine. Perhaps part of the explanation is that since testaments to a lesser and lesser extent included the transference of land and real estate, it was not to the same extent necessary for ecclesiastical institutions to preserve them. Against this it may be argued that, although the same is presumably the case abroad, many testaments have nonetheless been passed on. This leads us to another explanation. Many testaments from e.g. Italian, French and German towns have been passed on through civil registration and not through ecclesiastical archives. In Danish law, there was no requirement for civil authorities to register testaments. The only place where such a registration may be found is on the small island of Femern. With regards to ecclesiastical matters, this island belonged to the diocese of Odense, but because the island is geographically close to Lübeck, it became strongly influenced by the judicial conditions there, and the council in the main town of the island, Burgh, demanded knowledge of incoming testaments. Almost 10% of the preserved Danish testaments of the time thereby originate from this tiny town. These two factors put together are presumably the reason why so few Danish testaments from the middle ages have survived. However, in comparison to the other Scandinavian countries, there is a high frequency of testaments in Denmark.

As long as endowments and testaments are kept, either the original, a copy, or in an extensive account, the counting of them is fairly reliable. The real problems emerge if we involve the large amount of material known through registration or other reference. We could of course

---

7. Lars Bisgaard, '"Med slægtens samtykke" Det adelige testamente 1340-1559' ('By approval of the family', The testament of the nobility 1340-1559'), in Ingesman & Jensen (eds.), *Riget, Magten og Æren. Den danske adel. 1350-1650 (The Kingdom, the Power and the Glory)*, (Århus, 2001), pp. 191-213.

refrain from using such testimonies, but the result would be that the present investigation could at any time be rejected on the grounds of it's not being representative.

The deeds of gift still in existence only constitute a small portion of the ecclesiastical institutions' letters that we have knowledge of. Many of the ecclesiastical letter books have been written down at a late period and only note briefly what old or new letters are about. In the worst cases, the writer has abridged the content of a letter to who gave what and when. The gift book from the rich Benedictine convent of St. Peder's in Næstved from 1528 is a good example of this.[8] However, the situation is that we do not have the majority of the letter books from Danish convents in the middle ages, and the only registrations to have been kept are composed by royal officials some generations after the Reformation.[9] Such writers had an even more distant relationship to the content. The laconic formulation could for instance be "An old deed of gift in Latin. 1374."

In Table 2-4 below, this registration material is included and is listed in its own respective columns for deeds of gift and testaments referred to. The figures given have been found by listing registers in which the word "give" or variations such as "donate" and "grant" appear. The disadvantage is that more than just perpetual masses are thus registered. This concerns e.g. the sending of sons or daughters to monasteries or nunneries. The word "give" was generally speaking a word with positive connotations, and many acts which we would term differently could be either tailored to fit or else be already found within the basic meaning of to "give". An example of this could be the transference of land to a convent because the giver throughout his life has leased part of its land. Today, we would call this a rental agreement, but at the time it was an expression of friendship between two parties, and between friends only favours and gifts are exchanged.

The excessive figures on that account are presumably counter-balanced by the deeds of gift that are not recorded. This could be deeds and other transferences of land which figure under this name in the registers, but in reality may very well be related to the establishment of masses. The alternative would have been to include all deeds in the account and consequently have warned against too high and inflated figures.

Regarding the testaments, the imprecision is of a different nature. First of all, the term testament is not necessarily used when such an item

---

8. *SRD: Scriptores rerum Danicarum medii ævi*, I-IX, (Copenhagen, 1772-1878), IV.
9. *ÆA: De ældste danske Archivregistraturer*, I-V, (Copenhagen, 1854-1910).

is mentioned. A number of synonyms for this term exist, in itself a sign that its idea as such had caught on. These could be expressions such as his or her foremost/final wish. Such expressions are registered as a testament. It is worse the other way around when the registrar does not use a precise term, but merely refers to it as a deed of gift. This may in theory be a testament, but that would only be discovered if the writer e.g. at the same time mentions testament executors. In this sense, the figures listed for testaments are a minimum.

Secondly, and this is a much greater problem, the references to testaments are usually without precise dates. The testament referred to can in theory stem from hundreds of years before, and the issued letter's information relies exclusively on information from the church books, or on what the parish elders may remember. One such example is from Næstved Convent's gift book, in which a testament is mentioned during the year 1449. By drawing on other sources, it turns out, however, that in reality it was issued as early as the year 1315.[10] A delay of this extent is probably an exception, but the example shows clearly that it would be irresponsible to include such references in our count. The problem is solved here by letting them figure in a separate column. This column shows an *ante quam* date for testaments and other deeds of gift. Many undated deeds of gift in which the year of issue is unknown or cannot be narrowed down to within 25 years are not included.

THE DISTRIBUTION OF THE DANISH DEEDS OF GIFT

Based on the above mentioned principles and choices, in the period from 1360 to 1499, 1.496 deeds of gift are registered. To this we may add a number of undated letters which are not included in the count. Measured in decades, the distribution is as follows:

---

10. *SRD*, IV, p. 382.

Table 1: distribution of Danish deeds of gift per decade 1360-1499

		1400-09	111	1450-59	133
1360-69	48	1410-19	109	1460-69	137
1370-79	36	1420-29	99	1470-79	119
1380-89	85	1430-39	104	1480-89	130
1390-99	100	1440-49	148	1490-99	137

The early years up until the mid 1380s, are characterized by few preserved deeds of gift. Compared to the level in the 1370s which is as low as 36, the number of deeds of gift are tripled in the following decades. Up until 1439, there is a fairly constant number of approx. 100 to 110 deeds of gift per decade. After this, the figures rise again and there is a distribution of 120 to 150 deeds of gift per decade throughout the rest of the period. Since the number of letters generally rises dramatically in these years, and not least in the final decades of the 1400s, there is in actual fact a decline in the number of deeds of gift from 1470 to 1499. In terms of this investigation, the continual rising number of deeds of gift actually means that a large number of letters is not in itself an indication of the plague. The figures should constantly be compared with the difference between the single years in order to obtain an indication with any certainty.[11]

The most productive thing to do would therefore be to list the distribution of deeds of gift per year. This is done in the following tables. For the sake of clarity, the 140 years are divided into three tables, 40 years up until 1399 for Table 2, hereafter 50 years for Tables 3-4. The listed deeds of gift are distributed as follows:

---

11. Movements of less than 8 have not been considered.

Table 2: Distribution of deeds of gift pr. year 1360-1399

Year	Deeds og gift	Deeds of gift Mentioned	Wills	Wills Mentioned	Ante quam date	Total
1360	5	4	2	0		11
1361	2	1	1	0		4
1362	1	3	0	0	1	4
1363	1	2	0	2		5
1364	2	1	1	2	1	6
1365	1	0	0	0	1	1
1366	0	0	1	1		2
1367	0	2	0	1		3
1368	1	4	1	2	1	8
1369	2	0	1	1	1	4
1370	0	2	0	0		2
1371	3	1	0	0		4
1372	0	1	1	0		2
1373	0	0	0	0		0
1374	3	3	0	0		6
1375	0	0	0	1	1	1
1376	1	0	0	0		1
1377	5	2	2	0		9
1378	2	0	0	1	1	3
1379	2	2	1	3		8
1380	1	3	0	2		6
1381	5	2	0	2	1	9
1382	5	2	0	1	2	8
1383	4	0	0	0	1	4
1384	3	2	0	0		5
1385	3	2	0	0		5
1386	6	1	1	0	1	8
1387	5	7	0	0		12
1388	4	9	1	0		14
1389	9	2	0	1		12
1390	5	1	0	2	1	8
1391	7	4	1	1		13
1392	4	0	0	2		6
1393	8	3	0	0		11
1394	4	2	1	1		8
1395	5	2	0	0	3	7
1396	8	5	1	2		16
1397	4	5	0	0	1	9
1398	4	5	1	0	1	10
1399	2	10	0	0		12

Table 3: Distribution of deeds of gift pr. year 1400-1449

Year	Deeds of gift	Deeds of gift Mentioned	Wills	Wills Mentioned	Ante quam date	Total
1400	13	8	1	4	2	26
1401	3	3	0	0		6
1402	3	3	0	1		7
1403	1	4	0	0		5
1404	1	5	1	1	3	8
1405	7	7	0	1		15
1406	5	5	0	0	1	10
1407	6	7	0	0	1	13
1408	6	4	2	1	1	13
1409	2	5	1	0		8
1410	3	8	1	2		14
1411	6	4	0	0	1	10
1412	4	7	0	0	1	11
1413	2	4	1	1		8
1414	1	7	0	3		11
1415	10	5	1	2		18
1416	5	6	0	0		11
1417	2	5	0	2		9
1418	4	1	1	0		6
1419	5	6	0	0		11
1420	7	5	0	0	1	12
1421	2	4	1	0		7
1422	6	3	0	0		9
1423	7	2	0	1	1	10
1424	5	4	2	0	1	11
1425	3	5	0	0	1	8
1426	3	5	0	2		10
1427	5	5	1	1	1	12
1428	10	4	0	0		14
1429	2	4	0	2		8
1430	5	6	0	0	1	11
1431	5	8	0	0	1	13
1432	5	6	1	0	1	12
1433	4	3	0	1		8
1434	3	1	1	3	1	8
1435	6	4	0	0	1	10
1436	6	7	0	2		15
1437	2	3	1	0	2	6
1438	4	7	0	0		11
1439	4	5	1	0		10
1440	10	14	0	0	2	24
1441	11	7	0	0	1	18
1442	13	6	2	0	1	21
1443	7	5	0	1	1	13
1444	3	3	0	0		6
1445	4	5	0	0		9
1446	6	6	1	0		13
1447	8	8	1	1	2	18
1448	9	4	1	0	1	14
1449	6	5	0	0	1	11

Tabel 4: distribution of deeds of gift pr. year 1450-1499

Year	Deeds of gift	Deeds of gift Mentioned	Wills	Wills Mentioned	Ante quam date	Total
1450	5	9	1	0	2	15
1451	3	4	1	3	1	11
1452	8	5	0	1	4	14
1453	5	5	0	1	3	11
1454	13	6	0	2	2	21
1455	12	5	0	0		17
1456	5	7	1	0		13
1457	5	7	2	1	2	14
1458	3	5	2	1	1	11
1459	1	2	1	1	2	5
1460	8	10	0	0	2	18
1461	4	4	0	2		10
1462	5	8	1	4		18
1463	2	1	0	2	1	5
1464	14	4	1	0	2	19
1465	6	4	0	2	1	12
1466	7	2	3	2	1	14
1467	9	2	0	1	2	12
1468	7	7	0	3	3	17
1469	5	3	0	4	1	12
1470	3	8	0	0	2	11
1471	4	2	2	0		8
1472	4	6	1	7	1	18
1473	6	2	0	2	3	10
1474	9	6	3	2	2	20
1475	8	3	2	0	3	13
1476	4	2	0	0	1	6
1477	8	5	2	3	5	18
1478	8	1	1	0		10
1479	3	2	0	0	2	5
1480	4	3	0	0	1	7
1481	12	3	1	3	1	19
1482	6	5	1	0	1	12
1483	10	4	1	1	2	16
1484	8	6	1	0	3	15
1485	9	3	2	1	1	15
1486	2	7	3	2		14
1487	10	3	1	1	1	15
1488	5	3	0	0	2	8
1489	4	3	1	1		9
1490	2	4	1	1	1	8
1491	5	3	3	1	2	12
1492	7	6	0	0	3	13
1493	9	2	0	1		12
1494	11	3	0	4	4	18
1495	4	5	1	3	4	13
1496	11	7	1	0	1	19
1497	5	4	0	1	2	10
1498	6	9	1	1	6	17
1499	11	2	1	1	3	15

Shown as a bar chart, the distribution is as follows:

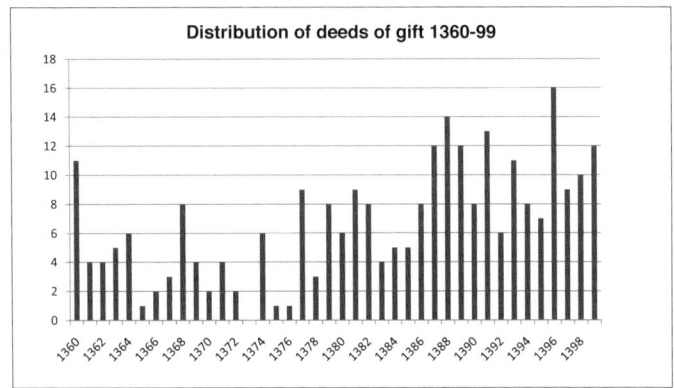

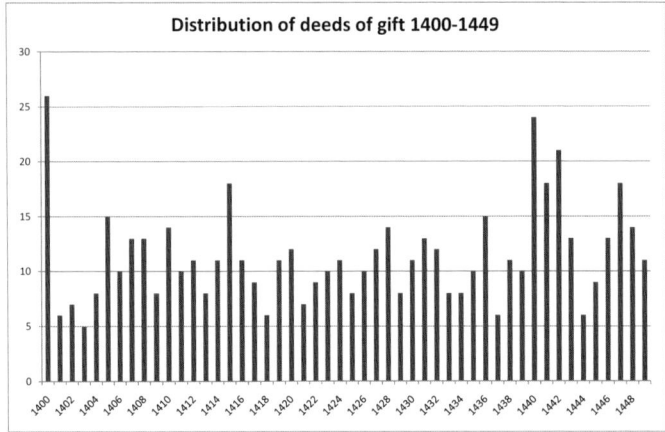

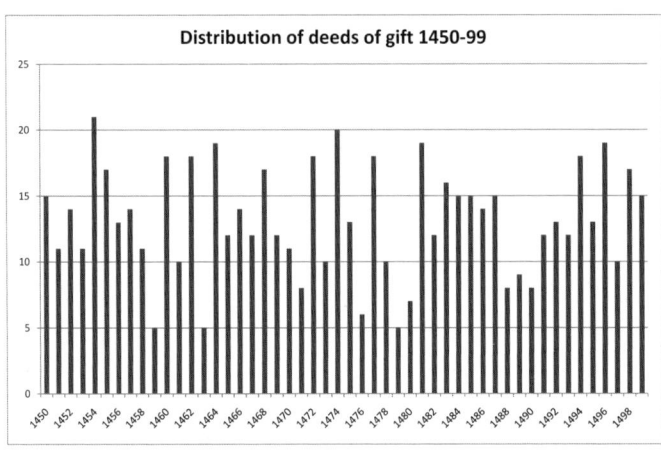

While the distribution of deeds of gift measured in decades fell into fairly fixed patterns, things look completely different when the count is annual. Here there are really significant oscillations from year to year. At times there are leaps equivalent to almost a doubling or even more. This is the case for the years 1360, 1368, 1377, 1396, 1400, 1405, 1440, 1454, 1460, 1464, 1472, 1474 and 1481. For other years the number of deeds of gift takes a leap and remains on a high level for two or three years, only to fall again after that. This is the case in the years 1387-89, 1440-42, 1454-55, 1481-87 and 1494-96. For 1440-42 and 1454-55 there is a conjunction with the years in which there is a significant raise in numbers.

Since the hypothesis in this article is that the apparition of sudden and significantly many deeds of gift may be an indication that the plague has ravaged, it would obviously be relevant to compare the years mentioned with the knowledge to be found concerning plague epidemics in neighbouring countries. The most reliable figures are based on studies of the more than 6,000 preserved testaments from Lübeck. Deviations in their numbers compared to references to plague epidemics in the town's chronicles have been looked into by Jürgen H. Ibs, who has furthermore found plague references for Holstein. Norwegian and Swedish conditions are investigated correspondingly, but the amount of obtainable data is much smaller here. In Table 5, the Danish years with a sudden high frequency of deeds of gift are listed and compared with known plague years for our neighbouring countries.

Table 5: Known plague years for countries neighbouring Denmark and high frequencies of Danish deeds of gift 1360 to 1499

Lübeck	Holstein	Sweden	Norway	Denmark
1358		1359-60	1360	1360
1367	1368	1368-69	1370-71	1368
1376		(1374-77)		1377
1388	1387*	(1389)	(1391-92)	1387-89
1396				1396
				1400
1406		(1405)		1405
1421	1420	1420-21		**
	1439-40	1439-40	(1438-39)	1440-42
1451	1448-50	1455	1452	1454-55
			1459	1460
1464	1464	1464-65		1464
		(1472-74)		1472, 1474
			(1479-80)	
1483-84	1484-85	(1484)		1481-87
		1495		1494-96

*refers to Hamburg, ** see the ensuing discussion, ( ) refers to uncertain years

The result of this comparison is a notable conformity. This does not merely concern a single year, but is valid for most by far of the years included. The apparent conclusion is that it is most probable that the oscillations found in the frequency of the Danish deeds of gift reflects that the plague has in some form or another circulated in the years concerned.

In this light it might be of use to take a closer look at the deviations. Here the year 1400 stands out significantly, because none of the neighbouring countries seems to have had the plague that year. The Danish figures are nonetheless hard to dismiss, since the increase is virtually explosive, and reaches the highest number in the 140 years that have been registered. However, if we look further abroad in Europe, the year 1400 is a known plague year: England, The Netherlands and Iceland were struck. This makes it plausible to maintain that there was also plague in Denmark in the year 1400. In the year 1420 Denmark stands out again, this time by not having been struck by the plague. However, if we consult the base figures in light of the new knowledge, it may be noted that the figures are actually almost doubled from 1418 to 1419. Since the numeric value is not significantly high, the year was overlooked first time round. The material therefore still leaves room for the possibility that there has been plague in the country that would, moreover, concur with the information provided by King Erik of Pomerania in a polemical pamphlet against the Holsteiners in the year 1421, that northern Jutland lay waste at the time, although he of course ascribed it to the Holsteiners' raids.[12]

In the latter half of the 15th century, a certain dispersion and greater incoherence between the figures may be noted. This concerns not only the Danish figures, but also the epidemics of the neighbouring countries among themselves. It is true that the figures are coherent in showing that in 1464, the epidemic struck the entire north-German and Scandinavian

---

12. *Dipl. Flensburg: Diplomatarium Flensborgense. Samling af Aktstykker til Staden Flensborgs Historie indtil Aaret 1559*, I-II, ed. H.C.P. Sejdelin, (Copenhagen, 1865-1873), I, p. 27: "wo greue Ghert ... vnde greue Hinric ... vnde greue Clawes ... dicte vnde to velen tiden loghen in Dennemarken myt walt vnde macht vnde roueden vnde branden vnde welde vnde walt deden, also it noch openbar schin ys in Nort Jutlande, des en grot dell dar aff noch wuste licht". I am indebted to Mogens Kragsig Jensen for having brought my attention to this.

region, but that is actually the only common feature. The plague in the beginning of the 1450s seems to have struck unevenly, or else the figures lie (more on this later), just as the Danish figures for the 1480s do not give a clear picture of any specific plague year. At the same time, one single epidemic seems only to have occurred locally for Denmark and Norway in 1459 to 1460. It is confirmed by a Danish Chronicle, calling it hard and severe.[13] The epidemics in the 1470s and the 1490s, however, concur with those of the Netherlands. This dispersal is relevant, since the data on which the figures rely is better and more extensive than previously.

In this situation it might be dangerous to try to bend and harmonise figures. Perhaps there is something else going on that differentiates the situation in the latter half of the 14th century. Thus we may note that from 1350 to 1449, Lübeck is struck by the plague six times, and each time, Denmark was hit either the same year or in the years just after. From 1450 to 1499, Lübeck seems only to have been struck by the plague twice. On the one occasion, Denmark is affected, on the other, a Danish plague year is not immediately determinable (more on this later). It may, however, be noted that the Danish plague epidemics concur to the same extent with those known from the Netherlands. Here there was plague from 1472 to 74 and from 1494 to 96, just as there was in England. To me, this seems to be a hint that Danish commercial relations with the Netherlands were of growing significance. Another issue is the nature of the epidemics. Based on general European material, Samuel Cohn has argued that the disease changed character during the course of the 1400s. Fewer people died as a consequence of the plague, and a pattern emerged in which it was exposed groups in particular that were hit.[14] The deeds of gift contain no information to either prove or disprove this assumption, but if Cohn's observations are correct, this may have a say in the distribution pattern and the consequences of the plague in northern Europe.

---

13. The Roskilde Chronicle 1448-1549: "Mcccclx oc thet aar hær nest wor alle wægne oc stæder en suar pæstelentze, saa mæste parten aff folcket bleff dødt, oc mindste parten leffde igien". *Monumenta: Monumenta historicae Danicae*, I, vol. 1-2, Holger Fr. Rørdam (ed.), (Copenhagen, 1873-1884), vol. 2, p. 311.
14. Samuel K. Cohn, *The Black Death Transformed. Disease and Culture in Early Renaissance Europe*, (London, 2002).

THE INDIVIDUAL EPIDEMICS

Tables 2 to 4 identify a number of probable plague years in Denmark. It might now be worth consulting the other source material to see if there are other items of information to be found on whether the plague might have struck in those years, just as supplementary information from the deeds of gift applied may be drawn in (See Appendix 1 regarding the sources).

Even Ulsig argued that 1360 and 1368 were plague years in a Danish context. His material was mainly obituaries from Cathedrals. They have not been applied in the above, which means that different material points in the same direction, thereby enhancing the credibility of the observation. To this we may add that the Cathedral in Lund had sent very urgent appeals to the Pope regarding exemption from expenses in the years 1368 and the archbishop dissolved various altars to create a better income for his canons.[15] There is reason to put our trust in the laments of Lund, since they form part of a pattern of similar cases from the latter half of the fourteenth century. Even the first bout of the plague in 1350 had led to complaints from the Cathedral in Ribe regarding disrespect towards the churches' property.[16] Hoards of self-appointed people had apparently made life unsafe. In 1361, a letter from Odense Diocese claims similar things. Here a parish vicar complains of a lack of income from the office,[17] and in 1377, the very year the fourth plague bout struck Denmark, a group of nobles gathered in Salling, situated on the Liim Fiord in Jutland to promise support of the church. The country had suffered ruinous damage, they stated,

> through murder and fire, through the infertility of the corn, through the cruelty of our enemy, through sudden death and through the destructive anger of God, through cattle death and the decrease in the number of fish,

---

15. *DD: Diplomatarium Danicum*, 1st ser., I -, (Copenhagen, 1938 -), 3rd ser., viii, no. 126 and 234. In 1373 (Ibid., ix, no. 302) the archbishop is asked by the Pope to secure that synods are held in his diocese.
16. First pointed out by H.F.J. Estrup in 1839 in 'Den sorte Død i Danmark' (The Black Death in Denmark), *Blandinger fra Sorøe. Et Tidsskrift*, pp. 50-51.
17. *DD*, 3rd ser., vi, no. 96: "cum dicta ecclesia totaliter sit destructa propter guerras et mortalites, ita quod nulli redditus de quo possit uivere".

and the conclusion was that our creator's revenge and cruelty had now been kindled "because the freedom of the people of the church had been reduced".[18]

About the same time the town lord of Copenhagen, the bishop of Roskilde, drew up a balance sheet of property in the city and of who lived where. This index to records is the oldest remaining one of the city.[19] Bearing in mind the presence of the plague yet again, this was an understandable and useful precaution against the forgetfulness that the church was forever confronted with. Another sign of crisis may be found in the negligible number of deeds of gift from that decade. Why should laymen pay gifts to the church in the form of land, because if the church could not protect its property, neither ensure that the reading of mass took place, then the gift would have been wasted. Other forms of gift thereby seem to have been preferable.[20]

The next four plague epidemics all fell within the reign of Queen Margret I (1387-1412). If we are to trust the geographical dispersion of the deeds of gift, then in 1387 to 89 the plague spread from east to west with a pivot around the Sound, and there was a Jutlandish one in 1388 to 89.[21] One of the earliest ordinances from a priest guild to have been preserved is from 1388. This is probably no coincidence, since this association of priests enjoyed the trust of the laymen in several ways. First of all they allowed a comparatively large lay influence upon the actual diocese, since laymen were members of the guild on equal terms with the

---

18. *DD*, 4th ser., i., no. 183: "Effterdi wi haffue befundet det arme Danemarchis rige och henndis inndbygere att haffue lit forderffuelig skade aff roff och brand, af kornenss wfructsommelighed, aff fiennderniss grumhed, brad død och Gudz forkomene wrede, aff feedød och fiskens formindskelsse, befrycte wi oss, at woriss skabers heffn och grumhed mod oss och forbemeltte rige optenndt er, fordii att kierchenss och kierchens personners friheder dennom forkorttet er".
19. *KD: Kjøbenhavns Diplomatorium*, I-VIII, O. Nielsen (ed.), (Copenhagen, 1872-87), vol. 1, pp. 92-114. The balance sheet is dated approximately to the years 1375-89. It is normally interpreted as the bishop's counteract against King Valdemaar IV, who unlawfully during his reign had kept the revenue from the city.
20. There is a corresponding argument by Myrdal, who interprets a low number of surviving letters as a sign of crisis. Myrdal 2006, pp. 145-46.
21. For instance there is only one Scanian deed of gift from the whole of 1389 compared to five and six in 1387 and 1388 respectively.

priests. Secondly, it is of course the case that in these guilds there would never be a lack of priests.[22]

During the next three epidemics at least two out of three letters derive from Zeeland and Scania, but since these are also the parts of the country from where most letters from ecclesiastical institutions have survived, it would be somewhat bold to conclude anything from that.[23] The havoc wreaked by the plague is, however, mentioned in Odense in the beginning of the 1400s without our being able to decide whether the document is from 1400 or 1405.[24] The town's shoemakers were given permission to break away and form their own guild, something which occurred on the grounds "that a massive death governed the world which we call the most terrible pestilencia".[25]

It is worth noting that the number of surviving deeds of gift rises dramatically during the reign of Margret I. There is an indication that trust in the ecclesial institutions had begun to return. If this was indeed the case, a significant reason would be the great efforts this strong-willed queen made. She seems to have been a forerunner in all areas. There is not space here to go into detail on this matter, but according to the standards of the time, these were really large institutions. They were established in all of the country's eight Cathedrals, as well as in many of the convents. This is that much more noteworthy in light of the fact that no royal donation letters exist from those years in the investigation which

---

22. *DGLM*: *Danmarks gamle Gilde- og Lavsskraaer fra Middelalderen*, I-II, C. Nyrop (ed.), (Copenhagen, 1895-1904), I, pp. 301-06. For the significance of priest guilds see Bisgaard, 'Det middelalderlige kalente – et bindeled mellem kirke og folk' (The Calente of the Middle Ages – a Link between Church and Laymen), in: Arnórsdóttir, Ingesman & Poulsen (eds.), in: *De to øvrigheder. Kirke og kongemagt i danske senmiddelalder (The Two Heads, church and royal power in the Danish late Middle Ages)*, (Århus, 2007), pp. 443-470.
23. I had planned on using the geographical distributions for each recurrence of the plague, but since many of them are erased and the figures are too low, the geographical perspective is only drawn in when the distribution appears unambiguous.
24. I must therefore reject Bjørn Poulsen's criticism with regard to attributing statutes to the year 1400. See 'Tilbagegang og vækst i senmiddelalderens danske by (Recession and development in Danish towns of the late middle ages), in S. Bitsch Christensen (ed.), *Middelalderbyen (The Medieval Town)*, Danske Bystudier 1, (Århus, 2004), p. 231.
25. *DGLM*, II, p. 15.

lay within her father's reign (1360-1375).[26] This can only be interpreted as a clear change in the royal plague policy. Her strong position meant that she was supported by particular noble families. Again, there is not space here to go into further detail. Finally, it was a sure sign of new times that convents were again established in Denmark. The first one seems to have been what was later known as the Tvilum Convent between Viborg and Århus, which must originate from the 1390s.[27] Shortly after followed the joint venture of Lady Ida of Gladsaxe and Queen Margret which became Gavnø.

The possible epidemic in 1419-20 has previously been mentioned. An epidemic from 1427 to 28 cannot be dismissed either, since the figures are high, but we lack the clear-cut rise compared to the level of the previous year. Plague is mentioned in German countries, Poland, the Baltic States and Sweden in 1427. The plague of 1440, on the other hand, clearly meets the criteria, and may be characterized as reasonably certain. It is mentioned in the 1439 chronicle from Eiderstedt.[28] The geographical distribution of the deeds of gift shows a Jutland dominance in both 1439, 1440 and 1441. This is interesting since we know that at the same time there was great peasant unrest in northern Jutland. Juxtaposing plague and peasant unrest has only in recent years become a target for research, with the result that there seems to be a connection.[29] In Danish research on peasant revolts, such things have not hitherto been taken into consideration, but it would seem worth trying out.

In the early 1450s, the extent of the plague is hard to define precisely on the basis of the Danish deeds of gift. There are also large figures for the years 1450 and 1452, and both would fit the overall picture. There is no supplementary material to refer to apart from another speculative factor. This concerns the years of the issuing of the laws of the Danish guilds. 54 have been saved for the period from 1430 to 1499. In those years in which there seems to have been plague in Denmark, the figures are as follows:

---

26. Valdemar IV's testament from 1375 is referred to, but the content is unknown to us.
27. *DD*, 4th ser., iv, no. 110, dated between 1389 and 1404.
28. Most recently published by Jasper, Johannes (ed.): *Chronicon Eiderostandense vulgare oder die gemeine Eiderstedtische Chronik 1103-1547*, (St. Peter-Ording, 1977).
29. Samuel K. Cohn, *Lust for Liberty: The Politics of Social Revolt in Medieval Europe*, (Harvard, 2006).

Table 6: the issuing of the laws of the guilds in Danish towns 1430-1499 in possible plague years

1440-42	1450-52	1464	1472-74	1484-85	1495-96
2	9	0	3	3	7

This distribution shows a clear predominance of renewals in possible plague years. The connection would then be that in years with plague or in their wake, both the guilds and the municipal authorities had an interest in putting down on paper what had hitherto been either oral agreements or things which stood in old documents deserving credence, should secure storage become a problem. The aim would have been to avoid unnecessary dispute concerning what rules applied. Many of those who could remember the rules might have died as a consequence of the plague. This explanation would fit a situation in many statutes which we might otherwise be hard put to explain. Several statutes assert the obvious paradox that the rules which have been committed to paper are as they always have been, at the same time as it is stated that the guild is newly established. This is the case, for instance, for the well-known Corpus Christi Guild (*Guds Legemes Lav*) from Aalborg in Jutland, whose activities we know of right back to the 1420s, but whose statutes were not put into writing until 1441 (a plague year), claiming that the guild was completely new.[30] If this interpretation is correct, the plague epidemic of the 1450s was earlier and was in accordance with the epidemic in Lübeck.[31]

The epidemic of 1464 is not to my knowledge certified in Danish annuals, but is, however, in those of Lübeck, which list the year 1464 for Denmark.[32] Møller-Christensen seemed certain that the plague did not strike Denmark until 1466, but on the basis of the distribution of the deeds of gift, this must be rejected.[33] The deeds of gift for 1464 come from the entire country, and there is no backlog for any specific part of the country in either 1465 or 1466.

---

30. *DGLM*, I, pp. 613-706.
31. Ibs 1994, p. 116 gives the information that there was plague in Halland 1452.
32. Ibs 1994, p. 117. Compare note 13. The words of the chronicler indicate that the plague of 1460 continued somehow later.
33. Vilh. Møller-Christensen, 'Pest' (Plague), in *Kulturhistorisk Leksikon for Nordisk Middelalder*, XIII, (Copenhagen 1968), columns 238-41.

The plague from the beginning of the 1470s is mentioned in a letter from Scania from May 1473, which refers to "the great death of men" in the provinces.[34] Since plague often strikes in the autumn, this could indicate that the attack referred to is from 1472. If this is the case, it is not reflected in the geographical distribution of the deeds of gift from 1472-74, which, apart from being highest on Zeeland, is evenly spread over the entire country. This fits what Huitfeldt writes about the year 1474, in which there "was a severe pestilence over all of the Danish country and areas" (vaar en hefftig Pestilentz offver alle Danmarckis Lande og Stæder").[35] The important thing about having pinpointed the epidemic of 1472-74 is the connection there might have been between this and the king and queen's great journey to Rome, which began in 1474 and 1475 respectively. Partly it would have meant that the king was in greater safety abroad, partly such a trip to Rome would have made sense in relation to this sinister inter-Scandinavian background.[36]

The deeds of gift do not unambiguously point to a specific plague year for Denmark in the 1480s, and the written testimonies are on just as uncertain ground. The 18th century church historian Erik Pontoppidan seemed certain, supposedly with reference to a now lost annal, that there was a shocking outburst of the plague in the year 1484.[37] He is supported by the Roskilde Chronicle.[38] In contrast, an inscription in Århus Cathe-

---

34. *Repert.* 2, *Repertorium diplomaticum regni Danici mediævalis. Fortegnelse over Danmarks Breve fra Middelalderen med Udtog af de hidtil utrykte*, 1. ser., I-IV, Kr. Erslev et a. (eds.), (Copenhagen 1894-1912); 2nd ser., I-IX, William Christensen (ed.), (Copenhagen, 1928-39), no. 3253.
35. Huitfeldts Bispekrønicke, p. 24. Quoted here from *Danske Magazin,* 1st ser., vol. 1ff., (Copenhagen, 1745ff.), II, p. 19. The Roskilde Chronicle states that from the year 1472 and onwards plague and war hit Europe. *Monumenta,* I, vol. 2, p. 314.
36. It is often proclaimed that King Christian I wore a suit of penance in Rome. The Cardinals ascribed it to his great piety. Perhaps the union king wished to atone for the plague in his kingdoms?
37. Pontoppidan, Erich*: Annales Ecclesiæ Danica diplomatici, oder nach Ordnung der Jahre abgefassete und mit Urkunden belegte Kirchen-Historie des Reichs Dännemarck,* I-IV, (Copenhagen, 1743-55), II, p. 680.
38. 'Thet samme aar oc thet aar nest, som wor 1484, wor ald som suariste folcke dødt oc pestilentze besynderliig i Walland oc Tyskeland', *Monumenta,* I, p. 319. The year 1481 had seen plague among cattle (p. 318).

dral states there was plague in 1487.[39] These statements are not mutually exclusive, but the inscription in itself is not that definite and is open for interpretation. It is not quite clear whether the plague took place in 1487, when some vaults were completed at the cathedral, or during the years these vaults were being erected.[40] If the latter reading is correct, the apparent contradiction has disappeared. This would be in accordance with the geographical distribution of the deeds of gift. If we compare the number from Jutland for 1484 and 1487, there are twice as many in 1484 as in 1487. In 1484, they make up over half of the entire number of deeds of gift, while the number of deeds of gift from Zeeland and Scania are at their highest in 1487.[41]

This leaves us with the concentration of deeds of gift in the mid-1490s. There are no notices in annals from this time regarding the plague in Lübeck, and for the same reason, the testament statements have not been consulted by Ibs. It is therefore not possible, strictly speaking, to determine whether the town has been struck by a minor epidemic which has escaped the attention off the annals due to the many other areas in Germany being in contact with the plague in the mid-1490s. In Sweden, the plague is also well attested, among other places in a correspondence by letter with nobles in Denmark.[42] Quite a few Danish guilds renewed their regulations in 1495-1496, which may also be seen as a sign of the plague. The geographic distribution of the deeds of gift 1494-96 is also of interest, since Zeeland and Scania account for 80-90 % of all deeds of gift in 1494, while Jutland, interestingly enough, accounts for almost half

---

39. *Danmarks Kirker (Denmark's Churches)*, Århus Stift, 1, (Copenhagen, 1969), p. 444.
40. The inscription consists of two pair of hexametres and runs as follows: 'Post nataliciam cristi de uirgine pura Mcd anno septem cum bis quadraginta/ progenie clarus Eylerus episcopus arusiensis hoc opus expleuit dum pestis maxima seuit'.
41. In 1484 Northern Jutland account for eight deeds of gift out of 13, in 1487 merely four out of 15. Southern Jutland has as many as five out of 14 donations in 1483, which must be considered in extension of the fact that this part of the country, along with Funen, are those areas which have fewest surviving letters from spiritual institutions. Put together, this information indicates that the plague came from Lübeck, striking in both Southern Jutland and Zeeland in 1483.
42. *Missiver. Missiver fra Kongerne Christiern I's og Hans's Tid*, I-II, William Christensen (ed.), (Copenhagen, 1912-14), II, no. 112, 2nd Dec. 1495. The disease is refered to as "the great pestilence". See also Myrdal 2006, p. 154.

of all letters in 1496. Regardless of the risk of over-interpretation, I may add that the only pilgrimage of King Hans that we know of took place in the very year of 1494.⁴³ It was to The Holy Blood in Wilsnack in northern Germany in the month of July. 1494 was also the only year of a 30-year period in which the great Sct. Lucii guild in Roskilde on Zeeland did not hold an annual gathering.⁴⁴

CONCLUSION

The use of the number of deeds of gift as an indication of the plague has proven to be a relevant approach. The years in which a high degree of frequency coincide with great oscillation in relation to preceding years, are years where there is plague in countries neighbouring Denmark. The credibility of this investigation is further strengthened by the fact that it is based on almost 1500 deeds of gift. The danger of circular argument is present, given that other countries use similar methods to define likely plague years. Here it is a considerable strength that the figures from Lübeck are based on such sound data as they are.

The preconceived fear that the endowments would to a further extent than the testaments spread the concentration of deeds of gift has not affected the investigation in any significant way. Apart from the 1480s, the distribution is at no time greater than three years, and it has hardly been unusual for the disease to hibernate and thus re-emerge the following summer. Although the material is scarce, the geographical distribution at least indicates that many of the epidemics have been active for more than one season. During an epidemic in Copenhagen in 1553, the king stayed away for all of 1554, which is a sign that they knew the plague could re-emerge the year after. The king, at least, was not taking any chances.⁴⁵

The most notable change during the 140 years occurred during the reign of Queen Margret. The number of deeds of gift rose considerably during her era, and everything point towards that masses for dead greatly increased as a safeguard against the plague. Apparently, the church re-

---

43. *Danske Magazin*, 2nd ser., ii, pp. 315-16.
44. *DGLM,* I, p. 372.
45. Tre breve (Three Letters) (n 2), p. 70.

covered but the price paid, as has been shown[46], was a considerably high element of lay influence on the endowments.

The result of the investigation is indirectly a salute to the royal scribes of the 1600s, who went through the old letters of the convents and briefly surmised their content, since it to a large extent relies upon their work. When they used the word "give" in a descriptive fashion, they probably did so in loyalty towards the old letters. Another result is that the Danish-Dutch connections have been steadily strengthened in the latter half of the 1400s, since the patterns in Danish plague epidemics at this point begin to resemble the Dutch just as much as those of Lübeck. Up until 1450, however, the old Danish proverb seems to hold true: "Death comes from Lübeck".

---

46. Lars Bisgaard, 'Kirken og pesten i senmiddelalderen' (Church and the Plague in the Later Middle Ages), *Personalhistorisk Tidsskrift* 2008, pp. 172-193.

Appendix

Documents referred to in years of plague (Tables 2-4)

1360	DD 3:5, 282, 337, 338, 364, (384-85), 388, 390, 393, 398, 399, 410.
1368	DD 3:8, xxx, 161(+ testament), 213, 235, 254, 255, 257, 455 (cf. 168).
1377	DD 4:1, 283, 284, 296, 303, 307, 322, 352, 451, 454 (cf. 9. March 1382).
1387-89	DD 4:3, 194, 216, 223, 232, 241, 246, 254, 283, 283, 290, 306, 307 / 333, (368-70), 390, 396, 407, 418, 427, 444, 451, 452, 455, 456, 458, 463/ 4:4, 23, 30, 47, 50, 59, 74, 81, 93, 139, 145, 147,170.
1396	DD 4:6, 4, 1. Febr., 12, 33, 67, 128, 131, 147, 164, 3. Nov., 180, 192, 195, 242, Repert, 1 4055 (4246), 4085.
1400	DD 4:7, 210, 245, 258, 2. March, 272, 280, 288, 306, 313, 332, 353, 354, 364, 373, 395, 421, 450, 491, 494, 497, 514, 518, Testamenter 74, Repert. 1, 4330, 4402, 4403.
1405	Cod.Esrum. 237, Repert. 1, 6025 (4672), 4680, 4707, 4711, 4716, 4730, 4733, ÆA I 173, II 242, III 168, IV 167, 231, 253, SRD 1, 319.
1419-20	Dueholm No. 23, SRD 1 323, IV, 382, V 518, Danske Magazin. III, 268, Terpager 112, Repert. 1 5816, ÆA III, 259, 271, 299, 303 / Repert. 1 5830, 5837, 5838, 5840, 5851, Dueholm, No. 38, 90, SRD VI 515, ÆA 1 171, III 122, 262, 268.
1440-42	Repert. 1 7056, 7066, 7079, 7091, 7096, (7106-07), 7125, 7126, ÆA II 205, III 138, 153, 276, 278, 289, 293, 300, IV 10, 94, Regesta 3646, SRD IV 365, VI, 513, HardDipl. 28, Aarsberet. II 71, Dueholm (1-2) / Repert. 1 7157, 7165, (7172-73+ 7466), 7173s, 7180, 7182, 7191, 7198, 7202, 7214, Ribe Oldem. 84 (= 17. Aug. 1441), KS 4:1 58, Dueholm No. 81 p. 49 and p. 83, ÆA III 162, IV 150, 216, 261 / DDL III 233, 244, Repert. 1 7228, 7232, 7235, 7243(7409), 7266, 7268, 7294, 7296, 7300, Danske Magazin 5:2 183, KD II 72, 73, Aarsberet. II 21, Urkunden 2, Testamenter 90, ÆA III 129, 278, IV 160, 240.
1450, 1452	Repert. 7977, 8027, 8041, 8049s Westphalen IV 3187, Noodt, II, p. 29, Danske Magazin 5:2 187, Urkunden 4, ÆA II 79, III 138, 298, IV 115, 218, V 679, 712 / DDL III 350, Dueholm No. 89 p. 53, No. 102 p. 63, No. 118 p. 72, Repert. 156, KD IV 47, Danske Magazin. II 187, III 227, DaHel.kl. 21, ÆA II 274-75, III 179, 257(294), IV 226, 375.
1454-55	Dueholm No. 101 p. 62, No. 184 p 121, No. 30 p. 18, No. 18 p. 11, KD III 3, Repert 2 320, 321, 360 (+ testament), 366, 369, 414, DDL III 367, 368, IV 379-80 Aalb.Kl.hist. 84, ÆA III 22, 194, 262, IV 96, V 721 / DDL III 370, 371, IV 134, Repert. 2 463, 469, 510, 522, Danske Magazin 5:2 190, 191, SRD VI 183, Dueholm No 69 p. 41, Westphalen IV 3188, ÆA II 369, III 83, 149, V 681, 722.
1460	Repert. II 1101, 1109, 1112, 1184, Rørdam 53, Terpager 546, Dueholm No. 108, DaHel.kl. 29, ÆA II, 216, 377, 380, III 158, 264, 266, 288,289, IV 98, V 877.

1464	KD II 117, 118, DDL IV 38, 40, 41, Repert. 2 1735, 1750, 1815, Aarsberet.
	II 38(x2), III 139, AktFyen I 132, Danske Magazin 5:2 197, Dueholm
	no 124 p. 75, SRD VI 185, ÆA II 99, III 192, 193 (x2).
1472, -74	Aarsberet III 11, KD IV 105, Urkunden 10, Repert. 2 3061, 3070 (3088,
	3188), 3079 (3150), 3150, 3090, 3136, 3165, DaHel.kl. 43, DDL IV 145,
	153, 155, Dueholm no 141 p. 89, ÆA III, 193, V 1017, 1123 / Terpager
	62, 201, DDL IV191, 200, 204, 209, Repert. 2 3404, 3519, 3520, 3532,
	Danske Magazin II 16, KS 3:2 365, Dueholm No. 145 p. 90, DaHel.kl.
	48, ÆA II, 379, III, 271, 276 (291), 277, IV 123 (67, 145), V 725.
1483-84	Noodt II 113, Aarsberet. III 13, 14, Dipl. Flensburg. I 639, DDL IV 383,
	Repert. 2 5212, 5219, 5220, 5224, 5262, 5333, 5363, KD IV 190, ÆA II,
	365, 373, III 95 (105) / Repert 2 5406, 5416, 5514, 5572, 5601, 5614,
	Danske Magazin I 269, KD III 8, Hofm.Fund. IX p. 30, Urkunden 12,
	ÆA II (St. Hans Viborg), 316, III 210, 215, IV 267.
1494-96	DDL V 215, 219(224 + testament), 222, 223, 231, Repert. 2 7612, 7613,
	7620, 7631, 7636-37, 7713, 7743, 7747, 7762 (7847) ÆA III 223, 289, V
	1005 / Repert 2 7911, DDL V 252 (x 2), HofmFund. X 178, Terpager
	297, Aarsberet. IV 5, Danske Magazin VI 196, 267, DaHel.kl. 88, ÆA
	III 276, 295, V 655 (716), 723 / DDL V 291, SRD IV 371, VIII 157, KD
	IV 236, 237, 238, 242, Repert. 2 8184, 8206, 8230, HardDipl. 79, KS 4:6
	34, 35, DaHel.kl. 90, 91, ÆA I 191, II 245, III 9, 186.

FURTHER ABBREVIATIONS

Akt.Fyen. *Aktstykker, for største Delen hidtil utrykte, til Oplysning især af Danmarks indre Forhold i ældre Tid*, I-II, published by Fyens Stifts literaire Selskab, (Odense 1841-45).

Cod.Esrum. *Codex Esromensis. Esrum Klosters Brevbog*, O Nielsen (ed.), (Copenhagen, 1880-81)

DaHel.kl. *De danske Helligaandsklostre Fremstilling og Aktstykker*, J. Lindbæk and G. Stemann (eds.), (Copenhagen, 1906).

DDL. *Diplomatarium dioecesis Lundensis*, III-VI. Lunds ärkestifts urkundsbok, Lauritz Weibull (ed.), (Lund, 1900-1939).

Dueholm. *Dueholm Diplomatarium*. Samling af Breve 1371-1539, der i sin Tid ere opbevarede i St. Johannesklostret Dueholm paa Morsø, O. Nielsen (ed.), (Copenhagen, 1872).

HarDipl. *Harsyssels Diplomatarium*, O. Nielsen (ed.), (Copenhagen, 1893)

HofmFund. Hofman, Hans de: *Fundationer, I-X*, (Copenhagen, 1755-65).

KS. *Kirkehistoriske Samlinger*, 1. ser. ff., (Copenhagen, 1849ff.).

Noodt. Johann Fridrich Noodt, *Beyträge zur Erläuterung der Civil-Kirchen-und Gelehrten Historie der Hertzogthümer Schleswig und Hollstein*, xxx 1744-1756

Regesta *Regesta diplomatica historiæ Danicæ*. Chronologisk Fortegnelse over hidtil trykte Diplomer og andre Brevskaber til Oplysning af den danske Historie fra de ældste Tider indtil Aar 1660, med kort Angivelse af Indholdet, 1. ser. 1-2, (Copenhagen, 1847-1870); 2. ser. 1-2, (Copenhagen, 1889-1907).

RibeOldem. *Samling af Adkomster, Indtægtsangivelser og kirkelige Vedtæger for Ribe Dom-*

kapitel og bispestol, nedskrevet 1290-1518, kaldet Oldemoder (Avia Ripensis), O. Nielsen (ed.), (Copenhagen, 1869)

Rørdam. Rørdam, Holger Fr.: *Kjøbenhavns Kirker og Klostre i Middelalderen*, (Copenhagen, 1859-63).

Terpager. Terpager, P., *Ripæ Cimbriæ*, (Flensborg, 1736).

Testamenter. *Testamenter fra Danmarks Middelalder*, Kr. Erslev (ed.), (Copenhagen, 1901).

Urkunden. *Urkundensammlung der Gesellschaft für Schleswig-, Holstein- Lauenburg*, vol. 3-4, (Kiel, 1852-80).

Westphalen. Westphalen, E. J.: *Monumenta inedita rerum Germanicarum*, I-IV, (Lips., 1739-45).

AalbKlHist. *Aalborg Klosterhistorie. Bidrag til Aalborg Bys Historie i Middelalderen*, J.P. Stenholm (ed.), (Aalborg, 1904).

Aarsberet. *Aarsberetninger fra det kongelige Geheimearchiv*, I-V, C.F. Wegener (ed.), (Copenhagen, 1851-75).

The Course of a Mid-17th Century Plague Epidemic in Denmark

By Lise Gerda Knudsen, Odense

The history of plague is a fascinating one, and one that has intrigued people at all times. The tale of a disease so powerful and so deadly arouses a feeling, common to all mankind, that ill health is beyond our control. And even more so, since the threat of a dangerous epidemic disease does not just belong to the past – today's fear of diseases like Ebola, SARS and most recently the avian influenza makes that clear.

In the late 19th and most of the 20th century Danish research into the history of plague was not very extensive, and the plague was only dealt with superficially. The last 10-15 years though, this has changed. The increasing interest in the history of plague, which is now seen among Danish historians, has probably less to do with a general interest in the history of epidemic diseases and more to do with the fact that something all of us regarded a fact has been questioned. Namely that the Black Death was the same disease as the modern bubonic plague that occurred in e.g. India and China c. 1900, and that it therefore was spread by means of the black rat and its fleas.

It will be too comprehensive for this article to give the full story about how the retrospective diagnosis was slowly questioned. In brief, it has become increasingly clear that there are several discrepancies between what the source material tells us about the historical plague and the medical knowledge we have of the modern bubonic plague.[1]

---

1. Graham Twigg, *The Black Death: a Biological Reappraisal*, (London, 1984).

Figure 1. The Zealand archipelago

The uncertainty about the character of the plague aroused my interest and had me turn my attention to the Danish plague epidemics. Because of the hitherto lack of interest in the history of the plague, an excellent source material had been left unexamined, until I began a research project on the plague in Denmark in 2003.[2] The material consisted of just under a hundred parish registers, covering Zealand and the smaller islands Lolland, Falster, Møn and Bornholm, in the mid-17th century – at the time when one of the last plague epidemics struck Denmark. This amounts to one sixth of the parishes in the examined area. The registers cover 82 rural parishes and 14 town parishes. There are an equal number of large and small parishes in the examination.

---

2. Published in Lise Gerda Knudsen, *Pesten grasserer! En undersøgelse af pesten i Danmark i 1650'erne*, (Landbohistorisk Selskab, 2005).

In a number of ways the 1653-57 plague epidemic is an interesting object of study. First of all this is the earliest of the Danish plague epidemics that are covered by parish registers. Parish registers are the first relatively homogeneous quantitative sources for the history of the plague.

Secondly, this epidemic was actually the last in a series of epidemics that had struck Denmark regularly since the Black Death. The 1710-11 plague in Elsinore and Copenhagen can be considered an error, an accident, which happened after the end of the actual plague period. Thus more than 50 years went by between the two last epidemics. This is a much larger interval that between any of the other Danish plague epidemics.

Finally this mid-17th Century epidemic was part of a large Europe-wide outbreak of plague. Denmark was closely linked to the rest of the continent through commercial relations, wars etc., and it was therefore also affected by disease patterns in other countries. In this way a Danish plague epidemic might be able to shed some light on the question, which is inter-European: What was the plague?

The extent of the epidemic

The plague epidemic of the 1650s did not strike the entire country, but only the eastern islands. The reasons why no other parts of the country were hit are worth an additional investigation, but it must be closely linked to the countermeasures which were implemented in the second half of the 16th century and the first half of the 17th.

The first knowledge we have of Danish countermeasures against the plague is from c. 1520. These consisted of provisional orders and regulations, which all had only one goal; to protect the King and the royal family during outbreaks of plague. In the second half of the 16th century (during the reigns of Frederik II (1559-88) and particularly Christian IV (1588-1648)) the objective of the countermeasures changed; now it was a question of protecting the entire population. It became important for the central administration to be able to control and contain the plague, to keep it from spreading.[3]

The arrangements that the Danish authorities made in order to control the plague were hardly distinguishable from the countermeasures

---

3. More about the contoneasures against the plague, can be found in Lars Olsen, Pestlovgivningen i den danske magtstat 1500-1700 (unpublished thesis, University of Copenhagen 2005).

which were carried out in other European countries. They where mostly based on the isolation and quarantine of the sick persons. During the last Danish plague epidemic in 1710-11 the combating of plague was based on an extensive quarantine system, in which a number of smaller islands were used as quarantine stations for all suspicious travellers. The station at Saltholm between Zealand and Sweden is said to be the busiest one.[4] Measures like these must have been one of the reasons why the plague epidemic of the 1650s did not cross the Great Belt.

The mortality lists in the examined parish registers do not always tell what the deceased had died of. Actually it is very rare; e.g. it is only in 22 of the examined registers that plague is mentioned as the cause of death. Still it is safe to assume that plague was present in many more instances. To find out in which of the other parishes plague appeared in the 1653-57 epidemic I have examined the mortality in the surrounding years. This was done in order to map so-called mortality crises, which could be a sign of epidemic disease.

The way to recognize mortality crises in a population of an unknown size is to calculate the Crisis Mortality Ratio (CMR) for the individual parishes.[5] CMR measures the size of the mortality in a crisis year in proportion to the average mortality in normal years. Thus, CMR enables us to compare different mortality crises without knowing the sizes of the populations. It is a mortality crisis if CMR is above 3, that is, if the mortality is more than three times larger than in a normal year.

The plague often led to a mortality way larger than that, even though it varied a great deal. Gentofte parish, north of Copenhagen, was struck by plague in 1654. That year 182 people died. The average mortality in the parish in the years 1652-1666 was 15,4.[6] The CMR-number for Gentofte parish in 1654 is thus:

$$CMR = 182/15,4 = 11,8$$

---

4. Karl-Erik Frandsen, *Kampen mod pesten. Karantænestationen på Saltholm 1709-1711*, (Frydenlund, 2004).
5. Crisis Mortality Ratio has been used by – among others – Paul Slack, *The Impact of Plague in Tudor and Stuart England*, (London, 1985).
6. Gentofte Parish Register. Provincial archives of Zealand, Lolland-Falster & Bornholm.

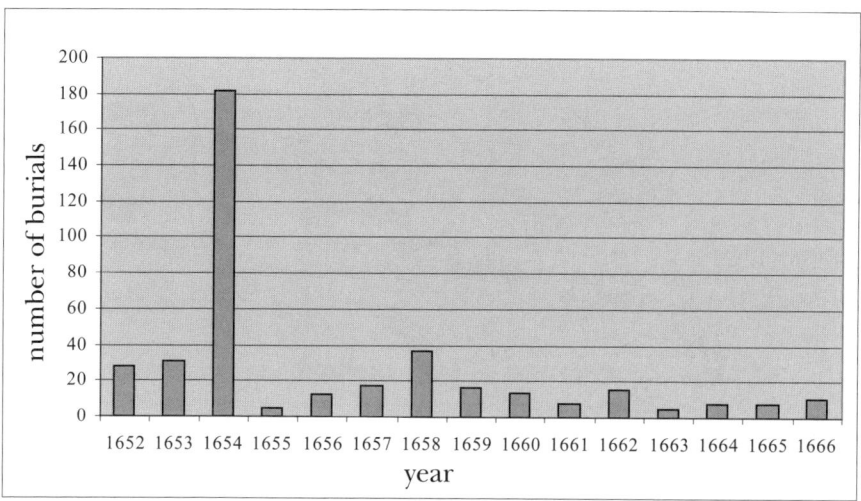

Figure 2. Number of burials per year in Gentofte parish, 1652-66
Source: Provincial archives of Zealand, Lolland-Falster & Bornholm, 1-131-1 Gentofte.

Mortality in the plague year was thus almost 12 times higher than in an average year (Figure 2).

In Horreby parish in the island of Falster the situation was completely different the same year. 11 people died from the plague; usually the mortality was 5,5 per year:[7]

$$CMR = 11/5.5 = 2.0$$

The size of the mortality is not enough to decide whether the plague had appeared in a parish. In the study I have defined parishes as plague-struck if the CMR-number in a given year in the plague period surpasses 3, or if plague is mentioned in the parish register or other sources such as royal letters and regulations. 59 of the 96 parishes examined were thus struck by plague during the epidemic of the 1650s.

---

7. Horreby Parish Register. Provincial archives of Zealand, Lolland-Falster & Bornholm.

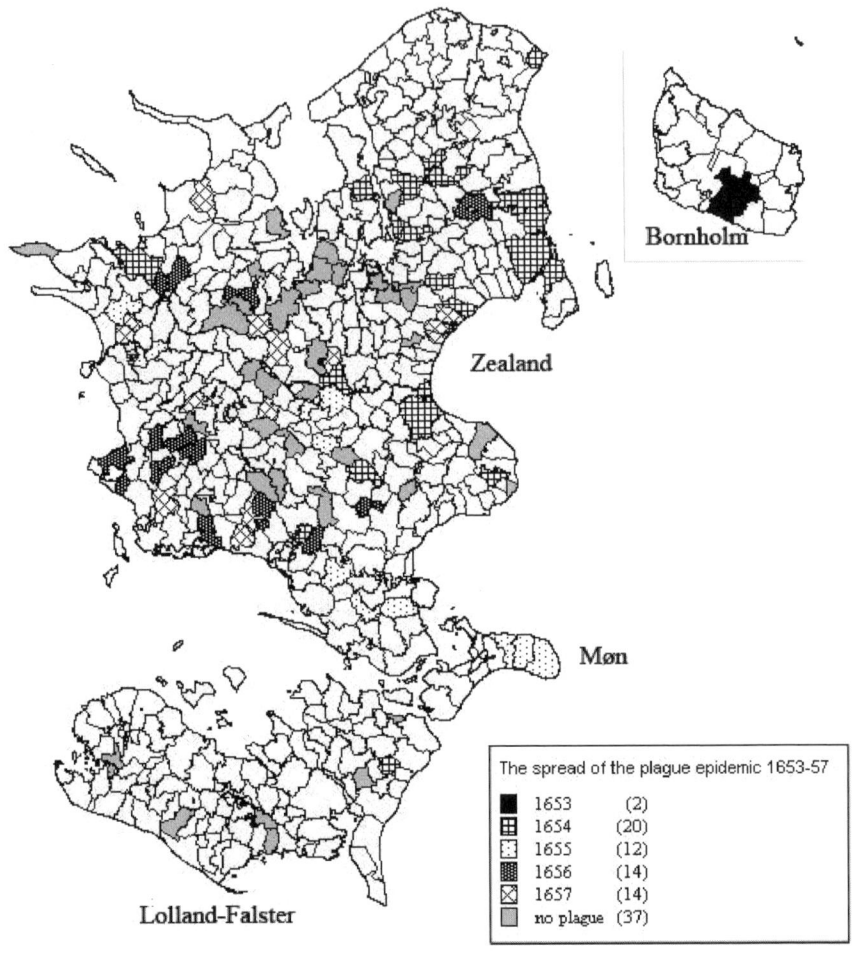

Figure 3. The spread of the plague epidemic, 1653-57
Source: Knudsen 2005.

THE SPREAD OF THE DISEASE
In order to establish what kind of disease the plague really was it is important to study how the disease spread both on the regional level and in the individual parishes. The modern bubonic plague is spread by means of the black rat (*Rattus rattus*) and its fleas (*Xenopsylla cheopis*). It cannot be directly transferred from one person to another. Those who lived in the time of the

plague, on the other hand, had a different view of the disease; they did not doubt that plague was a contagious disease, which could easily move from one person to another. That is the conviction that lies at the root of the isolation and quarantine measures in the fight against the plague.

A study of the regional spreading of the plague epidemic in the 1650s supports the contemporary idea of the plague as a contagious disease. After the first outbreak on the island of Bornholm in the autumn of 1653 the plague reached Copenhagen in the spring of 1654. From here the disease moved on to the rest of Zealand and the other islands. The chronological dispersion of the individual outbreaks shows clearly that the plague did not spread like ripples in a pond from Copenhagen outwards. On the contrary, it seems to have bounded randomly backwards and forwards between parishes (figure 3). There are plenty of examples of neighbouring parishes being hit with an interval of several years. The parish-of-ease St. Fuglede and Ll. Fuglede was afflicted by plague in 1657, even though two of the neighbouring parishes were struck already in 1655. It also often happened that one parish was struck hard, and the next not at all. The explanation for the apparent random spreading of plague might be that the disease was not spread by animal vectors, such as the rat flea in modern bubonic plague, but by the infrastructure. People brought the plague from place to place when they travelled the country.

On the local level it is even more obvious that human beings played an important role in the spread of the plague. During outbreaks of modern bubonic plague in India and China c. 1900 it was normal that only one from a household would fall ill from the disease, just as doctors and nurses would rarely get ill themselves. It has been said that the plague hospitals were actually the safest place to stay during an outbreak of bubonic plague, since none of those who worked in these places ever got sick.[8] Thus, it seems there was no danger of infection associated with the contact between healthy and sick. This fits in perfectly with a disease which does not transfer directly between humans, but only through an animal vector.

The situation was different in eastern Denmark in the 1650s. As soon as the plague had entered a household it was all but certain that several

---

8. R. Pollitzer & Karl F. Meyer, 'The Ecology of Plague', in Jacques M. May, *Studies in Disease Ecology*, (New York, 1961), p. 473.

members of the family would become sick. A couple of examples from the examined parish registers follow.

In most cases we have no knowledge of the size of the populations in the individual parishes. But for the parish of Sørbymagle in south western Zealand a 1645-census has been preserved, which makes it possible to study this parish a little more thorough! In a family consisting of 13 members at the beginning of the plague, only six were alive after the disease had been raging for a few months. The parents and four of the girls had survived.[9] In Jørlunde parish in north Zealand a father had to bury five of his children and his wife in the space of only two weeks.[10] There are plenty of examples.

A preliminary study of the plague mortality in a selection of parishes makes it positively clear that the plague usually hit more than one person in the families that were afflicted.[11] In the mortality lists of the parish registers it is usually mentioned who was the male head of the family of the deceased – that is the father or the husband. Through his name it is therefore possible to look closer at the situation of the individual households. In four of the 15 examined parishes 50-59% of the total number of deaths belonged to households where two or more died from the plague. In three others the amount was 60-69%. In seven parishes – almost half – 70-79% of all deaths happened in families with several plague deaths and finally in Fjenneslev parish 81.9% of the deceased happened in families, where two or more died from the plague.

There can be no doubt that this disease did indeed spread within families. The spreading pattern on the local level thus differs very much from that of the modern bubonic plague. Nonetheless it is not a surprising finding – we know from contemporary accounts and from other studies, both Danish and foreign, that this was the situation.[12]

---

9. Sørbymagle Parish Register. Provincial archives of Zealand, Lolland-Falster & Bornholm.
10. Jørlunde Parish Register. Provincial archives of Zealand, Lolland-Falster & Bornholm.
11. 15 parish registers have been examined for this study: Fjenneslev, Gundsømagle, Haslev, Hyllinge, Jyllinge, Jørlunde, Lundforlund, Marvede, Sneslev, Sørbymagle, Store & Lille Fuglede, Uggeløse, Uvelse, Venslev & Holsteinborg og Værløse sogne. All in the Provincial archives of Zealand, Lolland-Falster & Bornholm.
12. E. g. Susan Scott & Christopher Duncan, *The Biology of Plagues: Evidence from Historical Populations*, (Cambridge, 2001); Bodil Persson, *Pestens Gåta. farsoter i det*

A few years before the plague struck the eastern part of Denmark, the same area had been visited by another epidemic disease, namely dysentery. Dysentery is transmitted by means of infected drinking water and food, or by direct contact between infected and healthy persons. Because the dysentery epidemic struck almost the same area as the plague and because we know how it spreads, it is interesting to make a comparison between the two diseases.

The dysentery epidemic began in June 1652 and lasted throughout the year. The epidemic is known from contemporary correspondence from the authorities, who tried to fight it, and it can be found in the parish registers, since quite a few were killed by the disease. 59 of 90 examined parishes were afflicted by dysenteri 1652.

The chronological spreading pattern looks almost the same as the one for the plague epidemic to come a few years later. The first traces of excess mortality are seen in Hammer parish in southern Zealand in June. In July the disease had spread to eight other parishes nearby and to Copenhagen, which is somewhat further away. It is easy to explain why the dysentery spread to the nearby parishes, but Copenhagen is c. 50 miles from Hammer. On the other hand, Copenhagen was a large town with much trade and therefore also many travellers. One or more of these might have brought the dysentery to the capital from a trip to southern Zealand. Thus, just like the plague, the dysentery did not spread further and further from one entry point, but followed the paths of the man-made infrastructure.

The local diffusion of the dysentery was also somewhat similar to the spreading of the plague. The outbreaks did not have quite the same effect on the mortality, but nevertheless some excess mortality can be seen. And it is obvious that people living close together were more exposed to being infected than others. Very often several persons from one household are buried with very short intervals during the outbreaks. In Rye parish a married couple and their son were buried within a month,[13] and in the nearby market town Roskilde a father and two of his sons were buried in august 1652.[14] The examples – of which there are many more – show an

---

tidiga 1700-talets Skåne, (Lund, 2001); Felix Platter, *Beschreibung der Stadt Basel 1610 und Pestbericht 1610-11*, (Basel, 1987).

13. Rye Parish Register. Provincial archives of Zealand, Lolland-Falster & Bornholm.
14. Roskilde Domsogn Register. Provincial archives of Zealand, Lolland-Falster & Bornholm.

unmistakable pattern; the dysentery would spread within the families, killing people who lived close together with already infected persons. The spreading pattern of the plague is hardly distinguishable from that of dysentery, and it is therefore obvious to conclude that the plague was a disease directly transmitted from one person to another – just as we know dysentery is. The plague did not act as if it needed an external carrier of the disease in order to transmit it; it did not behave like the modern bubonic plague.

Mortality

The size of the plague mortality also tells something about the nature of the disease. When plague struck a town or an area it would often claim many victims – more than one would expect from a disease that wasn't able to transmit directly from one person to another. The British historian J.F.D. Shrewbury did not doubt, that the 'historical plague' was identical with the modern bubonic plague, and therefore he found it unlikely that outbreaks caused such a high rate of mortality. In his opinion it was impossible that such a large number of people were killed by a disease transmitted only by means of disease carrying rats and fleas.

> *Had [it] been in its entirety a disease with a malignity approximately equal to that of bubonic plague [...] that was spread by human contacts, a death-roll of one-third of the nation might conceivably have been achieved.*[15]

It involves some difficulties to speak about mortality in a period for which we have no certain knowledge about the size of the population. Nonetheless it is an important question when trying to establish which kind of disease the plague was. The first Danish census was made in 1787. Before this we have only fragmented and unreliable information about the population. On these ground estimates can be made of the number of people populating the Danish areas in different periods of time. In this article I will make use of the calculations made by the Danish historian E. Ladewig Petersen, which are based on a census made of persons liable

---

15. J.F.D. Shrewsbury, *A History of Bubonic Plague in the British Isles*, (Cambridge, 1970), pp. 123-124.

to pay taxes in 1645.[16] This census is not unproblematic as a source since it includes neither children below the age of 15 nor the non-taxpayers – that is the clergy, the nobility and the poor. Ladewig Petersen takes this into account, and his estimate that approximately 185,000 people lived in Zealand and the surrounding islands is absolutely credible.

In the mid-17th century by far most people lived in the countryside. It is therefore the mortality in the rural population that is most interesting. The following study of plague mortality is based on the remaining rural parish registers.

In order to find which percentage of the total population that lived in the areas of this study, I have used Henrik Pedersen's work with King Christian V's land register from 1688.[17] The register contains information about the number of farms and houses and the amount of land units in the Danish parishes.[18] This makes it possible to calculate how large a proportion of the total amount of farms, houses and land belonged to the examined areas. This has been done in figure 4.

	Zealand and surrounding islands total	Examined parishes	The examined parishes' part of total amount
Hartkorn land	144.374,53	26.247,30	18,20%
Farms	20.906	3.632	17,40%
Houses	6.885	1.002	14,60%

Figure 4. Farms, houses and land in the examined parishes, 1688
Source: Pedersen 1975 (1928).

The distribution of land is considered to be the most reliable measure for the distribution of people, in that parishes with much cultivated land would often have more inhabitants than parishes of a smaller extension.

---

16. E. Ladewig Petersen, *Dansk socialhistorie, vol. 3: Fra standssamfund til rangssamfund 1500-1700*, (Gyldendal, 1980), pp. 41-47.
17. Henrik Pedersen, *De danske Landbrug. Fremstillet paa Grundlag af Forarbejderne til Christian V's Matrikel 1688*, 2. edition (1. edition 1928, Landbohistorisk Selskab, 1975).
18. The amount of land is measured in 'hartkorn', which is an old Danish unit of measurement used to measure the value of a farm. 'Hartkorn' was 'hard corn', that is barley or rye. The measurement was connected with both the extent and the productivity of the land.

This assumption means that the population of the examined parishes constitutes c. 18% of the total population:

$$185{,}000 \times 0{,}18 = 33{,}300$$

4225 persons – of a total population counting 33,300 – were buried in the plague-struck parishes in the years 1653-57. This equals a mortality of a little less than 13% for the rural population in the Zealand archipelago during the epidemic in the 1650s.

Even though the study only covers a relatively small part of the plague-struck area, I see no reason why this mortality should not be representative for the total number of rural parishes. The parish registers examined vary both geographically and with regard to size. It is therefore not likely that the situation in the parishes from which no registers are preserved should differ much from what the study has shown. An investigation, similar to the present, set out to establish the plague mortality for an entire region, namely that of Castile in central and western Spain. A violent plague epidemic struck the area in 1596-1601 with a total mortality of c. 10% of the population.[19]

The plague outbreak in Copenhagen in 1654 is somewhat better known that the rest of the outbreaks during the epidemic. When plague entered the capital in February 1654 the population was c. 30,000.[20] In April the disease really began to rage, and the excess mortality, of which the parish registers tell us, did not ease off until October or November. It is generally believed that between 8,500 and 9,000 people were killed during the outbreak.[21] If this is correct the plague killed between one

---

19. Bartolomé Bennassar, *Recherces sur les Grandes Épidémies dans le Nord de l'Espagne à la fin du XVIe Siècle*, (Paris, 1969), pp. 10-13; Vicente Pérez Moreda, 'The Plague in Castile at the end of the Sixteenth Century and its Consequences', in *The Castilian Crisis of the Seventeenth Century*, (Cambridge, 1994), p. 46.
20. Ladewig Petersen 1980, p. 47. Frederik Hammerich estimates the population to be c. 35,000, Marcus Rubin to be c. 29,000; Frederik Hammerich, 'Præsident Hans Nansen den Ældre', *Historisk Tidsskrift* 3. ser., I, (1858-59), p. 191; Marcus Rubin, 'Bidrag til Kjøbenhavns Befolkningsstatistik i Hundredaaret 1630-1730', *Historisk Tidsskrift* 5. ser., III, p. 526.
21. F. V. Mansa, *Bidrag til Folkesygdommenes og Sundhedspleiens Historie i Danmark fra de ældste Tider til Begyndelsen af det 18. Aarhundrede* (Gyldendal, 1873), p. 402; Hammerich 1858-59, p. 191.

fourth and one third of the Copenhagen population in little more than six months.

Only two parish registers of Copenhagen are preserved; those of Holmen and Vor Frue (Our Lady) parishes. Holmen parish is not representative of Copenhagen, since it includes the property of the Navy. Still, the register gives us some interesting information. Of 2641 persons buried in the parish in 1654, the vast majority died of plague: all deaths from the plague have been marked with a capital P by the vicar.[22] The first recorded death by plague happened February 24th, when Karen Lauritzdatter, who was a servant girl, died just 20 years old. During the next couple of months there was a rise in mortality, until it peaked in June with more than 700 deaths, compared with a normal average of c. 35 deaths per month.

The register from the parish of Vor Frue, which is a relatively representative parish of Copenhagen, isn't complete for the plague year, as the recording stops already in august 1654.[23] In turn, the register contains information about the total mortality in Copenhagen in the years 1649-1653, which gives an idea of the average mortality in normal years (figure 5).

Year	Number of burials	Burials per 100 persons
1649	1188	4,0
1650	1146	3,8
1651	1169	3,9
1652	2559	8,5
1653	2110	7,0

Figure 5. Number of burials in Copenhagen, 1649-53
Source: Vor Frue Parish Register. Provincial archives of Zealand, Lolland-Falster & Bornholm.

In 1652, when the dysentery-epidemic was raging (see above), the mortality reached 8,5%. The following year also shows an above average mortality of 7,0%. It is unclear what caused this high mortality, but nearly half of the burials took place in Holmen parish, and maybe the excess mortality

---

22. Holmen Parish Register. Provincial archives of Zealand, Lolland-Falster & Bornholm.
23. Vor Frue Parish Register. Provincial archives of Zealand, Lolland-Falster & Bornholm.

had to do with naval activity. The remaining years show a mortality rate of c. 4% of the population.

When assuming that the plague killed c. 8,500 people, it means that more than one fourth of the burials happened in Holmen parish. In the parish register of Vor Frue parish it says that 26% of the deceased in 1649 came from Holmen parish. In 1650 it was 20%, in 1651 c. 30% and in 1652 c. 33%. As already mentioned nearly half the deaths in 1653 also occurred in Holmen parish. Even though the number varies somewhat, it is obviously not unlikely that 25% of the deceased in the plague year were buried in the churchyard of Holmen church.

8,500 dead in Copenhagen equals a mortality of above one fourth of the total population. This number is neither unlikely nor rare in plague outbreaks. During the plague in Basel 1610-11 half of the inhabitants were sick and one third died from the plague.[24] The outbreak in Marseilles 1720-22 killed about half the population,[25] and during the last Danish outbreak of plague – in Copenhagen in 1711 – 22,000 died of a population of c. 60.000.[26]

The high rate of mortality, which according to Shrewsbury among others would only be possible if the disease was transmitted directly from person to person, was present during the plague epidemic of the 1650s. This was a mortality far larger than what has been seen in the modern epidemics of bubonic plague. It has been estimated that c. 12 million people were killed by plague in India 1896-1914.[27] 12 million casualties in almost 20 years and out of a total population of ca. 300 million equals a cumulative mortality of 4%, while the average annual mortality was only c. 0,2 %.

SEASONALITY
The modern bubonic plague is dependent on fleas – primarily *Xenopsylla cheopis* – in order to spread, and the fleas are dependent on the right tem-

---

24. Platter 1987, p. 38.
25. Jean-Nöel Biraben, *Les hommes et la peste en France et dans les pays européens et méditerranéens*, (Paris, 1975-76), pp. 298-302.
26. Peter Christensen, '"In these Perilous Times": Plague and Plague Policies in Early Modern Denmark', *Medical History*, 47, p. 444.
27. David Arnold, *Colonizing the Body: State Medicine and Epidemic Disease in Nineteenth-Century India*, (Berkeley, 1993), pp. 200-203.

perature and humidity to survive. Thus, climate becomes very important for the course of an epidemic of bubonic plague. The ideal situation for *Xenopsylla cheopis* is a temperature between 20 and 25º Celsius (68-77º Fahrenheit). If it gets colder than 18ºC (64.4ºF) the fleas cannot reproduce, and by temperatures lower than 7ºC (44.6ºF) all flea broods die.[28] In the 1650s the mean temperature in Europe was just below 15.5ºC (59.9ºF) in July-August and just above 3ºC (37.4ºF) in December-February.[29] This means that the fleas would not be able to breed even in the summer, and they wouldn't survive during the winters in the temperate climate of Europe.

Going through the 60[30] registered outbreaks of plague during the epidemic of the 1650s, it becomes clear that most outbreaks occurred in the summer and autumn. 43 outbreaks were initiated in the period of July to October, and 28 of them ended in October, November, December or January. In 46 of the 60 outbreaks the highest rate of mortality was in the months of August-November (figure 6).

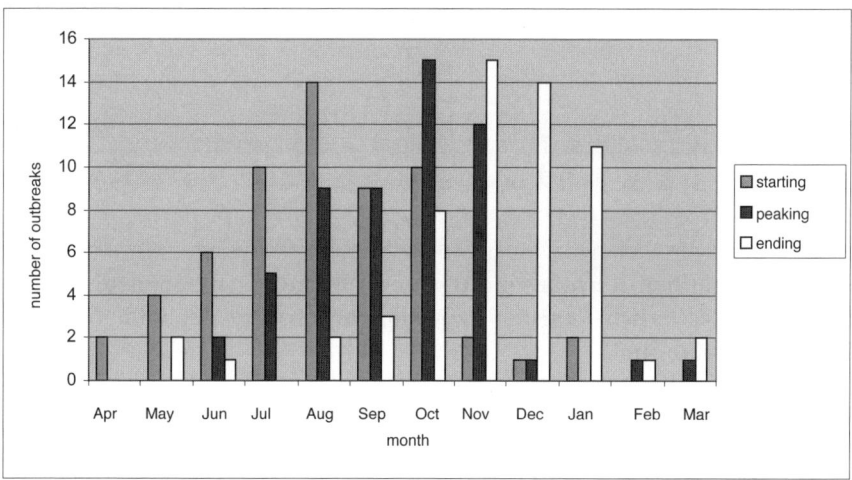

Figure 6. The seasonality of the plague epidemic of the 1650s
Source: Knudsen 2005, pp. 156-163.

---

28. Fabian L. Hirst, *The Conquest of Plague*, (Oxford, 1953), p. 273; Twigg 1984, pp. 115-117.
29. Twigg 1984, p. 119.
30. 59 parishes were struck by plague; three of them were hit twice (St. Taastrup,

This pattern thus follows the seasonality of the bubonic plague, but there are also a number of outbreaks which do not. 17 of the examined outbreaks of plague continued through the turn of the year, which means that the plague could in fact survive the cold season. This was the case in Borre parish on the island of Møn south of Zealand (figure 7). The vicar in Borre was a thorough man. When plague struck his parish in the autumn of 1655, he made a note of it in the register. He wrote that the previous vicar had died of the plague after having paid a visit in the vicarage in the neighbouring town of Stege, where they had plague. The disease was raging throughout the winter, and in February the vicar could count the losses. 154 parishioners had died.

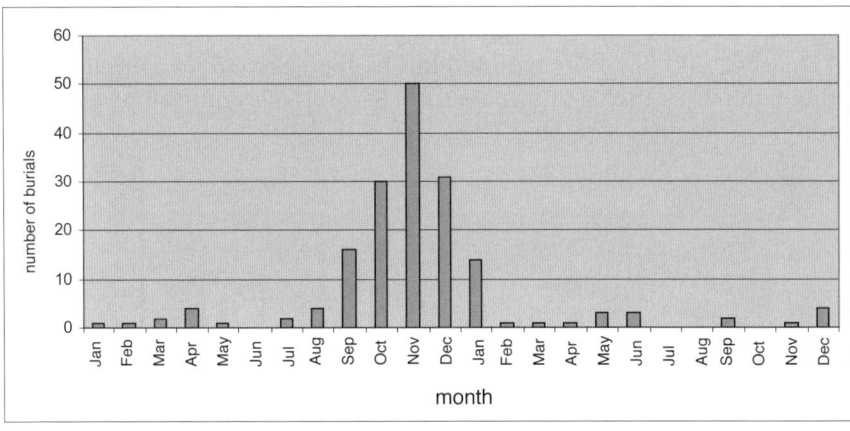

Figure 7. Number of burials per month in Borre parish, 1655-56
Source: Borre Parish Register. Provincial archives of Zealand, Lolland-Falster & Bornholm.

Other sources on the history of plague also tell us that this was a disease which could easily be found out of the summer season. In the family book of Rasmus Pedersen Thestrup we are told of an outbreak of plague that began in the spring.[31] Thestrup recounts how his parents and five of his brothers and sisters died during the plague of 1602. The first to die

---

 Bregninge, and Venslev). Two of the outbreaks (in Næstved and Jystrup) had no clear seasonality and are therefore not mentioned here.
31. Rasmus Pedersen Thestrup, *Stambog*, published by Helge Søgaard, (Aarhus, 1973), pp. 18ff.

was his brother Niels, who was buried March 29. After this Maren, Anne, Clemmend, Niels Fog and both the parents were buried within the next month and a half. In addition to the family, several of the servants in the farm also died; a total of 17 people died from the plague. Rasmus himself only escaped because he was studying in Lübeck at the time.

In the days of the plague, people knew very well that the disease could strike 'out of season'. Contemporaries were accustomed to fear the plague in any season. Christian Morsing, professor of medicine at the University of Copenhagen, wrote in his plague treatise about the plague that: "...at times she comes in the Winter / at times in the Summer / in the Spring or in the Autumn".[32]

As far as the seasonality is concerned the Danish plague epidemic of the 1650s was like the ordinary run of epidemics. The majority of the outbreaks happened in the warmest months, but there were always also outbreaks at times when the climate would have hindered it, if the disease had been modern bubonic plague. An explanation of this discrepancy between the source material and the retrospective diagnosis has been sought, but none of the theories are – in my opinion – satisfying.

First of all it has been claimed that the outbreaks of plague that happened in the winter were not plague at all. Shrewsbury was one of the spokesmen for this theory, and he thinks that the winter epidemics were really influenza, smallpox or typhus. The epidemic disease that struck Edinburgh in 1512 led to a new set of plague regulations; Shrewsbury therefore doesn't doubt that it is plague. But when the excess mortality continues through the winter, he argues that it is a typhus epidemic that 'takes over' from the plague, which could not survive the low temperatures.[33] There is nothing in the course of the epidemic that suggests a change in the disease, and contemporaries are certain that it is plague all the way through. In a study of the Scanian plague epidemic in 1710-13 smallpox and typhus are also used to explain overwintering epidemics.[34]

The assumption that contemporaries would mistake typhus for plague is not very likely, since to two diseases are very different. For instance, the

---

32. Thomas Bartholin, *Cista Medica Hafniensis* (originally published 1660, Copenhagen, 1982), p. 103 (translation by the author).
33. Shrewsbury 1970, p. 165.
34. Unni Løkkebø, *En epidemiologisk studie af pesten i Ivö og Kiaby Pastorat 1710/1711*, unpublished thesis, (Oslo, 1992), pp. 67-69.

period between the first symptoms and death is much longer in plague that in typhus.[35] Besides, the plague was a frequent visitor, and it was well known – just as a number of other diseases were. Shrewsbury himself tells of a letter to Cardinal, Lord Chancellor Thomas Wolsey, in which it is mentioned that people are dying of: "...small pokes, mezils, and the great sickness."[36] So people obviously did know how to distinguish between the different infectious diseases.

Another explanation of how the plague epidemics could survive the winter is climatic. It has been argued, that the rat fleas were able to survive mild winters and thereby carry on the disease. In Bodil Persson's study of the Scanian plague epidemic 1710-13 it is mentioned that the winter 1710-11 was extremely mild and moist, which may explain the outbreaks in Ivö and Kiaby this winter. At the same time Persson tells us, that the winter 1712-13 was so cold, that the Sound between Sweden and Denmark froze over as early as in January. This did not prevent several outbreaks of plague from going on throughout the winter months of 1713.[37]

In some cases the cold winters are even emphasized in the sources, as in the tale of the plague in the village of Eyam (in Derbyshire, England) 1665-66 where it is mentioned that the winter was particularly hard: "In December, a great snow is said to have fallen, with a hard and severe frost [...] The weather at the commencement of 1666 was exceedingly cold and severe."[38] The coldness didn't prevent the plague from striking the village, which suffered a severe outbreak of plague that winter.

It would have to be an extraordinarily mild winter, if it should be possible for the bubonic plague to survive; the temperature would have to be 18°C (64.4°F). In our part of the world very few winters live up to that. And the period of plague was not especially mild or favourable.[39]

---

35. Christopher Morris, 'The Plague in Britain', in Slack et. al. (eds.), *The Plague Reconsidered. A new Look at its Origins and Effects in the sixteenths and seventeenth Century England*, (Matlock, 1977), p. 39.
36. Shrewsbury 1970, p. 162.
37. Persson 2001, p. 367 and appendix 6.
38. Leslie Bradley, 'The most famous of all English plagues' in Slack et. al. (eds.), *The Plague Reconsidered. A new Look at its Origins and Effects in the sixteenths and seventeenth Century England*, (Matlock, 1977), p. 70.
39. Emmanuel Le Roy Ladurie, *Times of Feast, Times of Famine. A History of Climate since the Year 1000*, (London, 1972), p. 21.

Winter epidemics have also been explained as outbreaks of pneumonic plague. Such epidemics start out as an incidence of bubonic plague, which develops into pneumonic plague because of a pulmonary infection – this is called secondary pneumonic plague.[40] When the disease has reached the lungs it can easily be transmitted to others by means of coughing and vomited blood. This – of course – makes the fleas unnecessary as a host, which is why this theory is interesting in connection with the overwintering epidemics. If the fleas have no role to play, neither does the climate.

One of the spokesmen of the theory of the pneumonic plague is Christopher Morris.[41] He provides a series of references to outbreaks of plague in e.g. Southern Europe and in Ireland, in which bloody vomiting was one of the symptoms. Most of these refer to the Black Death, which is the one epidemic where it is certain, that some sort of pulmonary infection came alongside the plague. Spitting of blood is thus mentioned in a number of sources on this particular epidemic. Morris himself mentions that there are no references to bloody vomiting in any of the otherwise very rich English sources on the history of plague. The same goes for the Danish material. Those descriptions of symptoms that have been preserved till today mainly focus on boils and blisters on the skin.[42]

The mortality of the epidemics of modern pneumonic plague speaks against the theory. During the most thoroughly studied epidemic of pneumonic plague – in Manchuria c. 1900 – only 0.4% of the population died, despite the fact that the disease spread over large areas.[43] In Upper Egypt 88 outbreaks of pneumonic plague were registered in the period 1899-1913, but none of them were spread. The most severe outbreak happened in El Hamidad in 1911; 63 people were infected out of a population of 3728. This equals 1.69‰.[44] The low mortality is not consistent with our knowledge of the mortality during outbreaks of 'historic plague' (see above), and since there are no descriptions of pneumonic plague after 1400, I find it highly unlikely that the winter epidemics were outbreaks of pneumonic plague.

---

40. Hirst 1953, p. 222.
41. Morris 1977.
42. This is the case in the plague treaty of Christian Morsing 1546, and the treaty published by the Medical Faculty 1619/1654. Both in Bartholin 1982, pp. 105-106, 121.
43. Ole Jørgen Benedictow, *Plague in the Late Medieval Nordic Countries: Epidemiological Studies*, (Oslo, 1992), p. 27.
44. Twigg 1984, pp. 166-168.

A much more plausible explanation of the overwintering outbreaks is that the plague was actually an infectious disease, which could easily be transmitted from one person to another. Therefore it was also present during the winter. The clustering of plague outbreaks in the warmer months might be explained even just as simply.

The spreading of an infectious disease is dependent on inter human contact. The warm weather in the summer encourages outdoor activities, which automatically lead to more contact between neighbours in the individual towns and villages. The harvesting alone was a big social event, in that everyone in the village took part in the work. The large fairs, where people met from afar, were also held in the summer and autumn, when there was good chance of fine weather. All this meant that summer and autumn were the times when the danger of infection was largest, and thus the time when plague had the best chance of moving from one area to another.

In the winter, when the coldness made people stay inside, plague was primarily transmitted between members of the same family, who resided in the same rooms. This difference between summer and winter outbreaks is analyzed in a British study of the plague in Penrith (in Cumbria, England) in 1597-98.[45] The plague entered Penrith in the autumn of 1597, and in the months of October, November, and December 24 people died, all of them related by family, neighbourhood or the like. In the course of the winter the plague all but disappeared, only to flare up in March, when the social activities were taken up again.

The unequal seasonality of the plague might thus be a matter of exposure; in the summertime more people met each other, and they met more often. This led to a larger danger of infection with any disease that might be in circulation. The coldness of the winter kept the families indoors until the weather improved, and the plague would once again have the opportunity to spread. This distinction between human ways of life is repeated in the course of the individual outbreaks. Most summer outbreaks were short and violent, resulting in many casualties in a short time. The winter outbreaks, on the other hand, were rather long and had a lower mortality, simply because the number of susceptible individuals was lower.

---

45. Scott & Duncan 2001, pp. 177ff.

Concluding remarks

It might be said that not much new knowledge would appear from doing a single analysis of the course of a plague epidemic in Denmark in the 1650s. But this study is not alone; it is only one in a long series of investigations into the anatomy of plague epidemics in all areas of the European continent. Working with the original source material in all these different countries contributes to our collective knowledge of the plague. Was the plague an infectious disease, which was transmitted directly between humans? Or was it identical to the modern bubonic plague that exist even today, and which is spread by means of rats and fleas?

The analysis above indicates that the plague was indeed an infectious disease, and not one that was dependent on animal vectors to spread. And it seems almost impossible that the plague was identical to the disease which raged in India and China around 1900. That disease spread far slower than the plague, as it was dependant on the rats and their fleas. Moreover, the 'historical' plague spread in a completely different manner; very often – as was described above – whole families were more or less wiped out, if the plague entered the household. Even the size of the mortality differs from what is seen during outbreaks of modern bubonic plague. The study of the seasonality of plague outbreaks showed, that the plague could survive most climate conditions, but it was more easily spread during the warmer months of the year, when the inter human contact was most frequent.

Apparently it was not the modern bubonic plague that raged during the Black Death and the subsequent epidemics. But then, what was it? The comparison with the pattern of diffusion during the dysentery epidemic, which struck Zealand in 1652, indicates that the plague was also an infectious disease, transmittable directly from person to person.

The theory that plague was transmitted directly between humans answers a series of questions, which have otherwise puzzled several plague historians through the years. The extraordinarily high mortality rate, which was caused by the Black Death, and the overwintering epidemics, for instance, make perfect sense, if seen in this perspective.

Contemporaries had no doubt that the plague was contagious. Great efforts were made in order to stamp out the infection and hinder any contact between healthy and sick people. Quarantine, prohibitions against large gatherings, isolation of infected people either in their own homes or in the pest lazarettos were some of the precautions taken against the plague. All these restrictions, implemented by the authorities, were inspired by – or even copied from – the plague provisions of other European countries, mainly Italy and England. It is even possible, that it was the common efforts with quarantine stations, and isolation of infected people, which finally made the plague disappear from the European continent in the late 17th century.[46]

Thus, in my eyes there cannot be much doubt that the plague was an infectious disease. But precisely which disease it was, is a much more difficult question. And it might be a question of which we will never know the answer. Possibly, the plague was some sort of hemorrhagic fever like Ebola and Marburg Disease, which are known in present day Africa.[47] Hemorrhagic fevers are transmitted directly from person to person and are often very virulent; they have a pathologic course which is much more similar to the 'historical' plague than that of modern bubonic plague. But the truth is, we don't know what the plague was, we don't know which disease it was that killed so many people in the recurrent epidemics which ravaged Europe and the Middle East from the mid-14th century till the end of the 17th. But we can be almost sure that it was an infectious disease, which spread through direct contact between humans.

---

46. Christensen 2003, pp. 449-450.
47. Scott & Duncan 2001.

Behavioural Economics, the Black Death and the Labor Market

By Robert Braid, Paris

For well over a century, medieval economic historians have attempted to measure the impact of the Black Death on wage rates, either by compiling vast amounts of statistical data or by a close examination of narrative evidence. Although they differ in their interpretation of the source material, they all agree with the economic model that predicts that wage rates should have increased in the period of rapid depopulation. Modern economic theorists, however, have revised many of the paradigms that historians still use by focusing more on the behavior of economic actors and less on the traditional economic indicators. In this paper, I will first give a rapid overview of the historiography relative to the effects of the Black Death on the labor market. Then I will examine the new methods and concepts of modern economic theory. Finally, I will suggest ways in which economic historians could adapt their methodology by borrowing from behavioural and experimental economists.[1]

---

1. Although I focus primarily on English history and historiography in the article, a complete analysis based on source material and the work of economic historians from around Europe should certainly be pursued.

The effects of the Black Death on the labor market, an historiographical overview

One of the major debates in medieval economic history centers on the extent to which real wages increased in the post Black Death era. Although historians disagree about statistical evidence found for example in account registers, none brings into question the basic economic model that predicts that after at least a third of the population disappeared, there would have been a labor shortage which should have caused a sharp increase in real wages. Historians, however, differ in their interpretations of the data and in their explanations as to why this data does not correspond clearly to the paradigm.

Clear increase in real wages after the Black Death

On the one hand there is a group of historians who hold that there was a definite and tangible increase in real wages after the Black Death of 1348. Well over a century ago, James Thorold Rogers established price and wage tables for 6 centuries of English history. Looking at these charts, Rogers noted that wages doubled after the Black Death.[2] The epidemic, he observed, by wiping out one third to one half of the population, induced a "scarcity of hands", although this scarcity affected different types of work unequally.[3] In economic terms, then, the supply of labor dropped whereas the demand remained stable, inducing the price of labor to increase. Farm servants after the plague, he concluded, were in a "remarkably good position".[4]

Rogers's conclusions have been shared by a number of other historians. Similar studies led by Beveridge and by Brown and Hopkins have revealed the same trend of increasing real wages after the Black Death.[5]

---

2. James E. Thorold Rogers, *A History of Agriculture and Prices in England, 1259-1793*, 7 vols., (Oxford, 1866-1902), t. II, p. 265. See also J. E. T. Rogers, *Six Centuries of Work and Wages, the History of English Labor*, (London, 1912), pp. 217-219.
3. J. E. T. Rogers 1866-1902, t. II, pp. 261, 270-274.
4. Ibid., t. II, p. 689. One must not forget the purpose of his study which was to show the overall decline in condition for laborers of the 19th century. His observations are thus all tinted by a particular ideological lens. It may be for this reason that he ignored his own data which indicated that prices as well increased during the same period, keeping real wages stable.
5. William Beveridge, "Wages in the Winchester Manor", *Economic History Review*, 2nd ser., 7 (1936), pp. 22-43; "Westminster Wages in the Manorial Era," *Economic History Review*, 2nd ser., 8 (1955), pp. 18-35; E. H. Phelps Brown and Sheila V.

Michael Postan was so sure of the real wage increase that he used it as proof of continuing population decline.⁶ More recently, Richard Britnell has confirmed these findings with extensive evidence from Colchester. Wage rates after the plague, he observes, increased much more than prices, benefiting especially poorer families. Britnell concludes that "the conspicuous changes in money wage rates which had come about as an immediate result of the Black Death had proved to be of permanent effect."⁷ John Hatcher as well has shown statistical evidence from around England that shows that real wages increased "dramatically" after the Black Death.⁸

Similar trends have been observed in other regions. Citing the extensive data gathered by Charles de La Roncière, Richard Goldthwaite contends that there was an immediate and dramatic gain in the Florentine workers' real wages.⁹ Guy Fourquin, in his extensive study of account books from the Paris region, noticed a considerable rise in day wages after the Black Death and concludes that this increase was due to the numerical dearth of laborers.¹⁰

No significant increase in real wages after the Black Death
As is often the case, however, there is also a group of historians who disagree. Several historians have reexamined the statistical evidence found in account books and demonstrate the absence of an increase in real wage

---

Hopkins, "Seven Centuries of Building Wages", *Economica*, (1955), pp. 195-206; "Seven Centuries of the Prices of Consumables, Compared with Builders' Wage-rates," *Economica*, (1959), pp. 296-314.

6. Michael M. Postan, "Agrarian evidence of a declining population" *Essays on medieval agriculture and General Problems of the Medieval Economy*, (Cambridge, 1973), pp. 186-213.
7. Richard Britnell, *Growth and Decline in Colchester, 1300-1525*, (Cambridge, 1986), p. 147-148.
8. John Hatcher, *Plague, Population and the English Economy*, (London, 1977), p. 47-54.
9. Richard A Goldthwaite, *The Building of Renaissance Florence. An Economic and Social History*, (Baltimore, 1980), p. 334. Charles de La Roncière, *Prix et salaires à Florence au XIVème siècle, 1280-1380*, Rome, 1982.
10. Guy Fourquin, *Les campagnes de la région parisienne à la fin du Moyen Age*, (Paris, 1964), p. 278. See also Philippe Wolff, *Commerces et marchands de Toulouse, vers 1350, vers 1450*, (Paris, 1954), p. 455; Gérard Sivéry, *Structures agraires et vie rurale dans le Hainaut à la fin du moyen age*, (Lille, 1977), p. 429.

rates after 1348. Although nominal wages did indeed rise after the Black Death, prices kept very close pace causing real wages to remain stable.

Bridbury states, "the statistics of wages and prices do not indicate by the slightest movement that there was any change in the relative scarcities of land and labor until very near the end of the [14th] century."[11] Bolton observes, "The curious fact is that, although so many people died in the first outbreak, plague initially had few economic consequences," citing the fact that holdings were quickly filled, wages kept low and prices high.[12] Indeed, according to Bolton the economy recovered within only a few years after the Black Death.[13] The real change he notes did not take place until the 1370s, due to the subsequent outbreaks of plague. Lawrence Poos points out that although nominal wages did increase by a third between 1350 and 1380, this rise was muted by the high costs of grain. It was not until the 1380s, as grain prices dropped, that real wages were pushed up.[14] The author of the most recent and detailed analysis of English prices and wages, David Farmer, concludes that "it was not until the last quarter of the 14th century that both building and agricultural workers were clearly better off than they had been in the early 13th century."[15]

After a century of debate on the subject, economic historians still do not seem to agree on the movement of real wages after the Black Death. The only point that they all hold in common, the only thing that every economic historian who has attempted to analyze wage fluctuations in the 14th century can agree on, is that after the Black Death, in a context of dramatic population decline, real wages *should* have increased. Even those who find that real wages did *not* increase feel that they must somehow justify and explain why this is the case. Bolton considers his own observation relative to the stable real wages after the Black Death a "curious fact" as it does not correspond to economic logic.[16] There are two main arguments that historians use to account for the increase in real wages.

---

11. A. R. Bridbury, "The Black Death", *Economic History Review*, 2nd ser., 26, (1973), p. 578.
12. James L. Bolton, *The Medieval English Economy 1150-1500*, (London, 1980), pp. 61-62.
13. Ibid., p. 209
14. Lawrence Poos, *A Rural Society after the Black Death, Essex 1350-1525*, (Cambridge, 1991), p. 209.
15. David L. Farmer, "Prices and Wages (1350-1500)", *in* (ed.) Herbert E. Hallam, *The Agrarian History of England and Wales*, (Cambridge, 1991), t. III, p. 778.
16. J. L. Bolton 1980 (n 12), pp. 61-62.

Still enough people
Several historians hold that, although the population was diminished between a third and a half within the space of few months, this decrease was not sufficient to overturn the overpopulation in the pre-plague era and that there were still enough people available to work. Bridbury refers to the existence of "a submerged and pullulating throng" who simply replaced the dead.[17] Waugh speaks of a "huge surplus population".[18] Bolton dedicated an entire chapter of his book to the question and entitled it "the Overcrowded Island". "The countryside", he suggests, "was still full of people" creating a "continuing surplus of labor".[19]

This argument, however, is quite clearly wrong. First of all, there is a vast amount of narrative evidence from literary and administrative sources that indicates a dearth of workers after the Black Death. Even if contemporary accounts overestimate the demographic decline, there is no reason to believe that England was still full of people. Secondly, almost all demographic evidence points to the fact that the population was already in decline from at least the beginning of the 14th century. The overpopulation of the 13th century had already started to reverse its trend by 1300 as land and resources were overstretched. A series of famines wiped out a good number in 1315-1317, then again in 1321. And there is no sign that the population recovered in the 30 years before the Black Death. On the contrary, there is even evidence to show that the population continued to decline in the 1330s and 1340s.[20]

Finally, even without referring to all the demographic and narrative evidence to the contrary, we can refute this explanation on purely logical grounds. Any reduction in the competition for jobs would have had an influence on the wage rates. Even if there were still enough people to

---

17. A. R. Bridbury 1973 (n 11), p. 590.
18. Scott L. Waugh, *England in the Reign of Edward III*, (Cambridge, 1991), p. 89.
19. J. L. Bolton 1980 (n 12), pp. 61-62, 212-213.
20. Barbara F. Harvey, "Introduction: the 'crisis' of the early fourteenth century", and Richard M. Smith, "Demographic Developments in Rural England, 1300-1348: A Survey", *in* (ed.) Bruce M. S. Campbell, *Before the Black Death. Studies in the 'Crisis' of the Early Fourteenth Century*, (Manchester, 1991), pp. 1-24, 25-78; Edward Miller and John Hatcher, *Medieval England: Towns Commerce and crafts, 1086-1348*, (London, 1995), pp. 393-429. See also: David Herlihy, *Medieval and Renaissance Pistoria: the Social History of an Italian Town, 1200-1430*, (New Haven, 1967), pp. 64-66. David Herlihy and Christine Klapisch, *Tuscans and their Families: a Study of the Florentine Carasto of 1427*, (New Haven, 1985), pp. 62-63.

do the work, there was less competition for the jobs available. If there were ten workers for every job being offered, the wage could be negotiated down to a minimum. However, if there were only two workers for every job, the wages would not drop nearly as low. Moreover, according to their own argument, there were not two workers left for every job offer after the Black Death, but only one. For these same historians who claim that England was still full of people after 1348 also argue that the second outbreak of plague in 1361, an epidemic that only eliminated about 10% of the population, and mostly children for that matter, had a tremendous impact on the labor market because all the labor reserves had already been eliminated. So according to these very same historians, after the Black Death there were only just enough workers to do the jobs available. Logically then wages should have taken off as all the competition for the jobs had been eliminated. The argument that there was a sufficient number of workers after the Black Death to keep wages stable clearly does not hold true.

Effective enforcement of the labor statutes
The other argument used by economic historians to explain why real wages did not increase concerns the effective enforcement of labor statutes. Most historians recognize that the Statute of Laborers and subsequent labor ordinances had at least some effect on the labor market though they do not attempt to analyze exactly what the actual effects may have been. Only Nora Kenyon was of the opinion that "the Statutes of Labourers formed a despairing commentary upon a change which they were powerless to check."[21] Most other historians, however, temper this pessimistic view about the effectiveness of the statutes. Rogers stated that the statutes "may have induced some slight effect on the wages of farm labourers."[22] B. H. Putnam claimed that, although wages did not remain at their statutory level, the statute was successful at keeping wages lower than what they would have become in an unregulated market.[23] Although their aim was not at all to examine the effectiveness of such legislation, Penn and Dyer also asserted that the statute, "for all its patchy enforcement, may have inhibited the

---

21. Nora Kenyon, "Labor Conditions in Essex in the Reign of Richard II", *Economic History Review*, 2nd ser., 4 (1934), pp. 429-451, p. 430.
22. J. E. T. Rogers 1912 (n 2), p. 229.
23. Bertha Haven Putnam, *The Enforcement of the Statutes of Labourers During the First Decade after the Black Death 1349-1359*, (New York, 1908), p. 221.

demands of workers."[24] Scott Waugh considers that the statutes at the very least had a "chilling effect on workers' demands."[25] David Farmer found that whereas the first statute of 1349, he contends, "fell flat" in most of England, the second statute of 1351 was more effectively enforced.[26] But in the 1360s and 70s, even more vigorous action was taken by the justices to enforce wage limits, which is ironically the same time at which Farmer observes wages starting to rise, suggesting that wage legislation was not always an effective means to counter market trends.[27]

It is quite clear that the labor legislation of the 14th century had an effect on the market. This influence, however, is quite complex and cannot be reduced to mere numbers. If per diem money wages were kept lower than could be expected, many other practices were also modified. Employers tended to feed, clothe and house their workers, thus increasing their disposable income and improving their overall standards of living. Work hours as well were affected by the statutory limits on day wages. The relatively low and stable wages certain historians have observed are most probably due to the variations in the forms of payment that do not appear in account registers and possible shifts in work hours, and thus must not be used as an indication of standards of living. Although the labor laws of the 14th century had a profound impact on the labor market, one cannot simply reduce this impact to a quantitative analysis of the movement of real wages.[28]

Statistical evidence questioned
Neither of these attempts to explain why the statistical evidence does not support the economic model is entirely convincing. Other historians have questioned the reliability of the statistical evidence. In his well-known book on standards of living, Dyer noted that the Black Death resulted in only modest gains for many workers, but he remained extremely vague and did not at all commit himself to broad generalizations regarding overall

---

24. Simon A. C. Penn and Christopher Dyer, "Wages and Earnings in Late Medieval England: Evidence from the Enforcement of the Labour Laws", *Economic History Review*, 2nd ser., 43 (1990), pp. 356-376, p. 374.
25. Scott L. Waugh, *England in the Reign of Edward III*, (Cambridge, 1991), p. 112.
26. Farmer 1991 (n 15), p. 484.
27. Ibid., p. 485.
28. For a detailed analysis of the effects of various royal labor policies on the market, cf. Robert Braid, "*Et non ultra*: Politiques royales du travail en Europe occidentale au XIVème siècle,» *La Bibliothèque de l'Ecole des Chartes*, 161 (2003), pp. 437-491.

real wage movements.[29] A year later, he and Simon Penn remarked that the evidence of a rise of cash and real wages after 1348 may seem "well established" (referring to Rogers, Beveridge, Brown and Hopkins and Hatcher). But highlighting the various forms of retribution for labor (such as payment in kind, etc.) which do not appear in the account books, they go on to conclude that the extensive series of wages rates no longer seem certain.[30] In fact, a major conclusion of their study is their acknowledgment of "our ignorance of many aspects of wage earning."[31]

Attempting to buttress his initial observation, John Hatcher assembles a wealth of narrative evidence that indicates that real wages did indeed rise after the Black Death, independent of any indication in account books to the contrary.[32] Many contemporaries complained of the rising wages, and that laborers were developing consumption habits which were previously economically impossible, but now only socially unacceptable. Numerous laws were enacted and enforced to halt the wage inflation. Hatcher argues that it would be absurd to contradict the general consensus among contemporaries that real wages had increased. He considers that the statistical evidence of price and wage fluctuations gathered from account registers is in fact rather unreliable.

Snooks also questions the statistical evidence, but to support the notion that real wages remained low. He criticizes historians who support the notion of rising real wages after the Black Death based on the price and wage charts of Rogers and Beveridge, by claiming that the image given in these charts is but "a statistical illusion". "Accordingly," argues Snooks, "they are forced to develop ingenious, but totally unrealistic, arguments to support untenable empirical relationships." The building wages used in these charts are not representative of medieval workers on the whole. He develops instead a theoretical model, complete with graphs, to demonstrate that decreased capital stock and static technology caused real wages to drop in the years following the Black Death. But even Rogers' data relative to agricultural wages do not corroborate his model. He is consequently driven to the conclusion that one must dismiss over a cen-

---

29. Christopher Dyer, *Standards of Living in the Later Middle Ages: Social Changes in England, c. 1200-1520*, (Cambridge, 1989), p. 218.
30. S. A. C. Penn and C. Dyer 1990 (n 24), p. 356.
31. Ibid., p. 372.
32. John Hatcher, "England in the Aftermath of the Black Death", *Past and Present*, 144 (1994), pp. 3-35.

tury's worth of meticulous archival work and suggests that, should some enterprising historian start the same research from scratch, he would certainly find that the correctly amassed statistical evidence supports his theoretical model.[33]

The economic model
Although it is clear that there are problems with the statistical data compiled by historians over the decades, it would be unwise to entirely dismiss them as useless. One could of course advance an entirely different, and quite simple, argument on purely theoretical grounds to support the idea that wages remained low after the Black Death. After the Black Death, there was not only a decreased supply of labor on the market, but there was also a proportionate decrease in the number of consumers and thus also in the demand for the basic commodities. One must remember that the wage inflation that historians, legislators and chroniclers refer too is in the sector of the basic staples (food, wine, clothing), for which demand was rather inelastic, and not of luxury goods. Although there would have been an initial imbalance on the market, prices and wages would have quickly adapted. Fewer mouths to feed and backs to clothe means less need to produce. Employers would not have been able to sell as many goods as they were selling before the Black Death so would need to hire fewer people to produce them. Thus, even according to the traditional economic model of supply and demand, the rapid mortality caused by the Black Death would *not* have caused a dramatic increase in real wages in the long run. The stable wage rates after the Black Death that Bolton observes is thus not a "curious fact" as he remarked, but totally logical according to the basic economic paradigm.

However, I am not entirely satisfied with this argument, not because it does not clearly fit the economic model, but rather because it relies too heavily on this model and does not take into account the complexity of reactions that one can observe while studying the 14th century labor market. Other medieval historians have already pointed out the weakness of applying traditional economic paradigms to historical subjects, but they do not propose any new model or solution to replace it. Indeed, they continue themselves to use the same line of reasoning. Guy Bois has observed

---

33. Graeme Donald Snooks, *Economics without Time. A Science blind to the Forces of Historical Change*, (London, 1993), pp. 259-264.

that "medievalists wrongly borrow capitalist models and reasoning."[34] As Edouard Perroy has also pointed out, "scholars have certainly laid too great an emphasis on both the depletion of the labour market owing to the Black Death and subsequent epidemics, and on currency debasements, two factors that ought to have sent prices and wages soaring."[35] He argues instead that wages were low because trade and industry were in decadence, especially because of the insecurity caused by the war in France. Brown and Hopkins, looking at wage and price indices over seven centuries expressed their perplexity at the trends they observed: "For a century or more, it seems, prices will obey one all-powerful law; it changes, and a new law prevails; a war that would have cast the trend up to new heights in one dispensation is powerless to deflect it in another."[36] Guy Fourquin was also puzzled by certain of his own findings as they are "contrary to economic logic"; but Fourquin simply leaves it at that rather than question the relevance of "economic logic".[37]

In order to help resolve in part this dilemma, I have chosen to turn directly to economic theory and see how specialists in this field have dealt with similar issues. In the next section of this paper, I would like to trace the origins of the notions that many economic historians take for granted and also look at how they have evolved in recent years among economic theorists.

Economic theory

Traditional economic paradigms, initially elaborated in the 18th century, have always taken for granted the assumption of *homo oeconomicus*, and it was not until about fifty years ago that economic theorist have started to question whether human beings actually react in a purely logical and self-interested fashion. Medieval economic historians, however, still tend to adopt the very traditional paradigm of economic man and have not yet incorporated recent research in economic theory into their conception

---

34. Guy Bois, *La grande dépression médiévale XIVème et XVème siècles. Le précédent d'une crise systémique*, (Paris, 2000), p. 21.
35. Edouard Perroy, "Wage Labour in France in the Later Middle Ages" *Economic History Review*, 2nd ser., 7 (1955), p. 238.
36. E. H. Phelps Brown and Sheila V. Hopkins, "Seven Centuries of the Prices of Consumables", p. 305.
37. Guy Fourquin, *Les Campagnes de la région parisienne*, (Paris, 1964), pp. 304, 493.

of the medieval economy. I would thus like to trace rapidly the evolution of the notion of economic man, focusing in particular on the developments of economic theory over the past fifty years or so, to see which new theories economic historians could possibly use to resolve the problem of the effect of the Black Death on the labor market.

Origins of Economic Man
The theory of economic man has often been ascribed to Adam Smith, who is considered the grandfather of economic theory. This attribution is only partly justified. For although Smith's work does rely in part on the notion of self-interested economic actors, its use in neoclassical economic theory varies greatly from Adam Smith's original concept. Moreover, the notion that man is inherently egotistical was far from an earth-shattering concept in 18th century Europe.

Although the idea that men are self-interested beings concerned only with satiating their lower appetites is part and parcel of Judeo-Christian morality, it was perhaps Thomas Hobbes who launched the debate in mainly philosophical terms. In 1651, Hobbes published *Leviathan* in which he elaborated, among other ideas, his notion of *homo homini lupus* (man is a wolf to man).[38] Man is inherently a self-interested being, seeking individual gain and security at the expense of all those around him. The natural state of man is thus bloodthirsty chaos, and the only way to avoid such a state of affairs, according to Hobbes, was to eliminate men's ability to act according to his independent judgment and to impose absolute power. This of course sparked quite a debate, and much of late 17th and early 18th century moral philosophy had to do with the natural state of man, or human nature.

Another major influence on 18th century thought was Isaac Newton, who in 1687 published his *Mathematical Principles of Natural Philosophy* in which he exposed his theory of universal attraction.[39] It was Newton's theory of gravitation that made it possible to base on a single law a complete science of nature. In the century following Newton, scientists continued to seek universal principles that determine how entire systems work. Moral philosophers were not immune to this tendency and they too sought to reduce human nature to basic axioms that can be used to

---

38. Thomas Hobbes, *Leviathan*, (ed.) Richard Tuck, 2 vols., (Cambridge, 1991).
39. Isaac Newton, *Mathematical Principles of Natural Philosophy*, 2 vols., (London, 1729).

explain how people act. As Newton sought to understand the invisible rules that govern the physical world, so moral philosophers, such as David Hume and later Adam Smith sought to comprehend human nature and society as a system, a mechanism, based on a few simple laws.

Hume overtly sought to imitate Newtonian methodology in his *Treatise of Human Nature*.[40] Rather than seeking the mechanisms of human nature in the physical world around him, he observed human behavior through history to discover the universal principles that govern the system. He also recognized the impossibility of experimenting on the human subject, as his intervention would disturb the natural principle he sought to observe. Moral philosophers have merely to observe, and preferably through history, as it would be impossible to influence the course of what has already happened.

Adam Smith was a close friend of David Hume and heavily influenced by him, although he did not agree with many of Hume's ideas. He was primarily influenced by Hume in his method of observing through history and in his search for the universal principles of human nature, the machinery that is human nature. One must not forget, however, that Adam Smith was originally professor of logic then of moral philosophy. As such, he was very familiar with classical authors. He borrowed heavily from Stoic philosophy, notably Epictetus, Marcus Aurelius and Cicero, but attempted to reconcile this philosophy with Christian ideals.[41] Indeed, his first major work was the *Theory of Moral Sentiments* (first edition in 1759 but continuously revised up until Smith's death in 1790) in which not self-interest but sympathy was the driving force behind man's relations with other people. After a few years in France and contact with physiocrats such as Turgot, he came back to Scotland and wrote the *Wealth of Nations* (1776), from which has stemmed much of classical economic theory. For Adam Smith, however, the economic activities of man were only one part of a much more complex human system. The two basic forces driving human nature, sympathy as outlined in *Theory of Moral Sentiments*, and self-interest in the *Wealth of Nations*, were not diametrically opposed. Instead, they were two complementary aspects of human nature that kept balance in society.

---

40. David Hume, *Treatise on Human Nature, being an attempt to introduce the experimental method of reasoning into moral subjects*, 3 vols., (London, 1739-1740).
41. Gloria Vivenza, *Adam Smith and the Classics. The Classical Heritage in Adam Smith's Thought*, (Oxford, 2000).

Indeed, the very first words of *Theory of Moral Sentiments* question the Hobbsean premise that humans are basically self-interested. "How selfish soever man may be supposed, there are evidently some principles in his nature, which interest him in the fortune of others, and render their happiness necessary to him, though he derives nothing from it except the pleasure of seeing it."[42] Human history shows a tendency towards organization and order, it must also be true that there exists a sympathetic sentiment that keeps this self-interest in check. For Smith, man was *not* a wolf to man. Even the "greatest ruffian [or] the most hardened violator of the laws of society" is not entirely without sympathy.[43] The goal of the *Wealth of Nations* was to provide an understanding of the nature and operation of the economy in order to justify and facilitate systemic reform, namely of the mercantilist system. Smith's main objective was to do away with the artificial monopolies created through mercantilism and which served the interest of only a few. In order to convince governments to liberate the economy, he had to set up an organized balanced system which leads naturally towards peace and order. This is the basic notion behind the *Wealth of Nations*.

This conception of human nature, however, did not last very long in economic theory, primarily because it lacked clarity. Allen Oakley calls it "the imprecise and mixed methodological legacy left by Smith".[44] Indeed, even Jean-Baptiste Say, who was otherwise rather admirative of Smith's work, was also rather critical of his method. "His work, [*Wealth of Nations*], is but a confused assemblage of the most healthy principles of *political economy* supported with brilliant examples, and the most curious notions of *statistics* mixed with instructive reflections; but it is not a complete treaty of one or the other. His book is a vast chaos of correct ideas, mixed up with positive knowledge."[45] Say himself, in his *Treaty on Political Economy* (1803) looks for fundamental principals of economics through observation, and recognizes the impossibility of divorcing economic theory from economic reality. Economics is a human science and must remain empirical.

---

42. Adam Smith, *The Theory of Moral Sentiments*, (eds.) D. D. Raphael and A. L. Macfie, (Oxford, 1991), Part I, Section I, Chap. I, p. 9.
43. Ibid.
44. Allen Oakley, *Classical Economic Man. Human Agency and Methodology in the Political Economy of Adam Smith and J. S. Mill*, (Hants, 1994), p. 118.
45. Jean-Baptiste Say, *Traité d'économie politique, ou Simple exposition de la manière dont se forment, se distribuent et se consomment les richesses*, (Paris, 1803), p. vi.

After Say, however, the notion of economic man fell into the hands of philosophers who sought to make economics a science as pure as mathematics, based again on fundamental axioms, but entirely abstract. Moreover, theses philosophers took only the Hobbsean half of Smith's original conception of human nature and from that elaborated purely mathematical models. These abstract models were developed by James Mill, *Elements of Political Economy* (1826)[46], and David Ricardo, *Principles* (1817)[47]. James Mill went beyond the Newtonian metaphor of seeking fundamental principles and spoke of economics in geometric terms. James Mill's mathematical and geometric approach infiltrated even his *Analysis of the Phenomena of the Human Mind* (1829).[48] No psychological or even human aspects were introduced into his economic philosophy, which some scholars have identified as rather a "dogma".[49]

Modern Economic Theory
Although there were indeed varying opinions and great developments, it is this tradition of abstract economic theorizing, based on the fundamental principle of economic man that dominated the study of economics until the 1950s. It was thanks to the ground-breaking work of George Katona, who was the first person to use cognitive psychology in economic research that the underlying principle of economic man was first brought into question. In his own words: "Psychological economics considers economic processes as manifestations of human behavior. [...] Although economic behavior is elicited by the environment and its changes, human beings do not react to stimuli as automatons. Their motives and attitudes, even their tastes, hopes, and fears, represent intervening variables that influence both their perception of the environment and their behavior. In order to understand economic processes, psychological considerations and subjective variables must be incorporated in the analysis."[50]

---

46. James Mill, *Elements of Political Economy*, 3rd edition, (London, 1826), reprinted by Hildesheim, (New York, 1971).
47. David Ricardo, *On the Principles of Political Economy and Taxation*, (London, 1817).
48. James Mill, *Analysis of the Phenomena of the Human Mind*, 2 vols., (London, 1869).
49. For more detailed analysis of the notion of economic man in classical economic theory, see Allen Oakley, *Classical Economic Man* ; Patricia H. Werhane, *Adam Smith and His Legacy for Modern Capitalism*, (Oxford, 1991).
50. George Katona, *Psychological Economics*, (New York, 1975), p. 3.

Complementary to this approach of incorporating psychological considerations into economic analysis and equally responsible for the revolution in economic science these past decades, is the method of using laboratory experiments to test behavior. Isaac Newton, one must remember, was an astronomer and observed the physical world from afar. Early moral philosophers and economic theorists, such as David Hume, Adam Smith, J.-B. Say, Thomas R. Malthus, Karl Marx, etc., have generally adopted the astronomer's approach to observation, especially retrospective observation through history. Behavioural psychologists, however, use laboratory experiments to test economic behavior. In this sense, economics becomes less like astronomy and more like chemistry in that scientists set up controlled environments and test basic reactions.

These two advances in economic methodology have opened up a flood of new theories that demolish the basic principles that had been holding up neo classical economic paradigms. Neo classical economists had traditionally assumed that actors systematically chose an action that increases gain based on available information, or as some theorists would say, "that maximizes expected utility". Thus decision making is more a process of solving an equation than actually responding to a complex set of stimuli. Cognitive psychologists, on the other hand, think in terms of an interactive process in which many factors affect decision-making, such as perception, beliefs, emotions, cultural values, and memory. Behavior is not only subjective (relying on each individual's perception, experience and value systems) but adaptive (depending on the context) and transitory (changing over time). Even experimental economists tend to stress the universal nature of their findings, basing their experiments on hypothetical monetary gain and repetition to extract standardized patterns of economic behavior. Cognitive psychologists tend to concentrate more on the process or "framing" of decision making, rather than the result of the decisions.[51]

Various findings of modern economic theorists
In order to appreciate the variety and importance of recent research by cognitive and behavioural psychologists in economic theory, it is useful to give a brief description of some of their results. One of their findings

---

51. Daniel Kahneman, "New Challenges to the Rationality Assumption", *in* (eds.) Daniel Kahneman and Amos Tversky, *Choices, Values and Frames*, (Cambridge, 2000), pp. 758-774.

concerns the "heuristic probabilistic judgment", or in other words mental short cuts. Unable to absorb and properly process the vast amount of available information necessary to make a critical judgment, people tend to make quick generalizations and vast assumptions, connecting the dots between bits of data to make a decision. Some might consider this instinct or intuition or feeling, but the vast majority of economic decisions are based on such a process.[52]

Another finding is based on the notion of "availability". According to experiments, people generally evaluate the accuracy of information based on personal experience and memory rather than on objective criteria. For example, people who have been attacked or know people who have been attacked, grossly overestimate crime statistics. Also, information that has been frequently repeated, regardless of the source or reliability of that information, is perceived as more accurate than conflicting information which comes from a more reliable source but which is much less repeated.[53]

The concept of utility has also been broadened. Traditional economic theory holds that an economic actor will seek what is useful or desirable for that person. The desirableness or usefulness of a commodity is called its "utility". D. Kahneman, however, points out that people do not always know what they will like and may seek things that end up undesirable or useless. This is the notion of "predicted utility". Moreover, people do not always remember correctly what they enjoyed. This is the concept of "real-time" and "retrospective utility".[54]

Other modern economic theorists conclude that human decisions are the result, not only of a flux of impulses, but also on a system of filters, and that there are a variety of different filters in the human brain such as emotion, habit, and cognition.[55] People's decisions are often affected by variables seemingly unrelated, such as the way weather affects the stock market.

Experimental research has also been able to elaborate a conceptual framework (called "prospect theory") for understanding irrational be-

---

52. Daniel Kahneman, P. Slovic and Amos Tversky (eds.), *Judgement Under Uncertainty: Heuristics and Biases*, (Cambridge, 1982); George von Furstenburg (ed.), *Acting Under Uncertainty: Multidisciplinary Conceptions*, (Boston, 1990).
53. Amos Tversky and Daniel Kahneman, "Availability: A heuristic for Judging Frequency and Probability", *Cognitive Psychology*, 5 (1973), pp. 207-232.
54. D. Kahneman 1982 (n 52), pp. 758-774.
55. Roger A. McCain, *A Framework for Cognitive Economics*, (London, 1992).

havior, such as driving a long distance just to save a few dollars on a small item while refusing to make the same trip for the same discount on a more expensive item. Prospect theory has also made it possible to predict what would otherwise seem to be irrational consumption patterns or decision-making mechanisms that are in stark contradiction to earlier assumptions of rational self-interest. For example, the fact that people often prefer to lose $5 if someone they dislike will also lose $5, rather than winning $5 and letting the other person also win $5.[56]

All these findings point to the notion that man does not always act rationally and in his own self-interest. As J. Meeks states in his introduction to *Thoughtful Economic Man*: "Rational economic man has sometimes been very narrowly conceived as a crudely calculating self-interested maximizer."[57] Moreover, as McCain points out, "the evidence that actual human decisions are biased away from neoclassical optima and that some of the biases are to some extent hard-wired in the human sensorium (rather as visual illusions are), certainly undermines neoclassical economics as it stands."[58] Thus, human judgment violates the basic principles of rational decision-making that is the cornerstone of traditional economic theory.

MEDIEVAL ECONOMIC HISTORY AND MODERN ECONOMIC THEORY

Ironically, although historians are quick to recognize that pre-industrial societies were not capitalistic, and sometimes use the regrettable term "primitive" when referring to pre-industrial economies, very few ever really bring into question the notion of economic man when analyzing these pre-industrial economies. Not all economic historians, however, are entirely cut off form the world of economic theory. Several of the most brilliant economic historians also publish in journals of contemporary economics and are aware of the effects of behavioural patterns on labor productivity. Ian Blanchard demonstrated that English miners in the 15th

---

56. Daniel Kahneman and Amos Tversky, "Prospect Theory: An analysis of Decision Under Risk," and "Advances in Prospect Theory: Cumulative Representation of Uncertainty", *in* (eds.) Daniel Kahneman and Amos Tversky, *Choices, Values and Frames*, (Cambridge, 2000), pp. 17-43, 44-65.
57. J. Gay Tulip Meeks, "Introduction", *in* (ed.) J. Gay Tulip Meeks, *Thoughtful Economic Man. Essays on Rationality, Moral Rules and Benevolence*, (Cambridge, 1991), p. 1.
58. R. A. McCain 1992 (n 55).

and 16th centuries would work to obtain a given level of income.[59] "Work intensity" he concluded, "was conditioned [...] by the conscious decisions of the miner embodied within a specific work psychology."[60] According to Blanchard, however, the level of income was determined by one's place in village society and was quite stable. He does not consider in this article the possibility of external forces acting on one's income expectancy.

Karl Gunnar Persson astutely acknowledged that "when you discuss the historical relationship between work effort and consumption you have to relate it – nonetheless – to socio-psychological properties of men".[61] Unfortunately, he totally ignores these socio-psychological properties in the rest of the article. In fact he goes on to make vast generalizations that seem to reflect clichés rather than research: "Humans inherently avoid wage-labour as it is associated with subordination and lack of freedom that violate the modest standards of human dignity."[62] Moreover, he arrives at the same conclusions as all other economic historians: "The rise in nominal wages was evidently caused by the immense labour shortage following the demographic disaster associated with the Black Death and subsequent pests."[63]

Christopher Dyer dedicated an entire article to work ethics in the 14th century, in which he rejects Blanchard's opinion that peasants and day laborers accepted their lot and preferred leisure.[64] Highlighting women's increased participation in the labor market and an overall rise in per capita output in the second half of the 14th century, Dyer suggests that "medieval workers maximized their earnings, rather than opting for leisure."[65] In this article, he also summarizes the main texts relative to the problem of

---

59. Compare with Colin F. Camerer, Linda Babcock, George Loewenstein, Richard H. Thaler, "Labor Supply of NYC Cab Drivers: One Day at a Time," *in* (eds.) D. Kahneman and A. Tversky, *Choices, Values and Frames*, pp. 356-370.
60. Ian Blanchard, "Labour Productivity and Work Psychology in the English Mining Industry, 1400-1600," *Economic History Review*, 2nd. ser., 31 (1978), pp. 1-24, p. 3.
61. Karl Gunnar Persson, "Consumption, Labour and Leisure in the Late Middle Ages," in *Manger et Boire au Moyen Age, Actes du colloque de Nice (15-17 octobre 1982)*, 2 vols., t. I «Aliments et Société», (Paris, 1984), pp. 211-223, 211-212.
62. Ibid., p. 213.
63. Ibid., p. 216.
64. Christopher Dyer, "Work Ethics in the 14th century", *in* (eds.) James Bothwell, P. J. P. Goldberg and W. M. Ormrod, *The Problem of Labour in 14th century England*, (New York, 2000), pp. 21-41.
65. Ibid., p. 38.

attitudes towards work, both by contemporaries and historians. Unfortunately, he does not look at the direct effects of the Black Death on these attitudes and makes generalizations relative to workers' psychology that span half a century.

John Hatcher examined workers' attitudes as described in literary sources to bring into question the conventional historical wisdom that laborers' gains in the aftermath of the repeated outbreaks of plague in the 14th century were only modest. He contends that we have no reason to doubt contemporaries' observations that the working class was living better than before. These improved living conditions of workers in this period of high real wages "enhanced their self-esteem and encouraged them to question authority and tradition."[66] It is certainly true that the attitudes of laborers changed due to their economic situation, but it is probably equally true that their attitudes also influenced their economic condition. Moreover, the picture he paints of worker psychology reflects the long-term effects of the plague. Although rising living standards would no doubt in the long-run positively influence workers' self-esteem, it is also necessary to examine the short-term effects of a major catastrophe on economic behavior. As we should not question contemporaries' views that workers were living better in the second half of the 14th century, nor should we question their observations that point out the extreme psychological distress that they felt by witnessing their friends, family and neighbors die a rapid and painful death during the plague and the effect of this distress had on attitudes towards labor.

Leisure
Some economists and historians have asserted that workers in general have a "fixed income expectancy", meaning that once the basic necessities could be obtained for the wages earned, laborers tend to stop working rather than work more to increase their income. Other historians, however, have contended that laborers were actually working more after the plague than before. Workers continued to maximize their earnings by working hard, picking up extra cash whenever the occasion presented itself. It was this extra disposable income that allowed them to consume more goods. Prior to the epidemic, when there was a glut of people seeking work, forced unemployment was the lot of many. After the plague,

---

66. J. Hatcher 1994 (n 32), p. 33.

though laborers could not accept all the work that was being offered in this context of a labor shortage, so the argument runs, they were still spending more time working than their pre-plague predecessors. With their higher wages, they preferred to consume better foods and wear better clothing, not take more time off.

Contemporaries, however, complained of the laziness of workers after the Black Death. Boccaccio observed that, rather than taking care of their herds or reaping their crops, people sought only to consume what was already acquired. Land was not only left fallow, but crops were not even harvested. Peasants and townspeople alike "became lax in their ways and neglected their chores as if they expected death that very day."[67] John Gower remonstrated peasants for being "sluggish" and observed that "scarcely a rustic wishes to do [agricultural] work; instead he wickedly loafs everywhere."[68] William Langland's Piers Plowman complained about workers who preferred drinking to laboring.[69] Summarizing post-plague literature, Knighton observed that workers served their masters worse and worse every day.[70]

Labor ordinances, whether at a local or national level, also deplored the new attitudes of workers after the plague. In the year after the Black Death, Edward III observed that many workers were "willing to beg in idleness, rather than labor to get their living."[71] In Paris, King John the Good observed that both men and women remained idle, refusing to expose their bodies to perform any form of work, some roaming about the town, others spending their time in taverns and whore houses.[72] A Spanish statute issued after the Black Death as well indicates the prevalence

---

67. Giovanni Boccaccio, *Tutte le opere de Giovanni Boccaccio*. t. IV : *il Decameron*. (ed.) Vittore Branca, (Milan, 1976), pp. 14-18.
68. John Gower, *The Major Latin Works of John Gower: The "Voice of One Crying" and the "Tripartite Chronicle"*, (ed.) E. W. Stockton, (Seattle, 1962), pp. 208-209.
69. William Langland, *The Vision of Piers Plowman*, (ed.) A.V.C. Schmit, (London, 1978), passus VI, p. 100.
70. *Chronicon Henrici Knighton*, (ed.) J. R. Lumby, 2 vols., (London, 1895), t. II, p. 62.
71. *Statutes of the Realm*, 23 Edw. III (1349), t. I, pp. 307-308. See also 25 Edw. III (1351), *Statutes at Large*, London, 1618, t. I, p. 90; and *Statutes of the Realm*, t. I, pp. 311-313.
72. Bibliothèque nationale de France (BnF) ms fr. n° 2879 f° 1-32. BnF, ms. fr. n° 24070, ff. i-xxxii r° or ff. 42-73. Published in *Ordonnances des rois de France de la troisième race*, t. II, pp. 350-386 (30 janvier 1351). See also the second labor ordinance of John the Good in 1354: *Ordonnances*, t. II, pp. 563-566.

of healthy-bodied people simply roaming about the countryside rather than harvesting crops that were left to rot in the fields.[73]

Historians sometimes try to reconcile the incongruence of contemporary accounts with their own findings explaining that authors were no doubt stuck by the refusal of workers to accept employment and did not bother to notice that laborers were actually working more after the plague than before. It is too simple, however, to dismiss contemporary accounts as biased and inexact. Just as their views that workers were living better than before cannot not reasonably be dismissed, nor should their insistence on the laziness of workers in the wake of the plague. Indeed, it has been demonstrated that laziness amongst workers was not an issue prior to the plague and that contemporaries were not merely repeating an age-old trope.[74] Contemporaries complained not only that laborers refused to accept contracts at "reasonable" wages, but that they did not work as hard when employed as they did before the epidemic. It is certainly plausible to think that laborers were simply less motivated to exert themselves after the plague as contemporaries describe them. Not only did they (perhaps) have greater job security in the post-plague era but, as observers who had lived through the same experience witnessed, they were not convinced that they had been definitively spared by the plague. It is not unreasonable to think that the widely perceived threat of imminent death may have lowered worker productivity.

Consumption patterns
The same is true about the contemporary accounts relative to consumption patterns. There are some historians who hold that product variety was too limited in the Middle Ages to allow consumption patterns to fluctuate. There is ample evidence, however, to show that people bought and consumed more and more varied items in the post plague era. As Christopher Dyer points out, "the living standards of wage-earners before 1349 gave plenty of room for improvement."[75] Workers, he demonstrates,

---

73. *Cortes de los antiguos reinos de Leon y Castilla*, (ed.) Real Academia de la Historia, 5 vols., (Madrid, 1863), "Ordenamiento de menestrales y posturas" (1351) t. II, pp. 75-124. See also a statute issued in 1369 by Don Pedro's successor, Enrique de Trastamara, *ibid.*, pp. 164-184.
74. Indeed, laziness amongst workers was not a issue prior to the plague and contemporaries were not merely repeating an age-old trope.
75. C. Dyer 2000 (n 64), p. 36.

showed no sign of lowly consumption ambitions; they ate better types of grain, consumed more meat and ale, adopted new styles of dress and acquired a wider variety of manufactured goods. Dyer attributes these consumption patterns to increased disposable income, a direct result of higher wages.

It would be wrong, however, to ascribe these new consumption patterns solely to heightened purchasing power. First of all, many contemporary accounts indicate that the shift in attitudes towards consumption was a direct result of the epidemic. Matteo Villani noticed that no sooner had the plague ceased than the common people sought out the dearest and most delicate foods for their sustenance.[76] Boccaccio also observed this tendency to consume frivolously immediately after the mortality. Whereas some people lived soberly, others abandoned themselves to drink and to pleasure, frolicking about town with a song on their lips, granting every satisfaction possible to their passions and sought to "taste every pleasure and joy that the present can offer."[77] Agnolo di Tura remarked that, as a result of the plague, everyone in Siena "tended to enjoy eating and drinking, hunting, hawking and gaming."[78]

This phenomenon was not limited to Italy, nor did it disappear immediately after the plague. John Gower claimed that lowly workers demanded "things for his belly like a lord". Servants he complained had acquired an appetite for luxuries.[79] Before the plague, however, workers ate poor quality bread made of beans, not wheat, and they drank water; cheese and milk constituted a feast for the working class. But these "happy times of old have been wipe out". Piers Plowman complained that laborers no longer drink penny ale nor eat simple bacon. They prefer fresh meat or fried fish.[80] Labor ordinances as well deplored such consumption patterns. Many authorities even tried to halt the tendency. Edward III sought to keep common people from wearing "the outrageous and excessive apparel [...] against their estate and degree to the great de-

---

76. Matteo Villani, book I, ch. 5, cited in Millard Meiss, *Painting in Florence and Siena after the Black Death. The Arts, Religion and Society in the Mid-Fourteenth Century*, (Princeton, 1951), p. 67.
77. G. Boccaccio, *Il Decameron*, pp. 10, 19.
78. Agnolo di Tura del Grasso, *Cronache senesi. Rerum italicarum scriptores* , (ed.) A Lisini and F. Iacometti, (Bologna, 1932), vol. xv, pt. 6, pp. 555-560.
79. John Gower, *The Major Latin Works of John Gower*, pp. 58, 210.
80. William Langland, *The Vision of Piers Plowman*, pp. 109-110.

struction and impoverishment of all the land."[81] Although it is certainly true that heightened purchasing power would have allowed the working class access to such goods, it is equally true that an epidemic that pushes some people to wander about from town to town flagellating themselves, others to massacre entire communities of Jews, and still others leave their worldly possessions to embark on pilgrimages, may also be responsible for inducing people to spend more income on finer foods and clothing.

Production patterns
Perhaps one of the main reasons for the dramatic increase in wages offered on the labor market in the year following the Black Death stems from the demands, not of the workers, but of the employers. As mentioned in the first section of this paper, after the Black Death, there were not only fewer workers, but also fewer consumers. The demand for commodities, and therefore the need to produce, would thus have decreased proportionately to the decrease in the population and the supply of labor. In other words, as there were fewer people to consume basic products, there was less of a need to produce them. However, it is not certain that producers (who were also in many instances employers) would have realized that they would not have been able to liquidate all their produce. For centuries prior to the Black Death, employers had always been in a frame of mind that pushed them to reap the fields down to the last stalk, leaving only a few seeds for the elderly to glean, confident that there would always be someone willing to buy the produce. During the plague, they do not seem to have realized that there were no longer enough consumers to buy the harvest and they still wanted to hire as many workers as necessary to sew and harvest all the fields.[82] In other words, they improperly calculated their predicted utility. The initial increase in wages thus is not only linked to the decrease in the number of workers, but also to the fact that employers did not adjust their production habits to the demographic situation. Considering the context, however, their reaction is hardly surprising.

* * *

---

81. *Statutes of the Realm*, 37 Edw. III (1363), t. I, c. 8, pp. 378-383.
82. The average price of grains in England dropped by 45% in 1348-1349, a clear result of the decreased demand due to the drop in population. Cf. D. L. Farmer.

For over 50 years, economic theorists have begun accepting the fact that economic trends are heavily influenced by the behavior of economic actors, and that the observed behavior is far from the classical assumptions of economic man. Economic historians, on the other hand, are only starting to approach their subject from this angle, analyzing perhaps how the economic situation influenced the attitudes of individuals. The few historians who do look at how attitudes affected economic behavior rarely address the issue of the evolution of such attitudes, as if economic behavior were immutable. Even though social historians have long recognized the profound impact of the Black Death on the collective psychology of medieval society,[83] few economic historians have paid much attention to the effect that this catastrophe may have had on attitudes and economic behavior. They thus continue to support the notion of economic man as described by classical economic theorists, despite the vast body of research carried out by cognitive psychologists and behavioural economists over the last few decades.

An individual's behavior is not simply determined by the potential to "maximize expected utility". Decision-making, as has been demonstrated through experiments by cognitive psychologists, depends on a broad range of variables. And although the choices one makes are inherently individual, they are not totally independent of their social setting. As Katona has observed, although it is impossible to predict how any one individual will react to a given setting, it is not impossible to predict how 1000 people react.[84] At the same time, one cannot assume that there are fundamental principles that determine the mechanisms of human nature and dictate how economies work. Economic theorists should thus attribute greater weight to the precise cultural influences on economies and avoid prescribing universal panaceas to economic ills.

---

83. Yves Renouard, "La Peste noire," *Revue de Paris*, (1950), p. 107; Elisabeth Carpentier, *Une ville devant la peste : Orvieto et la Peste Noire de 1348*, (Paris, 1962), pp. 195-196; Philip Ziegler, *The Black Death*, (London, 1969), pp. 275-279; Jean Delumeau, *La peur en Occident, XIVème - XVIIIème siècle*, (Paris, 1978), pp. 132-187; Samuel K. Cohn, "Piété et commande d'oeuvre d'art après la peste noire", *Annales HSS*, 3 (1996), pp. 551-573; D. Herlihy, *The Black Death and the Transformation of the West*, (Cambridge MA, 1997), chapter 3; Francine Michaud, "La peste, la peur et l'espoir. Le pèlerinage jubilaire de romeux marseillais en 1350", *Le Moyen Age*, 104 (1998), pp. 399-434.
84. George Katona, *Psychological Economics*, pp. 53-58.

Economic historians should not only incorporate into their qualitative studies a broader spectrum of evidence which would shed light on the complexity of human behavior on the market place, but also concentrate on shorter-term phenomena to observe how these actors reacted to a particular set of stimuli, especially by analyzing economic patterns in different social, political and economic contexts. One would no doubt find that economic actors behave quite differently after, say, a famine than after an epidemic although the demographic patterns are quite similar. By looking solely at quantitative data in the second half of the 14th century, rather than at the reactions of people in the wake of a major epidemic, one cannot help but search for *homo oeconomicus,* when we should be looking for *homo sapiens.*

Saints as Protectors against Plague: Problems of Definition and Economic and Social Implications

By Heinrich Dormeier, Kiel

The Black Death of 1348 was truly one of the greatest catastrophes in the history of mankind. From the late 14th until well into the 18th century further regional epidemics continued to pose a constant threat to whole cities and communities as well as to the individual. From a historical point of view, two aspects are especially noteworthy: on the one hand, the short-, medium- and long-term effects of these epidemics and, on the other hand, the relationship between plague defence, social structures, and the general mentality. Studies on these topics seem to present themselves as prime examples for the research into collective awareness and behaviour patterns of that time.

These studies attempt to compare the despair and panic of those affected, the high number of plague victims, the helplessness of the physicians, the inadequate sanitary conditions, the – mostly futile – diversionary tactics provided by the authorities, and the patterns of explanation and rituals of appeasement propagated by the church. Relevant macro studies (e.g.w. within the history of mentality) on the history of fear, the history of death, etc., often give the impression that in 14th to 18th century Europe the reaction to the threat posed by the Black Death was always the same regardless of time and place. Thus, did people pray more in those times of despair? Did they turn to God and the Saints more often than usual? Or did they just hold more penitential processions? If this was true, then, of course, the enquiry into the piety practices of the individual, of groups, and of communities would prove only a marginal aspect of the history of the Black Death.

But on closer inspection and through a comparison of the various forms of religiosity during times of need, both in different countries and different towns, as well as throughout history, the contrary impression emerges. Thus it becomes clear why both economic and social history so far did not manage to bring forward satisfying results in the analysis and pinpointing of the crucial effects of the Black Death. Even in the case of the city of Florence, which boasts a comparatively high abundance of historical records, and whose economic evolution has been the focal point of researchers for years, it has been difficult to grasp the social consequences of the plague epidemics. Religious defence mechanisms against the plague have left much more obvious traces than any of its economic effects. Within the religious realm church authorities as well as the faithful reacted with enormous sensitivity to the development of the epidemics. Consequently it is these diverse forms of piety which seem to offer the most effective seismograph for the reactions to the plague outbreaks.

I would like to outline these reactions on the basis of the veneration of saints. For this purpose, I will draw upon two case studies which lie at the beginning and the current stage of my own research into the history of the plague. Both are ideal examples of the enigmatic quality of the term "plague saint" and for the way in which the history of piety is closely linked to both economic and social history.

"Plague saints". Problems of definition

My very first research was conducted on the probably most spectacular testimonial for the plague north of the Alps: the Saint Roch altar in the church of Saint Lawrence in Nuremberg, donated by the merchant Peter Imhoff the Elder between 1484 and 1493.[1] At first sight, this altarpiece does not seem to pose any problems with regard to veneration of saints. The shrine features a wood carving of the plague saint Roch with the bubo on his thigh and with the angel who assures him of his intercession for the sick. The insides of both screen panels (four wings in total) are

---

1. For more details, further information and illustrations see H. Dormeier, 'St. Rochus, die Pest und die Imhoffs in Nürnberg vor und während der Reformation. Ein spätgotischer Altar in seinem religiös-liturgischen, wirtschaftlich-rechtlichen und sozialen Umfeld', in *Anzeiger des Germanischen Nationalmuseums* 1985, pp. 7-72; P. Strieder, *Tafelmalerei in Nürnberg 1350-1550* (Königstein im Taunus, 1993), pp. 98f., 235-238 no 85.

ill. 1. Nuremberg, St. Lawrence, altarpiece of St. Roch, with opened screenpanels. Photo (of 1935): Hochbauamt der Stadt Nürnberg (Nuremberg).

ill. 2. Nuremberg, St. Lawrence, altarpiece of St. Roch, closed screenpanels. Photo: Hochbauamt der Stadt Nürnberg (Nuremberg).

ill. 3a. Nuremberg, St. Lawrence, altarpiece of St. Roch, narrow side panels (on the left). Photo: Hochbauamt der Stadt Nürnberg (Nuremberg).

ill. 3b. Nuremberg, St. Lawrence, altarpiece of St. Roch, narrow side panels (on the right). Photo: Hochbauamt der Stadt Nürnberg (Nuremberg).

painted with numerous scenes from the life of the saint (ill. 1). Together with the image of Saint Roch the outsides show Saint Sebastian at almost equal status, Saint Sebastian (ill. 2), whose martyrdom is repeated in the carvings on the upper part (Gesprenge/Wimperg) of the altar. Directly above we can identify another plague motif in Christ as the Man of Sorrows (ill. 1).

The figures painted on the outsides of the narrow side panels have been largely neglected by art historians. However, these images are especially interesting with regard to our topic. The left hand side depicts two popes (ill. 3a), while on the right hand side Saint Martin and a bishop are shown (ill. 3b). Older literature has been content with the simple identification of Saint Martin and a vague reference to two popes and a bishop. How can we proceed from there? First, by observing more closely: next to the pope on the bottom image of the left side panel lays a bull. Therefore, the figure of the pope can only represent Sylvester I. (314-335), who brought a dead bull back to life and who, as stated in the Nuremberg world chronicle of Hartmann Schedel, "freed the city of Rome from the pestilence of a dragon".[2] Given this context, we can presume that Saint Martin is also depicted in his function as a plague saint. In many places people prayed to Saint Martin in times of plague outbreaks, by fasting (on water and bread) on the eve of the 11th of November. Thus it seems only logical that both the image of the second pope and that of the bishop also depict patron saints against the plague. In order to trace their identity, I had to examine a host of liturgical texts with regard to which saints were commonly called upon together in plague prayers and masses. Among others I came across a votive mass against the plague from Bamberg (1503-1509), which had been extended specifically to include prayers to the Virgin Mary, Sebastian, Fabian, Sylvester, Roch and Nicasius. (ill. 4).[3]

Thus it is possible that the unidentified second pope represents Saint Fabian, whose relics were kept in a bust which was used to decorate the altar's predella (ill. 1). The bishop could therefore perhaps be identified

---

2. H. Schedel, *Liber chronicarum* (Das Buch der Chroniken) (Nuremberg, 1493), fol. 128v; J. Braun, *Tracht und Attribute der Heiligen in der deutschen Kunst* (Stuttgart, 1943), col. 662, ill. 362; *Lexikon der Christlichen Ikonographie*, 8, 1976, coll. 353-58, especially 354/55; W. Pohlkamp, 'Tradition und Topographie: Papst Silvester I. (314-335) und der Drache vom Forum Romanum', in *Röm. Quartalschrift für christliche Altertumskunde und Kirchengeschichte* 78 (1983), pp. 1-100, esp. 5-10, 48-61.
3. Bamberg, Staatsbibliothek, Msc. theol. 225, fol. 2r-9r; Itemisation of the plague patronage of the mentioned saints in Dormeier 1985, p. 28s.

ill. 4. Bamberg, Staatsbibliothek (State library), Msc. Theol. 225, fol. 2v/3r. Photo: Bamberg, Staatsbibliothek.

as Nicasius of Reims. In any case, the Roch altar in Nuremberg's church of Saint Lawrence can be recognized as a "plague altar" in a much broader sense than assumed until now.

If we generalize the above observations, we can conclude that there was a need for as many patron saints as possible to serve as protectors against the plague. The same conclusion arises from the closer study of other altars, of plague sheets ("Pestblätter"), and prayers which were generated during the epidemics from the 14th to the 16th century.[4] Essentially one

---

4. Among the extensive literature cf. only R. Crawfurd, *Plague and Pestilence in Literature and Art* (Oxford, 1914); P. Heitz (Ed.), *Pestblätter des XV. Jahrhunderts*, mit einleitendem Text von W.L. Schreiber (Einblattdrucke des 15. Jahrhunderts, Bd. 2) (Straßburg, 1918); H. Mollaret/ J. Brossolet, 'La peste, source méconnue d'inspiration artistique', in *Koninklijk Museum voor schone Kunsten, Antwerpen. Jaarboek* 1965, pp. 3-112; A. Ronen, 'Gozzoli's St. Sebastian Altarpiece in San Gimignano', in *Mitteilungen des Kunsthistorischen Instituts in Florenz* 32 (1988) pp. 77-124; H. Dormeier, '"Ein geystliche ertzeney fur die grausam erschrecklich pestilentz". Schutzpatrone und frommer Abwehrzauber gegen die Pest', in *Das große Sterben. Seuchen machen Geschichte.* Ausstellungskatalog (Dresden, 1995), pp. 54-93; N. Bulst, 'Heiligenverehrung in Pestzeiten. Soziale und religiöse Reaktionen auf die spätmittelalterlichen Pestepidemien', in *Mundus in imagine*.

can distinguish between three or even four groups of protectors against the plague:

1. First and foremost, Christ and Mary Mother of God were called upon. These two are portrayed as protectors against the plague more often than generally assumed. Some examples are: depictions of Christ as Man of Sorrows, the popular portrayal of God the Father with the three arrows (war, famine, and pestilence), pictures of the Holy Trinity, and especially depictions of Mary as the Virgin of Mercy. However, if representations of these holy figures are truly references to the plague can only be deduced from the study of supplementary texts or the iconographic context, for example the presence of other unmistakable plague saints.

2. The classic plague saints Sebastian and Roch.

3. The large group of auxiliary saints, who were "recruited" as plague saints for different reasons and were worshipped nationwide. Many of these had expanded their original "area of responsibility" for example several patron saints against disease: Anthony, who was no longer restricted to the protection against ergotism (the so called St. Anthony-fire), Valentine, patron saint against falling sickness (epilepsy), the silent sufferer, Saint Job, himself affected by leprosy, or the physician saints Kosmas and Damian.

Apart form those, patron saints against the so-called "sudden death" – when a dying person could not be given the last rites – were appropriated as plague saints: the saints Christopher, Barbara, George, The Three Magi, etc. Other saints like Gregory the Great and also the (around 1500) immensely popular Saints Anna or Martin of Tours were worshipped because their prayers had once liberated people from the plague. Depending on social background, personal preferences and hagiographical knowledge of the person seeking help, this circle of patron saints could be further extended, as done by Karl Borromäus after the Tridentine reform.[5] Nevertheless, one should not arbitrarily label these additional patron saints as "plague saints", unless the circumstances are clear.

4. Often in times of the plague people also called on local and diocesan saints, personal patron saints or saints whose feast day was approaching.

Bildersprache und Lebenswelten im Mittelalter. Festgabe für Klaus Schreiner (München, 1996), pp. 63-97; T. Esser, *Pest, Heilsangst und Frömmigkeit. Studien zur religiösen Bewältigung der Pest am Ausgang des Mittelalters* (Münsteraner theologische Abhandlungen 58) (Altenberge, 1999).

5. H. Dormeier, 'Il culto dei santi a Milano in balia della peste (1576-1577)', in G. Barone/ M. Caffiero/ F. Scorza Barcellona (eds.), *Modelli di santità e modelli di comportamento. Contrasti, intersezioni, complementarità* (Torino, 1994), pp. 233-242.

Thus, in principal any saint could be the addressee of help-seeking prayers from the faithful, without strictly being a "plague saint".[6]

We can draw the following conclusion from this attempt to bring some order into the large assembly of protectors against the plague: "plague saint" is not a copyrighted term, and thus it should be used with care. The horde of patron saints against epidemic disease and therefore also the number of plague references is more plentiful than generally assumed. But, that God and The Virgin Mary and the large crowd of the above mentioned saints which we encounter in prayers and pictorial references really were mainly invoked as protectors against the plague can only be said with conviction if the intercession or depiction concerned also invokes other definite plague motifs or well-known plague saints or if contemporaneous historical records about plague outbreaks in those areas are evident. Bearing this question in mind, one should examine altar patrons, images, plague sheets and especially the – mostly unprinted – texts of prayer-books, as well as hagiographical and liturgical texts about auxiliary plague saints, all the while taking into account regional differences as well as changes occurring through time.

The selection of saints that were called upon for protection during plague outbreaks differs quite significantly from region to region. South of the Alps the Virgin Mary plays the dominant role; here she can be found more often on the type of image known as Sacra Conversazione than north of the Alps, and in this context she also seems to be connected more closely to the saints surrounding her. Especially in Italy people turned to the local patron saints for protection more often than to the specific plague saints.[7] The selection and assembly of saints was mainly taken care of by the client

---

6. More detailed examination of the plague patronage of the mentioned saints in H. Dormeier, 'Laienfrömmigkeit in den Pestzeiten des 15./16. Jahrhunderts', in N. Bulst/ R. Delort (eds.), *Maladies et société (XIIe-XVIIIe siècles)* (Paris, 1989), pp. 269-306, especially 284-296.
7. For the forms of piety in Italy in relation to the plague cf. among others S.K. Cohn, *The Cult of Remembrance and the Black Death. Six Renaissance Cities in Central Italy* (Baltimore, 1992); S. K. Cohn, 'Piété et commande d'oeuvres d'art après la peste noire', *Annales* 51 (1996), pp. 551-573; L. Marshall, 'Manipulating the Sacred: Image and Plague in Renaissance Italy', *Renaissance Quarterly* 47 (1994), pp. 485-532; H. Dormeier, 'Pestepidemien und Frömmigkeitsformen in Italien und Deutschland (14.-16. Jahrhundert)', in M. Jakubowski-Tiessen/ H. Lehmann (eds.), *Um Himmels Willen. Religion in Katastrophenzeiten* (Göttingen, 2003), pp. 14-50.

and donator or the monks and clergy of the institution to which a donation was made. As an example one could cite the Umbrian Gonfaloni.[8]

But it is also necessary to look at chronological differences. On the plague altar of Nuremberg's church of Saint Lawrence and also in many other pictures, the two classic plague saints, Sebastian and Roch, are shown next to each other. Books providing a general overview tend to name these two saints in the same breath as protectors against the plague between the 14th and 18th century. However, this is not entirely correct. The fact is that wherever these two are depicted together, either on their own or in combination with other saints, it was done in the spirit of current, already conquered, or imminent plague outbreaks. Yet, this is where the first problems occur.

It seems to be taken for granted that the worship of plague saints showed a sudden, rapid increase under the devastating impact of the Black Death of 1348. However, if one examines the facts closely and disregards the irregularity of the historical records, it becomes clear that the Black Death of 1348 did not produce any new saints and only a few new sites of worship – like the votive chapel on the Campo Santo in Siena. It is probably even wrong to speak of an increase in the worship of the classic plague saint Sebastian. Exactly how Sebastian grew into this role still demands in-depth study.

However, Sebastian's cult also raises questions for another reason. Because of his martyrdom through arrows Sebastian was not only a plague saint, but also the patron saint of numerous archer fraternities. At the beginning of the 16th century his name was indeed mostly associated with the latter responsibility. The Reformer John Agricola (1499-1566), friend of Martin Luther and for a short while also working in Wittenberg, recalls the following episodes from his youth: "When I was afraid, I turned to the saints ... I would fast on the eve of Saint Barbara so that she would protect me and I would not die without being given the last rites, Saint Roch had to serve against the pestilence, Saint Sebastian against bowshots, Saint Anna when I lit her candle, and Saint Erasmus had to bring riches.

---

8. F. Santi, *Gonfaloni umbri del Rinascimento* (Perugia, 1976); R. Crawfurd 1914, pp. 136ff.; L. Marshall 1994, pp. 485-532; I. Tozzi, 'I gonfaloni perugini, testimonianza d'arte sacra e di devozione popolare', *Arte cristiana* 90 (2002) pp. 30-34; A. Dehmer, *Italienische Bruderschaftsbanner des Mittelalters und der Renaissance* (München et al., 2004).

That was where I turned in times of fear, but of Christ I knew nothing."[9] Thus, in some cases donations in honour of Saint Sebastian, especially those by archer fraternities, were not caused by the events of the plague. Also, as the name Sebastian was very popular at the time, some of the high regard this saint was held in could be explained by such external motives as a partiality for one's name patron.

Such reservations do not exist with regard to the cult of Saint Roch. This saint, who as legend has it, was born and died in Montpellier during the 14th century, was exclusively worshipped as a plague saint from the late Middle Ages to the early modern era. Nevertheless, authors of handbooks and readers on the history of the plague are completely mistaken when they declare this saint as a plague saint next to Sebastian already during the Black Death of the 14th century.

Saint Roch is a rather new saint, and more than that, among the varied forms of piety of the Late Middle Ages, the cult of Saint Roch is one of the very rare novelties which unambiguously and exclusively originated from the plague outbreaks of those times.[10] Thus, however indisputable it is that the "danse macabre" (death dance), the image of the three living and the three dead, as well as other motifs of death and transitoriness together with scenes of suffering of all kinds were increasingly depicted after the Black Death of 1348, it is very difficult to verify when and for what reasons these themes were first chosen. Even if one does not find evidence for one motif or the other before 1350, due to the general ways

---

9. Quoted from G. Kawerau, *Johann Agricola von Eisleben. Ein Beitrag zur Reformation* (Berlin, 1881), p. 9; cf. ibid. p. 6f.
10. Initial evidence about Roch as the "new" saint of the 15th century in H. Dormeier, 'Nuovi culti di santi nelle città della Germania meridionale intorno al 1500', in P. Prodi/ P. Johanek (eds.): *Strutture ecclesiastiche in Italia e in Germania prima della Riforma*, (Annali dell'Istituto storico italo-germanico 16) (Trient, 1984), pp. 317-352; also H. Dormeier 1985, pp. 11-16; *San Rocco nell'arte. Un pellegrino sulla via Francigena*, Catalogo di mostra (Piacenza, Palazzo Gotico, 8 aprile – 25 giugno 2000), Milano 2000; about the early legendary tradition of the cult of Roch see P. Bolle, 'Saint Roch de Montpellier, doublet hagiographique de saint Raco d'Autun.Un apport décisif de l'esamen approfondi des incunables et imprimés anciens', in È. Renard et. a. (eds.), *"Scribere sanctorum gesta". Recueil d'études d'hagiographie médiévale offert à G. Philippart* (Brepols, 2005), pp. 525-572; see also articles by Bolle, Bulst, Dormeier, Godding, Rigon, Vauchez and others in the records of the conference in Padua (12-13 February 2004) about: *San Rocco, Genesi e prima espansione di un culto* (Bruxelles, 2006).

of recording this does not constitute definite proof for a correlation to the plague events, as most of the remaining frescos, paintings and altars originate from the 15th century – at least those that can be found in Germany.

In various articles I have managed, if not completely to solve all the puzzles, to at least shed some light upon the history of the worship of Saint Roch. The connection between its origin and the records of the legend are still unclear. In contrast to that, its chronology and the ways of the cult's dissemination have now become more apparent. Thus, Saint Roch was not, as legend and some hagiographical literature may have it, already worshipped during the 14th century, but at the earliest from the middle of the 15th century, in Germany probably only from circa 1480. In the following decades however, despite the critique from the humanists and reformers, Saint Roch was able to become one of the classic "plague saints" next to Sebastian and to rise to the ranks of the most revered saints of Christendom – an unprecedented case in the history of piety.

The economic and social implications of saint worship during plague outbreaks: the example of the cult of Saint Roch

So, we reach the economic and social implications of saint worship during plague outbreaks. The dissemination of a saint's cult does not happen automatically and can never be exhaustive. If anything it has to be spread by specific people, groups, or holy orders. For example, the Franciscan Order strongly propagated the worship of Saint Bernardin of Siena (1380-1444, canonized 1450), while the Augustinian monks promoted Saint Nicolas of Tolentino (1245-1305), a patron against diseases who was canonized in 1445.

With Saint Roch things are slightly different. This specific plague saint was not canonized officially, and instead of being propagated by church authority or one of the big orders, it was mainly the laity who circulated and spread his cult. This can be seen as one example of how especially during times of need the laity was able to use and expand its scope against the hierarchy of church authority. In view of the abundant records it is fairly straightforward to chart the evolution of the cult towards the end of the 15th century.

As an example we turn again to the free city of Nuremberg to take a look at the early history of the Roch cult. When the then new cult established itself in the mid-eighties of the 15th century, it was not straightaway supported

ill. 5: Alms book ("Almosengefällbuch") of Saint Lawrence, fol. 63v (Detail: August 1484). Photo: Staatsarchiv Nürnberg (Nuremberg).

throughout the city as one might expect in the face of the plague threat and the helplessness among the population. Instead, the beginning of the cult was only propagated by one of the two town parishes, and therefore remained within the prescribed framework of church policy. Within the church of Saint Lawrence Roch quickly became one of the most popular saints; as we can learn from an extremely informative and – in view of the history of the Roch cult – highly interesting record, namely the so-called "Almosengefällbuch", the alms book of Saint Lawrence, which charts the results of the collection during Sundays and feast days between 1454 and 1516.[11]

In the year 1484 we can find the first record for collections on the day of Saint Roch (ill. 5)! Remarkable are the early date of mention, the solemn observance of the day through vigil and the presentation of the relics, and the extent of the revenue, which showed a distinct increase during the years of the plague. In the years 1492-93 the revenue during the feast day of Saint Roch were higher than during Christmas and Easter, and were only surpassed by those of the feast day of the church's patron Lawrence, the church consecration days and the commemoration day of Saint Deocarus, whose relics were kept in the church.

At least as astonishing as the amount of the revenue is another detail: namely the mere fact that this day was added to the parish calendar as one of only very few new feast days during the second half of the 15th century. Testimony of the council's view regarding this matter is not known, which is unfortunate as the council was known to be otherwise vehemently opposed to the introduction of new feast days. Even the Bishop of Bamberg did not take the initiative in this case. Could the introduction of this new and until then almost unknown saint only be explained by the shock implanted on people by the plague years of 1483/84? It is conceivable that the above mentioned altar of Saint Roch had been planned or even already been completed during those years.

In any case, it was not the parish clergy who was responsible for the astonishing success of the new plague saint, but probably the merchant family Imhoff, who not only donated the above-mentioned altar, but also

---

11. Nuremberg, Staatsarchiv: Reichsstadt Nürnberg, Nürnberger Totengeläutbücher Nr. 1, 2. Teil, fol. 1* - 101*; for more details see H. Dormeier, 'Kirchenjahr, Heiligenverehrung und große Politik im Almosengefällbuch der Nürnberger Lorenzpfarrei (1454-1516)', *Mitteilungen des Vereins für Gesch. der Stadt Nürnberg* 84 (1997) pp. 1-60; H. Dormeier, 'Aspetti finanziari del culto dei santi: il libro delle elemosine (Almosengefällbuch) della chiesa di San Lorenzo a Norimberga, 1454-1516', in S. Gensini, S. Miniato (eds.), *Vita religiosa e identità politiche: Universalità e particolarismi nell'Europa del tardo Medioevo* (Fondazione centro di studi sulla civiltà del tardo Medioevo San Miniato, Collana di Studi e Ricerche 7) (Pisa, 1998), pp. 231-250; strangely researched without knowledge of these articles, but without any further findings by G. Weilandt, 'Heiligen-Konjunktur. Reliquienpräsentation. Reliquienverehrung und wirtschaftliche Situation an der Nürnberger Lorenzkirche im Spätmittelalter', in M. Mayr (ed.) *Von goldenen Gebeinen. Wirtschaft und Reliquie im Mittelalter,* (Geschichte und Ökonomie, vol. 9) (Innsbruck-Wien/ München, 2001), pp. 186-220.

financed a prebend for the church vicar. Around 1500 more and more citizens of Nuremberg started to take an interest in the new saint and participated in the veneration through larger and smaller donations. However, the most impressive and extravagant measures in honour of Saint Roch were financed by the Imhoff family.

Around 1516/19 Peter Imhoff the Elder donated a separate feast day in honour of the saint. His stepbrother Konrad IV. Imhoff had the cemetery of Saint Roch with the chapel of Saint Roch laid out at the "Gostenhof" during the years 1517-1521. This was without a doubt by far the most costly project and thus even today this site tells of the financial strength of the Imhoff family around 1500.[12] In other words: a single Nuremberg family, the Imhoffs, has turned Saint Roch into their family's patron and virtually also into the patron saint of their own global trading company. Nuremberg had finally become the stronghold of the cult of Saint Roch in Germany.

How can we explain this astonishing commitment of the Imhoff family to Saint Roch? This dedication is probably closely connected to the family's business relations and trade interests. The company's economic heyday declines during the years around 1500. The Imhoff's company traded mostly spices, among these the extremely valuable saffron (from L'Aquila), which was among other things used for the production of the panacea Theriak. The Imhoffs owned offices in Lyon, Antwerp and other cities, but the most important trading centre among the many branches of this trading network was Venice.[13]

Within the Fondaco dei Tedeschi, the basis of the German merchants in Venice, the members of the family played a leading role during those years. Here Peter Imhoff and his brothers were able to get a personal impression of the growing veneration of Saint Roch in Venice. In 1478 the Scuola S. Rocco was founded. After the slightly dubious transfer of the alleged remains of Saint Roch from Lombardy to Venice in 1485, the fraternity experienced an unimaginable increase in members and by 1486 already had three hundred members. Thus, at the beginning of the 16th century they embarked upon the building of a new church above

---

12. Dormeier 1985, pp. 47-51.
13. About this and the following cf. Dormeier 1985, pp. 35-38; also H. Dormeier, Venedig als Zentrum des Rochuskultes, in V. Kapp/F.-R. Hausmann (eds.), *Nürnberg und Italien. Begegnungen, Einflüsse und Ideen*, (Erlanger Romanistische Dokumente und Arbeiten 6) (Tübingen, 1991), pp. 105-127.

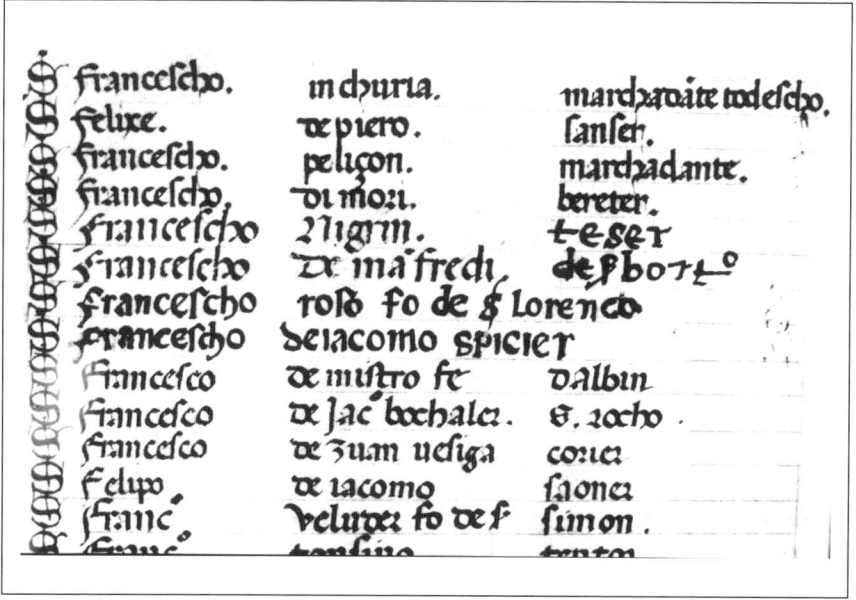

ill. 6. Venice, Scuola Grande di San Rocco, Mariegola (members list), fol. 72v. Photo: H. Dormeier.

the saint's tomb and a fraternity building, namely the Scuola Grande di S. Rocco, which is still in existence today.

Exactly what part the brethren played in the veneration of Saint Roch in Venice, and how economic contacts and lay piety were linked, is certified in all desirable detail in the biggest treasure of the fraternity's archive: the member's register, the so-called Mariegola, of the Scuola Grande di S. Rocco.

Many years ago, I was finally fortunate to consult this magnificent statute and the register of members. It records just about 1800 names of laymen, who became official members of the Scuola between 1490 and 1540, and on top of that more than 100 members of the nobility and 24 priests. Among those persons such as the Doge Antonio Grimani or the famous painter Titian can be found. Eventually I came across the name of the member for whose sake I had invested all this energy: *Ser Francescho in Churia, marchadante todesco* = meaning: Mister Franz in the courtyard, German merchant (i.e. Imhoff in its Latinized or Italianized form "in churia", "in the courtyard") (ill. 6).[14] Franz Imhoff was the half-brother of Peter, who donated the altar of Saint Roch.

It was not bound of happen, but also not just by chance, that specifically the Imhoff family, who for many years managed the altar prebend of Nuremberg's town patron Saint Sebald in Venice, turned to support the Venetian saint in Nuremberg with such reverence and claimed him as their personal patron saint. However, another aspect is of no less importance: the forms of lay piety practised in the large fraternity in Venice, which could have influenced the forms of piety in Germany. This does not necessarily have to be reflected through the foundation of new fraternities, but rather refers to the involvement of laymen and their initiatives within the religious realm. Venice might have been the model for the self-confident way in which the Imhoffs built up the cult of Saint Roch in Nuremberg, asserted themselves with the parish priests, and managed to hold on to their donations for quite some time even during the reformation.

That which can be observed in Nuremberg and Venice can be generalized – and this is where I would like to establish a connection to my current research. The large trading towns were not by chance the focal points of the cult of Saint Roch in Europe: besides Venice and Nuremberg above all the Flemish towns Bruges and Antwerp, followed by Cologne and maybe a little surprising – Lübeck.

Even in this city a whole series of initiatives in honour of the new plague saint were taken just before and after 1500. We come across the new plague saint in collections of the lives of the saints, in mass- and prayer-books, on altarpieces and on the sides of church pews. Still the best document of Saint Roch's rapid rise to popularity in Lübeck is the foundation of a fraternity in his honour and the establishment of a curacy *(vicaria)* for the fraternity in the cathedral of Lübeck at the beginning of the year 1511.[15] That way, Saint Roch registered more firmly with public

---

14. Venezia, Scuola Grande di S. Rocco, Mariegola, fol. 72v; cf. Dormeier 1991, pp. 111-119; F. Tonon, *Scuola dei battuti di San Rocco. Documenti sulle origini e illustrazioni dei capitoli delle mariegole* (Quaderni della Scuola Grande Arciconfraternità di S. Rocco n. 5) (Venezia, 1998); F. Tonon, *La Scuola grande di San Rocco nel Cinquecento attraverso i documenti delle sue Mariegole* (Quaderni della Scuola Grande Arciconfraternità di S. Rocco n. 6) (Venezia, 1999).
15. *Urkundenbuch des Bistums Lübeck*, vol. 4, ed. W. Prange (Neumünster, 1996), pp. 18-21 § 2185 (1511 Jan. 4); cf. M. Zmyslony, *Die geistlichen Bruderschaften in Lübeck bis zur Reformation* (Beiträge zur Sozial- und Wirtschaftsgeschichte 6) (Kiel, 1977), pp. 77-79.

awareness. In Lübeck several of the town's leading families cooperated in this case – similar to Italy, where indeed next to the fraternity it was often the town council who took the initiative, but very different from Nuremberg, where, as mentioned above, a single family virtually monopolized the new saint. Still, even in Lübeck the cult was conveyed via the trading routes and merchants. Both the trading connections with the West and those with Nuremberg and the South could have served as a gateway for the new cult.

An exemplary personification of this connection between trade and cultural promotion was a man who provided an extraordinary presence for the saint in the first parish church of the Hanseatic town: the merchant and banker Goddard Wiggerinck.[16] Wiggerinck, who was originally from Westphalia, had extensive trading, connections to Denmark and Livland, from where he imported copper, wax, fish and foodstuffs, and in return exported salt, pepper, rice and spices, part of which he obtained from his business associates in Nuremberg. Primarily, however, he sold copper and brass wire within the Baltic Sea region. After 1500 Wiggerinck became the principal business associate for the Fugger Company of Augsburg and Nuremberg the Baltic Sea region and his influence was essential in the Fugger Company's reorientation from trading in goods to trading in metals within the Hanseatic League. Money and credit transactions were conducted parallel to the goods traffic, which was also essentially guided by the interests of the influential tradesmen of the Fugger family and the trade connection between Nuremberg and Lübeck (via Erfurt). After 1504 Wiggerinck became the head of the Fugger company branch in Lübeck, and as the Fugger company's liaison man in Lübeck, he evidently took up the key position in their transactions from Scandinavia all the way to Rome.

This sophisticated tradesman set a permanent monument for himself in Lübeck's most important parish church in the shape of a magnificent

---

16. About the following cf. (including the itemisations) H. Dormeier, 'Immigration und Integration, Laienfrömmigkeit und Kunst in Lübeck um 1500: Der Großkaufmann und Bankier Godert Wiggerinck (+1518 April 24)', *Zeitschrift des Vereins für Lübeckische Geschichte und Altertumskunde* 85 (2005) pp. 93-165; for an abridged version: H. Dormeier, 'Wirtschaftlicher Erfolg, Laienfrömmigkeit und Kunst in Lübeck um 1500. Die Stiftungen des Bankiers und Großkaufmanns Godert Wiggerinck, in E. Bünz/ K.-J. Lorenzen-Schmidt (eds.), *Klerus, Kirche und Frömmigkeit im spätmittelalterlichen Schleswig-Holstein* (Studien zur Wirtschafts- und Sozialgeschichte Schleswig-Holsteins, Bd. 41) (Neumünster, 2006), pp. 275-297.

ill. 7. Lübeck, Church of St. Mary. Funeral monument of Goddard Wiggerinck, († 1518 april 24). Photo: Lübeck, Museum für Kunst und Kulturgeschichte.

ill. 8. Lübeck, Church of St. Mary, choir screen. Photo: Lübeck, Museum für Kunst- und Kulturgeschichte.

bronze renaissance memorial slab from Nuremberg's Vischer-Manufactory (ill. 7). Beyond that he also managed to leave his mark on the interior of the church of Saint Mary before the Reformation.

Among other things he financed the reconstruction of the choir screen of the Church of Saint Mary together with the soon-to be council member, Hans Salige (ill. 8). By doing so, he delivered at the same time an unusual example of plague iconography. The choir screen was designed between 1510 and 1520 and kept its shape until its destruction during the Second World War.[17] The artistic highlight on the west front of the choir screen structure were without a doubt the sculptures by Benedikt Dreyer. The north side was the responsibility of Hans Salige, as can be guessed by the selection and arrangement of the coat of arms. The Saints Anna, Michael and John the Baptist next to the Virgin Mary

---

17. Description including overall and detail illustrations of the choir screen which was destroyed in 1942: *Die Bau- und Kunstdenkmäler der Freien und Hansestadt Lübeck*, Bd. 2 (Petrikirche, Marienkirche, Heil.-Geist-Spital), eds. G. Schaumann/ F. Bruns (Lübeck, 1906), pp. 184-195; M. Hasse, *Die Marienkirche zu Lübeck* (München/ Berlin, 1983), pp. 157-161 inc. ills. 97-104; Tamara Thiesen, *Benedikt Dreyer, Das Werk des spätgotischen Lübecker Bildschnitzers* (Bau und Kunst, vol. 17), (Kiel, 2007), esp. pp. 87-147.

in the central panel were probably emphasized in their function as the church's patron saints, while John the Evangelist was probably the donator's name patron.

A little more surprising is the selection chosen by Goddard Wiggerinck and the executors of his will for the south face of the screen. On this side, both saints Anthony and Roch were added, apparently at Wiggerinck's explicit request (ill. 9); for the testator belonged to both, the fraternity of Saint Anthony in the convent of the Dominicans as well as to the fraternity of Saint Roch in the cathedral. It is conceivable that Anthony was placed right at the southern end of the row of statues to be closest to the church's southern portico, in front of which the brothers of the St. Anthony fraternity traditionally handed out alms. However, Anthony was not only the patron saint of the sick and poor and protector against St. Anthony's fire, but he was also worshipped as patron saint against the plague epidemics during the late Middle Ages. It would be for this latter reason that he is portrayed on the choir screen, where he can be found in immediate proximity to the two classic plague saints: Sebastian and Roch, who is emphasized in this assemblage for a good reason. Nearly at the same time the curacy (vicary) of the Roch fraternity was installed in the cathedral, namely "to honour the almighty God, the holiest Virgin Mary, his mother, as well as the holy confessors Roch and Anthony and the martyr Sebastian". Although Wiggerinck did not belong to the founding members of this new curacy, he was surely one of the first persons to join the new fraternity, as can be deduced from an early remark in his will of 1511. Therefore, it is clearly the personal preferences of the client which brought both the plague saints Anthony and Roch to be portrayed on the Wiggerinck side of the choir screen. As these two major saints on the southern side frame the above mentioned smaller figure of Sebastian, this area of the choir screen is clearly dominated by this nucleus of the three most important plague saints. From the eve of the Reformation to the Second World War visitors to the church of Saint Mary were confronted with this unusual combination of saints, and especially with the dominance of the protectors against the plague.

Of course, it was not self-evident that here the plague saints were so effectively emphasized and that preference was given to the new plague saint Roch over the more established Sebastian. The reference to Wiggerinck's membership of the Roch fraternity does not suffice as the sole explanation for the exposed position of the plague saint on the choir screen of the church of Saint Mary. After all, the members of the fraternity met in the cathedral, therefore it was not to be expected that the plague saint also took such a striking position in the church of Saint Mary.

ill. 9. Lübeck. Church of St. Mary, choir screen, detail: Saint Roch. Photo: Lübeck, Museum für Kunst- und Kulturgeschichte.

Apparently Wiggerinck must have had other reasons to place the plague saint in the limelight. Let us have another look at the banker's will from the year of 1511.[18] Strangely enough it is only at the very end of the document that he mentions his wish to be buried in the church of Saint Mary. He also requests a feast for the poor on the occasion of his funeral. This is not necessarily a singular notion, but it is also not necessarily a standard feature in the legacies of the well-to-do citizens of Lübeck. But Wiggerinck ties his request to a specific condition, which is remarkable:

> "And I wish my burial to be in the church of Our (Dear) Lady and afterwards, provided that I die not within times of plague ("dar ik buten pestilentie tiden in god vorstorve"), I wish for a traditional funeral meal and on the following day many of the pious poor shall receive a good meal and one shilling each in hand, so that they will pray to God for my poor soul."

The reference to a possible plague outbreak, which could foil the plans for a funeral meal, should not just be understood as a set phrase. As far as I can see, this phrase remains unique among the hundreds of testaments drawn up in Lübeck before and after 1500 – especially in passages referring to the remembrance meal. Wiggerinck's remarks must be directly influenced by specific personal experiences. Thus, when in later years he grants Saint Roch and his fellow protectors against the plague a special place within the iconography of the choir screen, we can surmise that this is first and foremost, as suggested above, evidence for the growing popularity of this particular plague saint, whose cult men like Wiggerinck, the St. Anthony brethren, and other business friends were interested in strengthening after the model of Nuremberg and Flanders. This is especially likely, as the donator himself was a member of the fraternity of Saint Roch and this would also explain why he had a strong interest in the post of the vicar of the Saint Roch chapel in the cathedral being filled with his brother-in-law. But at the same time it is probable that personal experiences with the plague had influenced or even determined his decision to choose Saint Roch and the group of plague saints for the choir screen of the church of Saint Mary.

---

18. *Lübeck Archiv der Hansestad*: Testamente 1511 July 19 (G. Wiggerinck), (ed.) H. Dormeier 2005, pp. 158-162.

When and on what occasion Wiggerinck might have had such encounters with the pandemic, one can only speculate. It may be that he only experienced how remembrance festivities at funerals had to be cancelled due to the threat posed by the plague. In those years cases of the plague are indeed rare in Lübeck. On the other hand, on his travels to Nuremberg, in the West and also to Rome, he probably was confronted often enough with fierce – although regionally restricted – outbreaks of the plague and panic-stricken flight from this incurable epidemic.[19] One should not, however, rule out the possibility that people close to him had fallen victim to the plague, or that even one or more of his wives – whose dates of death are engraved on his bronze gravestone – died of the insidious pandemic.

On balance the preliminary result of the preceding observations should be as follows:

1. The records and the saint worship of the 15th and 16th century invite us to both an examination and a new assessment of the main research focus up to now: Previous studies on economic and social history still tended to concentrate too much on the effects of the Black Death of 1348. In my opinion, one should instead take a closer look at the plague epidemics from the 14th to 17th centuries which although they were regionally restricted, nevertheless in the long-term showed graver consequences.

2. Even the evaluation of forms of piety, like the veneration of saints, can (and should) be on closer inspection and be more subtly differentiated than generally achieved. For even in modern monographs about the plague the two so-called classic plague saints Sebastian and Roch are named in the same breath with the most important patron saints during the plague outbreaks of the 14th and 15th century. Not only is this statement misleading but it also withholds the historically speaking most interesting point: namely that Saint Roch was only newly established and that he rather emphasizes the later plague epidemics, as it was predominantly laymen who supported the cult of this un-canonized saint. Even the otherwise correct statement, that the cult of Saint Roch was introduced to Nuremberg around 1480, does not take into account that a single family was the foremost driving force behind this deed, and

---

19. About the flight from the plague cf. H. Dormeier, 'Die Flucht vor der Pest als religiöses Problem', in K. Schreiner (ed.), *Laienfrömmigkeit im späten Mittelalter* (Schriften des Historischen Kollegs, Kolloquien 20) (München, 1992), pp. 331-397.

especially not that the cult was at the beginning only to be found in one of the two town parishes.

3. The cult of a saint does not disseminate itself, but is spread. Who took the initiative, who exactly was responsible for the introduction and circulation of the cult, and how the progress of the cult possibly followed the trade routes, are puzzles that due to favourable records can be solved more easily for the time around 1500 than for earlier periods.[20] As these first findings on the example of the cult of Saint Roch in Nuremberg and Lübeck show, the results could not only be instructive for the history of piety and the plague, but will also be important to economic and social history.

---

20. Cf. e.g. H. Dormeier 1989, esp. pp. 270-300. – For the translation into English I cordially thank Roya Shahr-Yazdi, London/Cologne, for further connotations thanks to Marina Loer and Janina Scheidl, Kiel.

The Black Death as Reflected in Scandinavian Art and Architecture

By Ebbe Nyborg, Copenhagen

This study is an attempt to incorporate some little-noted sources for the plague in the 14th century. The architectural and pictorial testimonies are indirect and difficult to handle. For that reason one ought perhaps to use them only when all other kinds of sources are more or less absent. This is very much the case in Scandinavia, especially as regards Denmark and Sweden.[1] In this article, the attempt will be made.

Our architectural and pictorial testimoni are probably substantial enough to give a general feeling that the plague actually was in Scandinavia and that both economic recessions and an atmosphere of apocalyptic fear were known here as well.

To illustrate this was not the original purpose of this article. The equally ambitious intention was to examine to what extent this kind of testimonies could be connected to more specific outbreaks of the plague. That, as will appear, is hardly possible. Nevertheless, this article will maintain that the problem of dating is quite essential. This seems to offer the best chance of testing the power of assertion and the possibilities of the material.

---

1. Among the more recent contributions to the history of the plague in Scandinavia may be mentioned E. Ulsig, 'Pest og befolkningsnedgang i Danmark', *Historisk Tidsskrift*, 1991, pp. 21-43; O. J. Benedictow, *Svartedauen og senere pestepedemier i Norge. Pestepedemiens historie i Norge 1348-1654* (Oslo, 2002); and J. Myrdal, *Digerdöden, pestvågor och ödeläggelse: Ett perspektiv på senmedeltidens Sverige* (Stockholm, 2003).

Fig. 1. Tronhjem cathedral seen from the north 1661. Copper engraving by J. M. Maschius. After Fischer.

Architectural Testimonies

It is a saying among architectural historians that a cathedral that had not been completed by the early 14th century was at risk of never being finished at all. A good example is the cathedral in Cologne whose immense High Gothic chancel was finished in 1322 while the low Carolingian nave was waiting for a similar rebuilding. In 1388, approximately 40 years after the Black Death, a part of the two western towers had been built, but otherwise the works had been at a complete standstill. And they were not resumed until the 19th century when the cathedral was completed as a monument to the growing German nationalism and industrialism.[2]

---

2. A. Wolff, *Der Kölner Dom* (Köln, 1974, 3. edition 1982). See also *Der Kölner Dom*

In Scandinavia there is a cathedral whose building history is quite similar to that of the cathedral in Cologne, namely the cathedral in Trondheim which was the seat of the Norwegian archbishops and provided the setting for the cult of the national saint St. Olav. As it appears from an engraving from 1661 (fig 1), the Middle Ages left only parts of the church in good repair, namely the parts that had been completed before the Black Death. The parts concerned are the 12th century transept and the chancel with the octagonal St. Olav's 'Corona' which had been built in the decades up to the middle of the 13th century. The nave that was begun afterwards is only shown on the engraving as a ruin. The nave remained in that condition until the national awakening of the 19th century when the cathedral was restored to its 'old' grandeur. The nave was reconstructed with inspiration from the so-called 'Angel Choirs' in Lincoln cathedral. And a west façade embellished with sculptures was erected, of which the two lower floors are more or less original, showing the considerable ambitions that were behind the original plans.[3]

Recently, Øystein Ekroll has attempted to illustrate the medieval building history of the cathedral in a number of stages (fig. 2),[4] which gives a good impression of the cathedral as a perpetual building site: Older parts of the building on the site are reused as long as it is possible and useful; new building plans are made, changed and given up, sometimes because a new master builder has been employed, sometimes for liturgical, economic or other reasons. Under such circumstances it is not easy to point out halts in construction that can be specifically connected with certain calamities such as fires, collapses or a plague with a subsequent lack of funds, labour etc. Strictly speaking, many of the difficulties in carrying out the building programmes are most likely due to the overly ambitious original plans.

The latter has almost certainly been a factor in Trondheim. The plans for a new nave that the archbishops initiated in the middle of the 13th century would have quite outshone all cathedrals in the rest of Scandinavia

---

    im Jahrhundert seiner Vollendung 1-2. Katalog zur Ausstellung der Historischen Museen in der Josef-Haubrich-Kunsthalle Köln, (ed.) Hugo Borger, (Köln, 1980).

3.   G. Fischer, *Domkirken i Trondheim. Kirkebygget i Middelalderen*, I-II, (Trondheim, 1955-65).

4.   Øystein Ekroll, *Med kleber og kalk. Norsk Steinbygging i mellomalderen 1050-1550* (Oslo, 1997), pp. 148-158. See also *Ecclesia Nidrosiensis 1153-1557. Søkelys på Nidaroskirkens og Nidarosprovinsens historie*, (ed.) Steinar Imsen, (Trondheim, 2003).

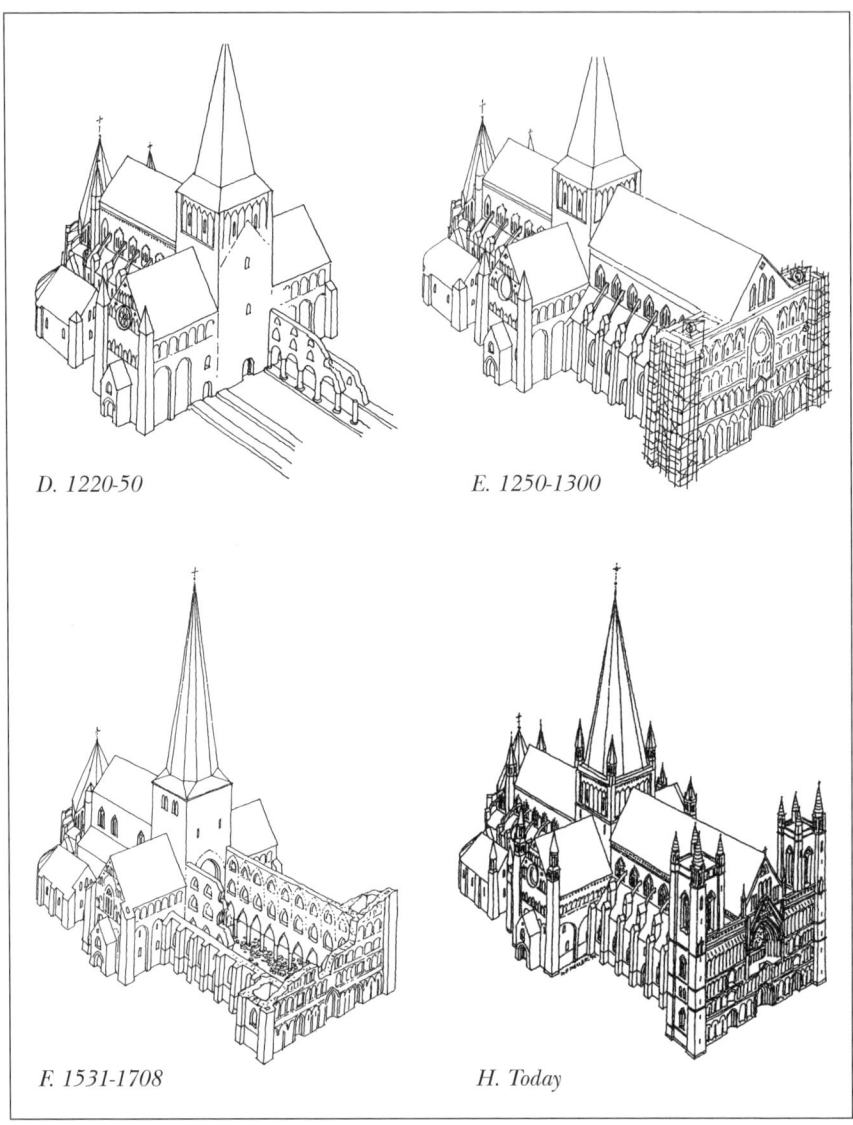

Fig. 2. Tronhjem cathedral, stages in the development of the building seen from the northwest. After Øystein Ekroll.

and Northern Germany. Øystein Ekroll has the work be almost completed around 1300 (fig. 2E), but he allows room for doubt by showing scaffolding around the west front and its towers. Actually, the works need not even have been completed in 1328 when a fire ravaged large parts of the cathedral, evidently the new nave in particular. Archbishop Eilif noted that not only did the roofs burn, but also the "stone posts", the pillars and the stone arches, so that the building needed immediate help. Most likely, those works had not been brought to an end at the coming of the Black Death 1349-50. Not only did Archbishop Arne fall victim to the disease, so did all but one of the canons![5]

If the nave had been finished at the coming of the plague, there would probably not have been any subsequent building problem for the post-plague community with its unquestionable lack of resources and labour. But the increasing late medieval decay (fig. 2F) must show that the nave had not been completed at the coming of the plague, or later, for that matter. Apparently, it has not even been possible to raise funds for the necessary maintenance of walls and roofs. All efforts were concentrated on maintaining the chancel and the transept into which the congregation had to crowd until the 19th century.

In that way, the plan for an immense cathedral in Trondheim apparently became the victim of its own grandeur, of the fire in 1328 and not least of the Black Death. When the plague broke out, the nave was probably almost completed. But even the limited remaining work seems to have been too much for the post-plague community. And then everything started to slide backwards.

A situation that was similar in several ways must have existed at the building of Odense cathedral on the island of Funen in Denmark. That too housed a national king and saint, St Knut. At the end of the 13th century it was still a cathedral built of travertine blocks with a crypt which was constructed by English monks around 1100 and which was now regarded as very outdated. The initiative in making a completely new building in the High Gothic style was taken by bishop Gisico (1286-1300) and commemorated in two inscriptions (in black glazed tile) under the battlements of the aisles. They mention Gisico as the founder of the building and seem to contain the date "1301" in poetic form.[6]

---

5. O. Krefting, *Om Trondhjems Domkirke* (Trondhjem, 1899), pp. 18-19.
6. See, also for the following, *Danmarks Kirker, Odense Amt*, vol. 1 by Hugo Johannsen and Birgitte Bøggild Johannsen (Copenhagen, 1990), and by the same authors,

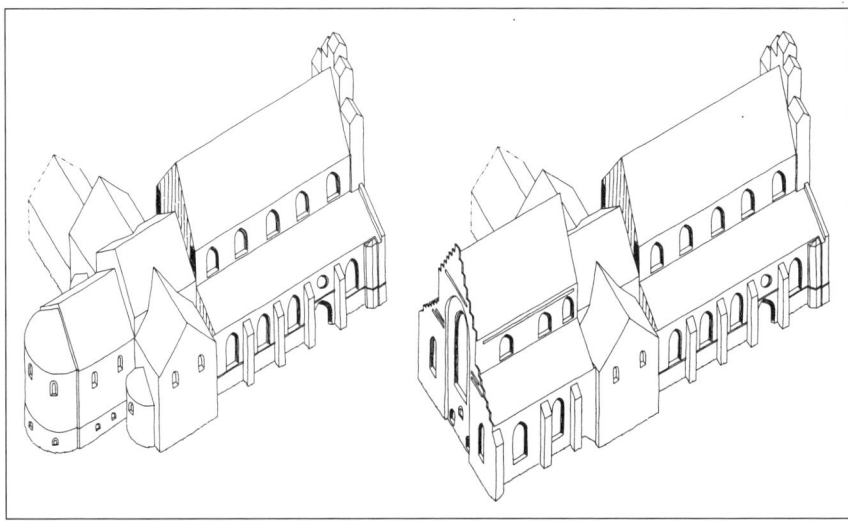

Fig. 3. Odense cathedral, stages in the development of the building seen from the northeast. To the left: The new building begun by bishop Gisico as it had progressed by app. 1350. To the right: The construction after the resumption 1400-25. The joining of the Gothic building parts was left out, and it took place app. 1475. After Danmarks Kirker.

As can be seen (Fig 3 to the left), Gisico's construction work was begun at the west end with a tall brick nave which joined the travertine transept to begin with. Some foundations for a three-sided Gothic end of the chancel east of the Romanesque apse (not shown on the drawing) may be contemporary with Gisico's nave and if so show that a new and ambitious ambulatory chancel was also being worked on. However that may be, these plans were never carried out.[7]

Letters of indulgence in favour of the construction of the cathedral from 1310 and 1345 suggest that the works continued well into the 14th century. At the arrival of the plague they had not progressed much further than shown on fig. 3 on the left. The Romanesque chancel and transept were

---

Sct. Knuds Kirke. Otte kapitler af Odense Domkirkes historie (Odense, 2001), especially pp. 42-58.
7. For a discussion of the importance of these foundations for the gothicization of the cathedral, see C. Lovén "Den första gotiseringen av Odense domkyrka. En omtolkning", *Fortid og Nutid* 2006, pp. 127-135.

still waiting to be succeeded by a monumental continuation eastwards. The cathedral looked like it might very well get into trouble.

It is fairly certain that there was practically no building activity in the first half century after the Black Death. Not until the years 1400-1425 were the works resumed, and that in a rather curious way, since the old transept was left standing as a kind of middle building while a new chancel was erected as a replacement for the Romanesque one (Fig. 3 on the right). All that was left now was to remove the transept and join the two Gothic building parts, which was done app. 1475. The church was completed.

But how to estimate the possible influence of the Black Death on the building of the church in Odense? Perhaps the resources of the bishop and the monastery were already pressed before the outbreak of the plague. Actually, the letter of indulgence from 1345 explicitly emphasises the poverty of the church and its insufficient income, which prevented it from completing the building begun long ago without help from the faithful. Of course, it must be noted that this is a standard form.

If not already before the plague, the planned chancel must have been given up soon after it, which entailed a substantial reduction of the plans. And it was hardly a coincidence that no work at all took place during the second half of the 14th century. These decades represent a low in every way when it comes to church building in Denmark. Only in the 15th century did the building begin anew – in Odense and elsewhere.

And here one may note an important difference from Norway where almost no stone buildings were constructed between the Black Death and the Reformation! The entire technique and the craft of working stone died out after the number of construction works had dropped below a certain critical mass.[8] This did not happen in the rest of Scandinavia, but in some areas it probably came close to happening.

---

8. Ekroll 1997, pp. 57-57. Here the consequences of the plague are probably not fully taken. Thus, a dendrochronological dating of the roof of Trondernes church in Northern Norway, which is supposed to date the building of the nave to app. 1400, is emphasised. However, the church must have been completed before the plague; but not until app. 1400 did they apparently have the means to roof the nave. See O. E. Eide, *Trondernes kirke. Fra 1200-tallet eller fra senmiddelalderen?*, (Trondernes, 2005).

If we reduce the scale of the churches a little and remain in the diocese of Odense, our attention turns to the Cistercian church of Holme (*Insula Dei*) which is now a part of the manor Brahetrolleborg. Here the construction of the church began app. 1250 and was drawn out until it was nearly finished in the first half of the 14th century (Fig. 4 on the left). The building was then a basilica with transept chapels. Only the top vaulting was missing, but it was prepared for five vaults. They were never built, however, and the room had a wooden ceiling until app. 1450 when four lower vaults were inserted instead (Fig. 4 on the right). Probably at the same time, the aisles as well as the transept chapels were given up, though the southern one was included in the monastery.[9] In Holme monastery as in Odense, we see that the construction works completely stopped after the middle of the 14th century, even if they were practically finished when the plague broke out. And when the work of finishing the church was finally begun, it was decided to give up large parts of the building that was already standing – presumably a long-term effect of the calamities of the 14th century. Something similar can be seen in Jutland (Western Denmark), for instance at the Franciscan church in Horsens where a new construction of the nave came to a halt during the 14th century and was never finished.[10] At another nearby abbey church, Asmild by the cathedral town of Viborg, reductions of the already standing building were also carried out, as in Holme. Here the three-aisled high medieval basilica has been deprived of its aisles and an unusually large Romanesque tower building with a west apse. It is not possible to say more precisely when the demolitions took place, and one reason for them may be an archaeologically proven fire in the middle of the 14th century.[11] In the light of our earlier examples, however, there is reason to assign to the plague a large part of the blame for the late medieval decline of Asmild abbey church.[12]

---

9. E. Hædersdal, "Holme Klosterkirke", *Bygningsarkæologiske Studier* 90 (Copenhagen, 1990), pp.7-32; J. C. Varming, "Holme Klosterkirke. Nye tanker omkring kirkens bygningshistorie og klosterkirkebyggeriets begyndelse", *Bygningsarkæologiske Studier* 91 (Copenhagen, 1991), pp. 7-12.
10. *Danmarks Kirker, Århus Amt*, vol. 9 by Hugo Johannsen and Birgitte Bøggild Johannsen (Copenhagen, 2004-05), pp. 5704-13.
11. H. K. Kristensen, *Middelalderbyen Viborg*, (Aarhus, 1987), pp. 62-64; J. Vellev, *Asmild Klosterkirke i 900 år*, (Højbjerg, 1990).
12. E. Nyborg, "Church and cloister", *Digging into the Past. 25 Years of Archaeology in Denmark*, (eds.) Steen Hvass and Birger Storgaard, (Aarhus, 1993), pp. 242-247.

THE BLACK DEATH AS REFLECTED IN SCANDINAVIAN ART AND ARCHITECTURE 195

Fig. 4. Holme abbey church, two stages in the development of the building seen from the southeast. To the left: The church in the first half of the 14th century with the preparations of four never completed vaults in the nave. To the right: The church app. 1450 with four lower vaults built in. Aisles and chapels have been given up. After Hædersdal 1990.

It is natural to see the reductions of the buildings in Horsens and Asmild in connection with an extensive closing down of parish churches which took place precisely in the Jutlandic area. Not less than 111 high medieval churches (or 10.4%) can be shown to have disappeared in the late Middle Ages (6) and during the Reformation period (44).[13] As it appears, a more precise dating is difficult here too. The churches have evidently been closed down in places where they were already lying very close to each other, and especially on the sandy soil in Mid-Jutland. The latter

---

13. N. Engberg, "Ødekirker", *Arkæologiske udgravninger i Danmark 1999*, (Copenhagen, 2000), pp. 7-17; and – with slightly different figures – J. Wienberg, *Den gotiske labyrint. Middelalderen og kirkerne i Danmark* (Stockholm, 1993), pp. 111-115.

shows that the churches have not normally been given up immediately after the plague because of a particularly large mortality in the parishes in question. The closings have usually taken place in the somewhat longer term as an adaptation to a new demographic situation.[14]

Nevertheless, examples of an immediate demolition are known. Thus, Sjællandske Krønike reports under 1357 that King Valdemar Atterdag at that time let 11 churches be demolished about the town of Randers in order to use their stones for the fortifications.[15] Such an unchristian act may not be unheard of from brutal rulers, but perhaps this one ought to be considered in connection with the fact that the surrounding area was more or less depopulated at the time as a consequence of the plague, which made the churches in question more or less superfluous? It was the same king who in 1354 actually declared a general amnesty for all punishments involving life and limb, involving to "the overly large lack of population in the realm of Denmark".[16]

It is a common characteristic for the Scandinavian parish churches that they were only to a very limited degree built on during the 14th century (cf. fig. 5). The only churches that were actually newly built to a significant degree in that century were the ones on the Baltic island of Gothland (Sweden). The exceptional wealth of the island is evident from its churches. During the 14th century a number of rural parishes made ambitious High Gothic new buildings on a much larger scale than the Romanesque and early Gothic churches they were to succeed. These 14th century buildings were mainly carried out by one master builder or 'Bauhytte' who was called 'Egypticus' because of his characteristic 'Hathor capitals'. Some of these new buildings were completed, but a remarkably large number were stopped halfway through and never completed.

Here, the problem is once again the dating, of course. It has been assumed that the earliest High Gothic building on the island, the large chapel by the Maria church in Visby, was to be dated to the year 1349 and the village churches consequently after that. This would lead to the conclusion that the interruption of the Egypticus constructions on Gothland

---

14. The same migration towards the more fertile Eastern Jutland can be seen after the outbreaks of the plague in the 17th century. Se N. J. Poulsen, "Randbøl sogns bebyggelse ca. 1570 til 1700. Et sydjysk sogn før og efter svenskekrigene", *Landbohistorisk Tidsskrift*, 2. ser., IV, 1982, pp. 125-181.
15. Ulsig 1991, p. 23.
16. Ibid., pp. 22-23.

Fig. 5. Fulltofta church in Scania, a typical Scandinavian parish church with a chancel and nave from the 12th or 13th centuries, porch and tower from the 15th century. Here, the social order seems to be disintegrating 1383, maybe as a consequence of the plagues: Until now, the residents had celebrated mass daily, waked and praised God in the holy Magnhild's chapel in the churchyard. But now it was only the gathering point for fiddle players and singers who promoted scandalous songs and dances, parties, drinking and adultery – all this to the insult of God, the danger of their souls and the resentment of many others". Photo Ebbe Nyborg 1972.

was probably caused by the Danish king Valdemar Atterdag's looting and conquest of the island in 1361. But in 1975 Gunnar Svanström was able to show that the testament which was supposed to be able to date the large chapel in Visby to 1349, in reality had nothing to do with the chapel.[17] Therefore the Egypticus works can now be dated more freely in relation to their architectural role models outside the island. To begin with, though, this has only led to a very wide frame of dating 1320-60.[18]

---

17. *Sveriges Kyrkor, Visby Domkyrka, Kyrkobyggnaden*, by Gunnar Svanström, (Stockholm, 1978), pp. 99-107, 154-164.
18. M. Ullén, 'Gotikens Kyrkobyggande', *Den gotiska konsten. Signums svenska konsthistoria,* (Lund, 1996), p. 80.

In the past decades, however, dendrochronology has been used to a larger extent, and we will look at some of the results even though some of them are controversial.[19] Like most churches on the island, Lärbro church dates from the 13th century, only the tower is an Egypticus work from the 14th century. Miraculously, its vault in the 2nd storey has preserved its scaffolding. And this woodwork, so directly connected to the completion of the building, now seems to be dated to 1339-41, a year that fits very nicely with the casting of the church bell in 1345.[20]

But what about the buildings that were never completed? Apparently, only two such works have dendrochronological datings that are reasonably unchallenged. One is Lye church (Fig. 6) which the Egypticus master has furnished with a large and high chancel, conceived as the first stage in a new building which was to have continued on westwards on the same scale. But that never happened, and the dating of the chancel says 1346.[21] Here, a close connection with the plague seems likely. There was probably a natural pause in the construction work after 1346 and it was never resumed after the ravages of the plague.

The other church is Vallstena with a very similar building history. However, the new building got a little further here, because a part of the nave has been erected as well, with a temporary roof and a connection to the old nave. Here one gets sense of a building that has been broken off at short notice. But the immediate reason is not likely to have been the Black Death, since the works on the new building can apparently be dated to 1320.[22]

One might wish for more and more certain dendrochronological datings. Until then the situation in Vallstena must be a warning against connecting the unfinished Gothlandic Egypticus buildings too generally and unambiguously to the Black Death. Buildings may have run into prolonged halts in construction decades before the arrival of the plague. And the halts may have become permanent not only because of the plague

---

19. A. Bråthen, *Dated Wood from Gotland and the Diocese of Skara*, (Højbjerg, 1995). Critique and corrections by E. Lagerlöf, T. Bartholin og R. Hauglid (plus reply from Bråthen) in *Fornvännen*, 1997-98.
20. Bråthen 1995, pp. 61-63, 118 and Lagerlöv (cf. note 14) with reference to dating by T. Bartholin. See also Ullén 1996, pp. 81-83 with note 38.
21. Bråthen 1995, pp. 77-78, 118. See also Lagerlöv (cf. note 14).
22. Bråthen 1995, pp. 81-82, 112.

Fig. 6. Lye church on Gothland seen from the south. To the right the large chancel building of the 14th century which has never been continued westwards with a new aisle. Photo Ebbe Nyborg 1972.

epidemics but also for other reasons, such as king Valdemar's looting in 1361 mentioned earlier.[23]

THE MACABRE PICTORIAL CULTURE IN SCANDINAVIA

We now move from the possible influence of the plague on the architecture – which appears to be negative only – to its possibly more creative and instigating significance for the so-called 'macabre' pictorial culture. Characteristic for the culture is its stark reminder of death, *memento mori*, in the shape of personal, physical death with detailed description of worms and toads consuming the dead body. Such an interest was unknown to the

---

23. Of course, economic and structural conditions may have been important. Jes Wienberg, "Gotlands guldålder – kyrkor, konjunkturer och korståg", *Från Stad till land. En medeltidsarkæologisk resa tillägnat Hans Andersson*, (Stockholm, 2001), pp. 229-240 finds the reason for the 'fall' of the Gothlandic churches too exclusively in the church builders' 'megalomania'.

High Middle Ages which regarded the 'second death' (Judgment Day) as the only one that mattered, and to which such a wallowing in physical death would have seemed almost unchristian.

It is not without reason that the macabre culture of the 14th and 15th centuries is so closely connected to our notions of the Black Death. But the connection is often seen as too causal. Essential elements of the macabre culture were present decades before the plague. An important element that is rarely mentioned in this connection is the crucifix of pain (*crucifixus dolorosus*), whose preconditions were not least the mystics of the late 13th century and their rather extreme identification with Christ's torment on the cross. Such crucifixes are widespread in Europe, and they are often termed "Pestkreuze" (plague crucifixes). But actually, they became common already about 1300.[24] Is it possible to imagine that any churchgoers of that time, having beheld their saviour in such extreme torment, might be moved to feel repentance for their own death and transitoriness by means of less harsh pictorial expressions? Here was a pictorial dynamic that apparently did not 'need' any plague.

In Scandinavia, crucifixes of pain are not easier to date than in the rest of Europe. They are quite numerous, not least in Sweden (fig. 7) and Finland.[25] In (present) Denmark, the approximately 110 crucifixes of pain from the 14th century seem to fall into two main groups, a southern one from the first decades of the century and a northern one which probably cannot be dated more accurately than the second half of the 13th century.[26]

Classic scenes in the macabre pictorial genre are motifs such as the Dance of Death, 'Frau Welt' (the princess of worldliness with a hollow, worm-eaten back), the wheel of fortune, the three living kings who meet themselves as ghosts, and the so-called "Transi" of the grave culture. The latter (of *trans eo*=cross over) are representations of the dead

---

24. For a discussion of the earliest appearance of the crucifixes of pain, see G. Hoffmann, "Der Crucifixus dolorosus in St. Maria im Kapitol zu Köln. Neue Erkenntnisse nach seiner Restaurierung und ihre Bedeutung für die Kunst des frühen 14. Jahrhunderts", *Colonia Romanica*, XV, 2000, pp. 9-82.
25. For Sweden, see L. Karlson, "Träskulpturen", *Den gotiska konsten. Signums svenska konsthistoria* (Lund, 1996), pp. 204-12; and C. Jacobsson, *Höggotisk träskulptur i gamla Linköpings stift*, (Visby, 1995), pp. 113-185.
26. S. Wenningsted-Torgard, "Kruzifixe des 14. Jahrhunderts auf Lolland-Falster und in Nordjütland" in *Figur und Raum. Mittelalterliche Holzbildwerke im historischen und kunstgeographischen Kontext*, (Berlin, 1994), pp. 70-80.

Fig. 7. Crucifix of pain in Hogstad church in Östergötland as seen from below, app. 1350. The glance is fearful, the figure is collapsed and beaten up and the blood hangs in heavy clusters from the wounds. Photo Ebbe Nyborg.

person lying as a worm-eaten body under his official 'living' effigy with all its regalia.

The macabre culture that was developed during the 14th century has been characterised as a 'guilt culture' which evidently originated from a need for deep personal penance and humiliation before an offended God.[27] It is quite obvious from written sources that such needs sprang from the Black Death and from the subsequent European outbreaks

---

27. A very good overview of the macabre culture and its expression is found in Paul Binski, *Medieval Death. Ritual and Representation*, (London, 1996), pp. 70-128. For the individual motif, see articles in *Lexikon der christlichen Ikonographie*, (ed.) E. Kirschbaum, (Rom, Freiburg, Basel, Vienna, 1968-72).

of the plague. But that does not mean that the epidemics created or shaped the macabre culture in such a way that conclusions can be drawn between the outbreaks of the plague and the memento mori motifs. The relationship between the outbreaks of the plague and the so-called 'plague themes' of the pictorial art was seemingly less causal than 'atmospheric'.[28]

The difficulties of establishing a more direct relationship between the plague and the macabre art is not least apparent when it comes to the Dance of Death, one of the motifs that are presumably younger than the Black Death. It is quite difficult to find examples dating from before 1400 of the motif, which moreover has a literary basis and must have developed from the legend of the three living and the three dead, maybe also from certain traditions involving an actual dance in the churchyards.[29] In Scandinavia the motif does not appear until the middle of the 15th century, for instance in the Finnish Ingå church and in the South Scandinavian churches Jungshoved, Nørre Alslev, Engtved and S. Petri in Malmö.[30]

On the contrary, the large majority of the *memento mori* motifs are significantly older than the Black Death, since they can be dated to the 12th and 13th centuries. Thus, though the plague cannot have been the cause of the emergence of these motifs, it may well have been of importance for their wider distribution and more markedly 'macabre' appearance from the 14th century. Likewise, outbreaks of the plague may of course lie behind concrete late medieval decorations with strongly appealing penance motifs.

In the following Scandinavian examples the emphasis will be put on the 14th century. Representations of 'Frau Welt' which have their roots in

---

28. For instance Franz Egger, "Mittelalterliche Totentanzbilder" in: *Todesreigen – Totentanz. Die Innerschweiz im Bannkreis barocker Todesvorstellungen*, (Luzern, 1996), pp. 9-33.
29. H. Rosenfeld, *Der mittelalterliche Totentanz – Entwicklung – Bedeutung*, (Köln, Vienna, 1974). For a critique of the frequent dating of the Dances of Death after concrete outbreaks of the plague, see Egger 1996.
30. E. Nervander, "Dödsdansen i Ingå kyrke", *Finsk Museum* 1895, pp. 65-82; *Danmarks Kirker, Maribo Amt*, ed. O. Norn and Aa. Roussell, pp. 1195-1197; *Danske Kalkmalerier, Sengotik 1500-1536*, (ed.) Ulla Haastrup, (Copenhagen, 1991), pp. 166-169; *A Catalogue of Wall-Paintings in the Churches of Medieval Denmark 1100-1600. Scania Halland Blekinge*, II, (Copenhagen, 1976), pp. 290-297.

Fig 8. The wheel of fortune, fresco from app. 1325-50 in Birkerød church on Zealand. Of the dead king lying under the wheel mainly the fallen crown is seen as well as a bit of his ribbon with the writing: "svm sine regno". In the middle of the wheel the king is shown confronted with himself in the shape of a worm-eaten skeleton. Photo Roberto Fortuna/Nationalmuseet.

the 13th century, are known in Scandinavia from Ängsjö church in central Sweden and Skibby church on Zealand in Denmark.[31] The first representation can be dated between 1346 and 1359 and might thus be connected to the plague. But the minor role of the motif in the total decoration of the church speaks against it. In Skibby the paintings are normally dated

---

31. Since none of the repesentations are sculptural, they lack the most macabre element of the figure, the hollow, worm-eaten back.

to app. 1325-50, which does not absolutely rule out a date of execution just after the Black Death.[32] Another early motif is the legend of the three living kings who meet themselves in the shape of worm-eaten ghosts who point out to them: "As you are, we have been, and as we are, you will become!" In Scandinavia we meet that representation for instance in the above-mentioned Skibby church[33], where the occurrence of several *memento mori* motifs might suggest that the decoration has been done at a time when they evoked a special response.

A third early motif is the wheel of fortune which already occurs in Denmark in the 12th century, but which reaches its wide distribution only with the Danish and Swedish frescoes of the 15th century. A couple of examples from the 13th century are found in Scanian and Zealand churches, in Norra Mellby probably from app. 1325,[34] in Birkerød from app. 1325-1350 (fig. 8), and in Bregninge from app. 1380. In the latter church the Three living and the Three dead kings are also seen as well as a rare image of death as an apocalyptic horseman (fig. 9). The latter has a contemporaneous counterpart in the nearby Højby church where a sumptuously dressed rider is seen on his horse, steadily pursued by death riding after him on an ox with his arrow ready to shoot.[35]

The real macabre motifs cannot be said to have played a particularly large role in the Scandinavian church art of the 14th century, in which they are to a large extent centred in the old Eastern Denmark (Zealand and Scania). Nothing suggests that these landscapes were particularly severely struck by the plague. Rather, one must see them as quite wealthy areas where new vaults were built in the churches even in the difficult 14th century, which offered a basis for some monumental painting. Not surpris-

---

32. Å. Nisbeth, *Ängsjö kyrka och dess målingar*, (Stockholm, 1988), pp. 113-114, 172-77; *Danmark Kirker, Frederiksborg Amt*, IV, (eds.) Marie-Louise Jørgensen and Hugo Johannsen, pp. 2675-2679; U. Kjær, "Hverken fugl eller fisk. En usædvanlig kvindefremstilling i Skibby", *Iconographisk Post*, 1985, no. 1, pp. 1-13.
33. *Danmarks Kirker, Frederiksborg Amt*, IV, (eds.) Marie-Louise Jørgensen and Hugo Johannsen, pp. 2673-2674.
34. *A Catalogue of Wall-Paintings*, III, pp. 6-7. The dating here to app. 1275 must be too early. In Norra Mellby the motif is unconventional by showing a wheel with the ages of man's life.
35. *Danmarks Kirker, Frederiksborg Amt*, II, (eds.) Erik Moltke and Elna Møller, pp. 929-931; *Danmarks Kirker, Holbæk Amt*, III-IV, (eds.) Marie-Louise Jørgensen and Hugo Johannsen, pp. 1735-36, 2148-2149.

Fig. 9. Death as the fourth apocalyptic horseman (Rev. 6,8), fresco from 1380-1400 in Bregninge church on Zealand. His ribbon probably reads: "I bring death with violence, I take young and old". To the right an allegory of Christ's sacrificial death, the pelican that pecks its own chest and feeds its young with its blood. Photo Ebbe Nyborg 1972.

ingly, the fresco painters would be able to execute the fashionable motifs of the time. It may be more remarkable that the *memento mori* motifs are practically unknown in the other Scandinavian areas with a living fresco tradition in the 14th century. The areas in question are Middle Sweden and especially Gothland.

Still, such differences are found all over Europe without being easily explainable. It must be pointed out as characteristic of the macabre motifs in Scandinavia that they do not include the most sophisticated and most obviously plague related themes. Thus, they do show death with a bow and arrow, as mentioned. But there are no examples of the pictures of the triumph of death, known from Italy and Central Europe, where his arrows hit the wretched people with large clearly marked buboes. Neither is any medieval Scandinavian transi grave monument known. The European appearance of the type is usually set to app. 1400, but new evidence suggests that a Swiss example in chapelle Saint-Antoine in La Sarraz, dating from 1363, can be established, and that this deeply

Fig. 10. Peder Oxe of Gisselfeld lying dressed in armour with his transi under him in the sarcophagus. Detail from the epitaph app. 1565. Photo Ebbe Nyborg 2004.

humble self-representation may thus have sprung more directly from the Black Death.[36]

In Scandinavia, transi graves are not known until the 16th century, e.g. Peder Oxe's wall epitaph from app. 1575 in Øster Broby church on Zealand (fig. 10). The late appearance of the type is probably evidence of the somewhat peripheral place of Scandinavia in medieval culture. But precisely this delay also shows how far-reaching an influence the macabre art and culture of the 14th century must have had in both time and space.

---

36. H. Körner, *Grabmonumente des Mittelalters*, (Darmstadt, 1997), pp. 160-162 with fig. 122; Jean-Luc Rouiller, "Les sépultures des seigneurs de la Sarraz" in C. Martinet, *L'abbaye Prémontrée du Lac de Joux des origines au XIVe siécle*, (Lausanne, 1994), on pp. 221-223 finds a dating of the monument to app. 1380-1400 likely.

Imagining Plague:
The Black Death in Medieval Mentalities

By Leif Søndergaard, Odense

The Black Death that raged in Europe in the middle of the 14th century was probably the greatest demographic catastrophe Europe has ever been exposed to. The Tuscan poet Petrarch wrote in a letter to his brother:

> Will posterity credit that there was a time when, with no deluge from heaven, no worldwide conflagration, no wars or other visible devastation, not merely this or that territory but almost the whole world was depopulated? When was such a disaster ever seen, ever heard of? In what records can we read that houses were emptied, cities, abandoned, countrysides untilled, fields heaped with corpses, and a vast, dreadful solitude over all the world?[1]

Despite the number of plague outbreaks through history *The Black Death* has achieved the status of not merely one plague among many others, but as *The Plague* – with the definite article. Petrarch was mistaken in his evaluation that in the centuries to come people would not believe that an epidemic could shake the whole world, kill a large part of the population and destroy cities and regions all over Europe. The Black Death of 1347-50 has become the epitome of plague in all times and in consequence

---

1. *Letters from Petrarch*, ed. Morris Bishop, Indiana UP, (Bloomington & London, 1966), pp. 73-74.

has attracted special attention from professional historians, authors and painters as well as the general public.

The medical causes of the plague, the pattern of dispersion, the death rate, the efforts of the authorities to constrain the contagion, the demographic consequences and the impact on the feudal economy and the labour market have been studied thoroughly through generations.

On the other hand there are only scattered remarks in most scholarly works on the *mentalities, notions and ideas* around the Black Death. What did people in fact think when they were confronted with the plague? How did they react? Philip Ziegler, Alf Åberg, David Herlihy and Dick Harrison in their overall views upon the Black Death have touched on this aspect.[2] There is evidence concerning the reactions of the population in different layers of society in contemporary sources, especially in Italy, but also from Britain and other countries.[3] From Scandinavia we have to include later sources from the next couple of centuries in order to give an idea of the mentalities dealing with the plague. I do not include the pictorial evidence in wall paintings, altarpieces etc.[4]

Another even more underestimated aspect is *the way the events were related* by various persons in various contexts. What narratives were told? What literary modes, metaphors, rhetorical and stylistic devices were used? What accounts from previous plague epidemics, especially in Antiquity, served as topical patterns?

The population was totally unprepared for a misfortune so disastrous and it must have been an enormous shock when it suddenly showed up. When Petrarch wrote that "almost all the earth was without inhabitants", that was his immediate impression. He had no opportunity to examine the death rates in various parts of Europe, not to speak of the world at large, so his hyperbolic expression must be taken as a reflection of the horrifying impact of the Black Death on him and his fellow citizens of Florence rather than a reference to any empirical investigation.

---

2. Philip Ziegler: *The Black Death*, Collins, (London, 1969); Alf Åberg: *Digerdöden*, (Prisma, Stockholm, 1963); David Herlihy: *The Black Death and the Transformation of the West*, (Harvard UP, Cambridge Mass, and London 1997); Dick Harrison: *Stora Döden. Den värsta katastrof som drabbat Europa*, (Ordfront, Stockholm, 2000).
3. I refer to the collection of source material, translated in Rosemary Horrox, *The Black Death*, (Manchester UP, 1994).
4. Ebbe Nyborg deals with this topic in his article in this volume.

The prevalent feelings were fear and insecurity and these feelings were intensified because nobody could give a satisfactory explanation of the exact causes, the way the plague worked, who would be affected by it, and what could be done against the disease. It seemed to pop up anywhere, to hit people accidentally in all layers of society, clerics as well as lay folk, children, adults and old people, sick and healthy persons, no matter what was done against it.

After a period rumours ran faster than the plague itself and travellers were able to tell about the effects in places where the Black Death had already ravaged. It only contributed to reinforce the horror and panic because the stories that travellers told were extremely horrifying, and the plague seemed to sweep over all countries in Europe – even though regions in the Eastern part of Central Europe and smaller areas around Milan and in the Pyrenees were not attacked.

A demographic catastrophe like the Black Death inevitably provoked concern and called for possible explanations. New and unknown phenomena were hard to cope with but people tried to *use the usual frameworks of understanding in order to explain what happened.* They endeavoured to adapt the unknown to the known. It is a normal cognitive procedure to endeavour to incorporate new events into the old system of experiences, explanations and beliefs, possibly with modifications. The Black Death caused severe problems in that respect and several attempts to come up with adequate answers were undertaken from various positions.

Most 14th century philosophers focused not on the specific features but on *the general idea* which was common for the phenomenon at all times and in all places. They tried to capture the essence instead of sticking only to the surface and a superficial knowledge of the phenomena. This way of thinking made it possible to confer from one age to another, so that descriptions from earlier plagues could be taken as general patterns. For instance Petrarch might have picked up the idea of the almost totally deserted world from Thucydides who had written of the plague in Athens that so violent an epidemic and so great a mortality had never been seen anywhere.[5] Another prototypical way of describing the plague was derived from the Apocalypse and the idea that the Black Death foreshadowed the Last Judgment.

---

5. Thucydides: *History of the Peloponnesian War*, (Penguin Classics, 1954), Book Two, Chapter Five, pp. 123-29.

The most reliable parts of the narratives were the descriptions of the symptoms: the buboes in the armpits and the groin, the black spots on various parts of the body (face, arms and legs); eventually how the lungs were affected and the patients were coughing blood. Also the way that the disease spread by human contact, the short time from the infection to the death and the immediate reactions in the population were recorded in a relatively precise and reliable way by Boccaccio and others. When it came to providing an explanation for the occurrence of the plague, placing it in a social or religious context and proposing appropriate measures to be taken against it, the ideas became volatile and fanciful.

People living in the 14th century endeavoured the best they could to find an explanation as well as a remedy for the terrible plague. Some reports were based on what they saw themselves or heard from eyewitnesses but often the point of view was coloured by the reading of descriptions of plagues in other places and other times. Their points of view might differ considerably, depending on the context from whence the authors derived. Clergymen tried to adapt their reports to what they had read in the Bible or theological tracts. Scientists used their astrological or medical skills in order to explain the ways the plague worked and to meet the challenges it posed. Ordinary people often built their opinions on rumours and anecdotes. They looked for scapegoats in order to get a hold on the catastrophe and find manageable solutions to the problem.

To us the explanations may look irrational and misplaced but they seemed without any doubt to be adequate for the people who offered them. Pious people might find comfort in the religious interpretation of the events as an extreme expression of God's will and judgment. Scientists gave what they regarded to be rational explanations on a scientific basis – even if in some cases the latter seemed to be speculative rather than building on experiences and exact knowledge.

This means that the descriptions of the plague might contain empirical observations, but at the same time the plague was seen in the light of the general ideas of the plague and influenced by religious or secular historical models. The mixture and the importance of the respective elements could vary considerably and of course literary style, personal preferences and other factors might contribute to the actual accounts in each case.

We have to be careful not to project our actual knowledge of the causes, procedures, remedies and consequences back onto medieval mentality, but to try as far as possible to understand it on the basis of their own society, their living conditions and the knowledge, available to them. We are not able to understand fully the mentalities of the mid-14th century, because we are caught in what Georg Lukács called a *necessary anachronism*, bound to our own time.[6] I would like to add that we are equally bound by a *necessary ethnocentrism* (our national scope) and *necessary sociocentrism* (the contexts in which we live and work). However these obstacles must not prevent us from trying to understand people on their own premises, to the extent that this can be possible.

A chronicle from Lübeck, probably written by the Franciscan friar Detmar at the end of the 14th century, records for the year 1346:

> The same year the great plague of humanity began, the sudden death, first in Jerusalem's countries beyond the sea and in heathendom; they fell and died by the half hundred, sixty, a hundred, a thousand, indeed innumerable people. This was not all that regrettable as they are God's enemies but later the same great plague came to Christendom.[7]

It was commonplace to distinguish between the Christians who might gain salvation of their souls and go to Heaven and heathens who would inevitably end in the sulphurous pit of Hell. It did not matter for Detmar whether heathens died or not because their lives were of no value whereas the attack of the plague on Christians prompted much concern. This ethnocentric – or maybe rather christianocentric – view was common among clerics in the Middle Ages.

Most chroniclers were associated with the Church and they were often especially worried about the loss of parsons in many parishes, partly because they were estimated as valuable persons of special interest to clerical chroniclers and partly because the death rate for clerics was above the average, due to their obligation to give the Extreme Unction to dying people, an obligation which however was not always fulfilled. In this respect parsons resembled doctors and lawyers who were often infected when they visited plague sufferers in their homes in order to cure them or take down their last will.

---

6. Georg Lukács: *The Historical Novel*, 1937, (Peregrine Books, Harmondsworth 1969).
7. "Af den Lybske Krønike", *Valdemar Atterdag. Udvalg af Kilder*, Ellen Jørgensen, (Det schønbergske Forlag, København 1911), p. 126. Translation by Tom Pettitt and Leif Søndergaard. All translations of texts from Danish and Swedish are by TP/LS.

In the framework of his *Decameron* (c. 1350) Boccaccio gave the most elaborate description of the Black Death in Florence. A part of the description derived from his own observations as an eyewitness:

> It is a remarkable story that I have to relate. And were it not for the fact that I am one of many people who saw it with their own eyes, I would scarcely dare to believe it (…) One day, for instance, the rags of a pauper who had died from the disease were thrown into the street where they attracted the attention of two pigs. (…) And within a short time they began to writhe as though they had been poisoned, they then dropped dead to the ground, spreadeagled upon the rags that had brought about their undoing. [8]

We have no reason to doubt that this is a reliable description of a specific situation in Florence during the plague there, even though Thucydides has similar descriptions of birds and animals dying after eating the infected bodies.[9]

In his *Historia de morbo* the Italian chronicler Gabriele de Mussis wrote of the plague that ravaged Russia's Crimean peninsula in 1346. In addition to realistic descriptions he related a particular episode. During the Tatar siege of the town of Kaffa where Italian merchants had taken refuge, the besiegers were suddenly overtaken by plague and began to die in large numbers. After some time they began to launch plague infected bodies over the town walls by catapults in order to spread the disease among the refugees, with success, insofar that the inhabitants and refugees were soon infected in large numbers.

The story seemed to be told by an eyewitness but in fact de Mussis never left his home town Piacenza so he must have relied on travellers and maybe inserted elements of his own experiences from the time when the plague ravaged Piacenza. We are not able to decide whether the catapult-story is right or built on a legendary anecdote because it cannot be confirmed by other sources.[10]

Even de Mussis is a barrister his narration on the Black Death resembles a sermon. He introduces dialogues between God and the Earth where God pronounces his verdict and between Death and the Genoese and

---

8. Giovanni Boccaccio: *The Decameron*, (Penguin 1972 /1995), p. 6.
9. Thucydides, p. 125.
10. Horrox 1994, pp. 14-26. Harrison 2002, pp. 75-76.

Venetians who were responsible for revealing the judgment of God as they carried the contagion with them to Europe. The dialogue is a well known genre in the Middle Ages between personified opposites such as the Body and the Soul, Wine and Water etc.[11] And de Mussis continues his vivid description in a dramatized way:

> Listen to the tearful voices of the sick: 'Have pity, have pity, my friends. At least say something, now that the hand of God has touched me.'
> 'Oh father, why have you abandoned me? Do you forget that I am your child?'
> 'Mother, where have you gone? Why are you so cruel to me when only yesterday you were so kind? You fed me at your breast and carried me within your womb for nine months.'
> 'My children, whom I brought up with toil and sweat, why have you run away?'
> Man and wife reached out to each other, 'Alas, once we slept happily together but now we are separated and wretched.'
> And when the sick were in the throes of death, they still called out piteously to their family and neighbours, 'Come here, I'm thirsty, bring me a drink of water.'[12]

His narration reflects the words of Christ when he was crucified so that Christ's crucifixion serves as a prototype for the death that the plague stricken victims suffer during the Black Death. This is combined with the tradition from Antiquity where the dissolution of all family bonds was described.

Of course the authors of most descriptions would have to draw heavily on what they had heard or could read in various accessible manuscripts. Mathias Neuenberger wrote a chronicle on the plague in Strasburg, and when he continued with descriptions of the plagues in Pfalz and in towns along the Rhine he simply reused a lot of episodes from his first text, for the greater part without changing anything but the place name.[13]

---

11. Jean-Claude Aubailly: *Le monologue, le dialogues et la sottie*. Essay sur quelques genres dramatiques de la fin de Moyen âge et du début du XVIe siècle, (Champion, Paris 1976).
12. Horrox 2002, p. 22.
13. Robert Hoeniger: *Der schwarze Tod in Deutschland*, (1882), Åberg 1963, pp. 17-18.

The pope in Avignon received information about the situation in various parts of Europe and conducted a correspondence with clerks in many places. Some of the letters from the pope were diffused and copied all over the Christian world. Many of the expressions of pain and complaint were repeated in the chronicles. In one of the letters from Avignon the exact expression went: "Mercy is dead and Hope is lost", and these words were repeated in the same form by many chroniclers.

The contagion was first brought to Messina in 1347 by seamen on a Genovese ship returning from the Crimea. According to Michele da Piazza no less than 12 ships came to Messina with the plague but this hyperbole and the typological number only served to underline the severe situation. Shortly after that the disease arrived in Marseille, also by ship. As transport by ship was the most usual over long distances it was inevitably a typical way for the disease to spread quickly. When ships arrived from affected areas with dead and ill seamen aboard and the local population contacted them the contagious plague could enter a new place and then spread to the inland areas.

The Icelandic parson Einar Haflidason in his *Lögmanns-annáll* (The Lawman's Annals) from 1360 on the basis of reports from travellers returning to Iceland from Norway, described how the plague first came to Scandinavia:

> At that time so devastating a plague came to Norway that no such had hit these lands since they first were settled. (…) a merchant's ship sailed from England and there were many people aboard. It docked in the harbour of Bergen and a small part of the load was unloaded. Then all the crew on the ship died. As soon as the goods from this ship were brought into the town the population died. Then the plague swept through Norway and caused such great destruction that not a third of people in the land survived. The ship from England sank with all the goods and the corpses without being unloaded. Several other ships sank or drifted away.[14]

The Icelandic parson was accurate in what he related about the clerks who died in the largest towns in Norway and thus reliable to a certain extent. It became a commonplace to describe the arrival in terms of a ship with

---

14. "Lögmanns Annal", *Islandske Annaler*, (1888), pp. 231-96. Harrison 2002, p. 350.

dead and ill seamen or indeed nobody aboard from which the disastrous disease could spread its deadly effects. From a realistic experience the symbolic *topoi* (pattern) was developed in which the ship assumed a form not far removed from that of the Flying Dutchman, i.e. a mythological ship. According to legend, the plague was first brought to Denmark by a ship that arrived in Northern Jutland with no living soul aboard.

The folk belief in Sweden saw the plague personified in two childish figures, a boy with a rake and a girl with a broom: Where they entered a village people would die in large numbers, it was believed.[15] We may imagine that when children were the only inhabitants surviving in a village they had to walk to the next village in order to get shelter and something to eat and drink. They might very well carry the contagion with them and thus spread the plague to this new place. Under these circumstances it seemed understandable and reasonable for the inhabitants to try to exclude the newcomers in order to avoid the spreading of the disease in the local community.

In Denmark another prototypical episode was common in folk belief. In one village the only surviving person was a young man. He mounted a church tower and started ringing the bells. This was heard by a young woman in the next parish who was the only person surviving in that village and she answered back, ringing the bells from the church tower in her village. The two youngsters met, formed a couple and founded a new population in that neighbourhood. This myth of redemption might likewise have its offspring in a concrete situation which was later mythologized. According to a similar Swedish myth only one woman had survived in a parish and when she saw smoke at a distance she walked there and found a man with whom she founded a new population.[16]

The contemporary Welsh poet Jeuan Gethin described the plague in poetic language deploying metaphors to make his description understandable to a broader audience:

> We see death coming into our midst like black smoke, a plague which cuts off the young, a rootless phantom which has no mercy for fair countenance. Woe is me of the shilling in the arm-pit; it is seething, terrible, wherever it may come, a head that gives pain and

---

15. Tillhagen: "Sägner och folktro kring pesten", *Fataburen. Nordiska Museets och Skansens Årsbok*, (1967), p. 218.
16. Ibid., pp. 225-26.

> causes a loud cry, a burden carried under the arms, a painful angry knob, a white lump. It is of the form of an apple, like the head of an onion, a small boil that spares no one. Great is its seething, like a burning cinder, a grievous thing of an ashy colour. It is an ugly eruption that comes with unseemly haste. They are similar to the seeds of the black peas, broken fragments of brittle sea-coal and crowds precede the end.[17]

He makes deliberate use of metaphors (death like black smoke, the boil in a shape like an apple or an onion, a seething like a burning cinder) and personification (the plague is represented as a phantom with a ruthless personality). He also deploys various points of view, in the beginning of the quotation a "we", including himself and other possible spectators beside him, but at the same time inviting the reader to take the same position, and later an "I" where he places his (fictionalized) ego in the position of a victim. His language is vivid and dynamic in order to give the reader a powerful impression of the terrifying disease.

In his letter to his brother Petrarch used traditional epistolary style deriving from Antiquity, and he refers deliberately to Cicero and Vergil in his opening remark. He is extremely well aware of the stylistic devices when he uses Petrarch's initial threefold repetition in the invocation of his brother and his exclamation (alas) reveals his perplexity and his concern and the rhetorical questions heighten the effect to desperation:

> Oh, brother, brother, brother. (That may seem a new way to begin a letter, but in fact it's very ancient; it was used by Cicero nearly fourteen hundred years ago). Alas, my loving brother, what shall I say? How can I begin? Where shall I turn? Everywhere is woe, terror everywhere. You may see in me what you have read in Vergil of the great city with everything tearing pain, everywhere fear and the manifold images of death.[18]

When Haflidason states that more than two thirds of the population died we have to take that as a literary expression for "an extremely large

---

17. Ziegler 1969, p. 190.
18. *Letters from Petrarch*, p. 73.

number of people". The French chronicler Jean Froissart in his *Chronicle* estimated the death toll to be about one third of the population. Both authors would know very well the description in *Apocalypse*, chapter 8, where the destruction of the world is described in thirds: a third of the world was burned up, a third of the rivers infected, a third of the sun, the moon and the stars became dark and a third of humanity were killed by fire and smoke and sulphur.

In a letter from April 1348 Louis Heyligen of Beeringen, who was attached to a cardinal at the papal curia in Avignon, stated that the plague had its origin in India. The plague there developed in three days and at that time it spread all over the world:

> On the first day it rained frogs, snakes, lizards, scorpions and many other similar poisonous animals. On the second day thunder was heard, and thunderbolts and flashes mixed with hailstones of incredible size fell to earth, killing almost all the people, from the greatest to the least. On the third day fire, accompanied by stinking smoke, descended from heaven and consumed the remaining men and animals, and burnt all the cities and settlements in the region.[19]

This description is reminiscent of the narrative in the *Apocalypse* of the evils leading to the destruction of the world: frogs, lightning flashes and thunder and heavy hail. In the *Apocalypse* we are told that the false prophet breathes out three demons like frogs, and later we are told that God let heavy leaden hail fall upon the earth.[20] Even when Louis Heyligen witnessed the plague in Avignon his description was primarily written on the basis of the *Apocalypse* rather than observations in India or Avignon.

For Boccaccio the great model was Thucydides and his account of the plague in Athens. Thucydides focused on the collapse of morals in the town. The experience that relatives and friends who undertook the care of the sick were the first to become infected, caused hopelessness and disillusion, so that the sick were often left to suffer and die alone. People took refuge in water reservoirs in order to relieve their pains or went to holy places, but no matter what they did, it was in vain. In consequence

---

19. Horrox 1994, pp. 41-42. Harrison 2002, p. 82.
20. *The Apocalypse*, chapter 16, verses 13, 18 and 20.

the situation became totally chaotic with dead bodies scattered in the streets, and all rules for burials were abandoned.[21]

Boccaccio expanded and elaborated on this description in his *Decameron*:

> It was not merely a question of one citizen avoiding another, and of people almost inevitably neglecting their neighbours and rarely or never visiting their relatives, addressing themselves only from a distance; the scourge had implanted so great a terror in the hearts of men and women that brothers abandoned brothers, uncles their nephews, sisters their brothers, and in many cases wives deserted their husbands. Bur even worse, and almost incredible, was the fact that fathers and mothers refused to nurse and assist their own children, as though they did not belong to them.[22]

His narrative develops from broader circles (citizens) to narrower and narrower circles (neighbours and then relatives) in order to culminate in the total dissolution of family bonds when parents abstain from taking care of their own children – with Boccaccio's remark: this is almost unbelievable. In the Avignon letter the formulation goes: "the father abandons his sick son and the son his sick father", and the break-up of family relations is developed in different ways in various chronicles.

The most common religious explanation said that man's sinful life was the reason for God's anger, and he sent the plague in order to punish humanity. The argument was often connected to the nostalgic idea of the good old days and the decay of morals in present times as formulated for instance by an anonymous English poet:

> Peace and patience are thoroughly plundered; love and justice are not at home. Men cuddle up to errors and vices; children die for the sins of their fathers.
> (…)
> Alas! Love and charity have grown cold in kingdoms. It is spite and harshness which blaze up in the people. Truth and faith are

---

21. Thucydides, pp. 33-34.
22. Boccaccio, pp. 8-9.

lukewarm in laymen and clerics alike. Nobility and renown are asleep in this realm.[23]

Virtues and vices are here represented as allegorical figures in a way which forebodes the 15th century moralities like *Everyman* and *The Castle of Perseverance*.

But not everybody accepted the explanation that the plague should be perceived as God's punishment. Konrad of Megenburg pointed to the problem that many good people succumbed to the plague whereas many evildoers survived. As he saw it that could hardly be the Lord's will.[24] This may be taken as an early example of the *Théodicé* problem: how could God allow the evil to hit pious people?

Sometimes the population developed the argument so that God's punishment became ascribed to the uncouth life of the clergy or was due to the lack of responsibility among the noble towards their copyholders. This version moved the focus from a general religious to a specific social context and it implied a potential for revolt against the existing religious and social order.

Konrad of Megenburg approached the question of why the plague should hit so hard in the late 1340s in a scientific way. He gave the explanation that the constellations of the planets favoured the outbreak. This argument was further developed by the doctors of the medical faculty at the University of Paris whom the French king, Philip VI, had ordered to compile a report on the plague, its causes and the precautions that could be taken to counter it. The professors considered the issue and published their evaluation:

> To attain this end we have listened to the opinions of many modern experts on astrology and medicine about the causes of the epidemic which has prevailed since 1345. However, because their conclusions still leave room for considerable uncertainty, we, the masters of the faculty of medicine at Paris, inspired by the command of the most illustrious prince, our most serene lord, Philip, King of France, and by our desire to achieve something of public benefit, have decided to compile, with God's help, a brief compendium of the distant and immediate causes of the present universal epidemic (as far as

---

23. Horrox 1994, p. 126.
24. Harrison 2002, p. 196.

these can be understood by the human intellect) and of wholesome remedies; drawing on the opinions of the most brilliant ancient philosopher as well as doctors of medicine.[25]

The professors in Paris invoked God's help and the French king's but this seems to be mere clichés. They rely on philosophers and doctors from Antiquity, first and foremost Aristotle and Hippocrates, as well as contemporary doctors of medicine. They distinguish distant causes and immediate causes. They calculated that on the 20th of March 1345 at 1 o'clock in the afternoon a special conjunction between Saturn, Jupiter and Mars had taken place in the house of Aquarius, and that this conjunction foreboded evil events (distant cause). People could protect themselves against dangerous evil air and stinking rain (immediate causes), for instance by setting fire to vines, laurels or other green trees. They advised eating certain foods and avoiding other things. A clyster was recommended in order to keep the body open, if necessary. It would be damaging to take a bath and "men ought to be coy, if they cared about their lives." The professors were careful to express a degree of uncertainty. Their tract became a model for others in the following years with explanations and advice.

Another observation was made in Paris in August 1348. A strong light, probably from some orb, was seen at the same place in the Western sky both during the day and night before it finally disappeared, and the omen was taken as a sign that a severe catastrophe was approaching. Some clerks like Thomas Brinton, Bishop of Rochester, rejected the arguments and stuck to a purely religious context. For him those who supported astrological explanations were sinners and heretics, and he argued that the actual sins were much more sophisticated and manifold than in Noah's days when God destroyed the whole world, so for him there was no doubt that the plague was God's punishment for all the sins committed in his time.[26]

Another way of explaining the outbreak of the Black Death was to focus on earthquakes and volcanic eruptions. A chronicler in the monastery Neuburg in Steiermark argued that a violent earthquake in the Austrian Alps on the 25th of January 1348 had let out fumes which had poisoned the air and hence facilitated the plague. This theory of polluted air could find

---

25. Horrox 1994, p. 158-63. Henrik Jensen: *Den Sorte Død og livet i senmiddelalderen*, (Gyldendal, Copenhagen 1987), p. 21.
26. George Deaux: *The Black Death*, (1969), pp 52-53.

support in the ancient miasma doctrine in which diseases were ascribed to bad-smelling air. Some scientists rejected this theory because earthquakes and volcanic eruptions were not always followed by catastrophic diseases – and disastrous diseases not always related to earthquakes.

A Danish treatise from the mid 15th century probably was derived from a French plague tract by John Jacobus in Montpellier, possibly through other manuscript version(s). It was reworked by Bishop Canute (Knud) in Arhus in the 15th century but had kept its typical plague tract pattern. It was divided into three sections on the tokens foreboding the plague, the causes for its emergence and the possible remedies against it.

The following signs that announced the coming of the Black Death were related: 1) the weather changes rapidly on a summer day, 2) its looks as if it will rain but it does not do so, 3) there are many flies, 4) stars are often falling, 5) a comet is seen, 6) many lightning flashes and thunder, 7) strong winds from the south.[27] This mixture of meteorological, astronomical, empirical and possibly other arguments was typical for the medieval mentality.

Theories of contagion in the air were first developed by Arabic doctors and philosophers and their opinions were adopted in wider circles. Immediate observations reinforced the impression that the disease was transmitted through direct physical contact or via the air. In spite of this the majority of doctors inclined to the antique miasma theory that bad air, caused by volcanoes or rotten substances in the vicinity, was the direct cause of the disease. The difference might seem unimportant but nevertheless it created agitated disputes.

Dick Harrison 'resolved' the problem in a pragmatic way. In his opinion nobody in the 13th century could in fact find any important differences between the two explanations that incorporated either small invisible organisms or likewise invisible devilish emanations.[28] Harrison may be right from a modern, rational point of view but the important thing is what people thought at that time. Probably ordinary people could or would not distinguish the causes but for learned people the question was

---

27. *Biskop Knuds Bog om Pesten*, (Bishop Canute's Book on the Plague) Fr. Hallager (ed.), (Copenhagen, 1919), pp. 32-33. Horrox ascribes the text to Bengt Knutsson in Västerås, even the tract itself states that it was made by "the most expert doctor in physic the bishop of Arusiens in the realm of Denmark." (Horrox 1994, p. 173).
28. Harrison 2002, p. 211.

important. Even though the manner of transmission through the air and the fatal consequences were the same, the explanatory framework differed significantly: invisible organisms pointed to a scientific context whereas the devilish emanations involved a religious interpretation.

If the contagion or miasma was transmitted by bodily contact or through the air the adequate way of avoiding the disease would after all be to stay away from the infected persons, towns and areas if they were not able to keep the disease away. This method was adopted by several people. In Boccaccio's narrative seven young women and three young men fled from Florence during the plague in order to enjoy themselves far away from the infected areas in the town.

The Swedish king Magnus Eriksson in the year 1350 when the plague reached Sweden travelled around in his kingdom and in Norway to places which had not yet been attacked by the plague or where the plague had already passed, and in that way he avoided the contagion. The Pope Clement VI isolated himself in his palace in Avignon where he had fires in all the rooms of the castle with herbs like rosemary, aloe, musk and amber in order to cleanse the air. Later plague doctors used long beaks in which they carried aromatic oils or the like in order to keep away the damaging odours.[29]

More systematic initiatives were taken during the period of the Black Death in some Italian towns and orders and prohibitions were issued to prevent the plague from entering the towns. When the plague reached the region near Pistoia all travellers from the plague stricken Lucca, Pisa, and other places were banned from the town. Nobody was allowed to visit and come back from plague-infected places. Old clothes could not be taken into the town. In every quarter of the town sixteen men were elected to carry the coffins to the graves and nobody else was allowed to participate. If people tried to avoid the job they were severely punished. Venice used one of the islands in the lagoon as a burial place and paid for a boat and people to transport them at an extremely high price. In Florence infected persons were immediately expelled from the town. Other towns followed with similar measures. From 1377 the authorities in Ragusa (Dubrovnik) were the first to keep in-coming ships in quarantine until they were sure that the crew did not carry the disease into the town.[30]

---

29. Åberg 1963, pp. 77, 28.
30. Herlihy 1997, p. 71; Åberg 1963, pp. 51-52; Harrison 2002, pp. 115-120.

Traditional medicine saw diseases in the light of the four bodily fluids: blood, phlegm, black and yellow bile and the respective temperaments: the sanguine, the phlegmatic, the melancholic and the choleric. Diseases would break out when there was an imbalance between the various body fluids. Doctors who were used to Galen and his medical system would recommend blood-letting, also as a cure against the plague. Sometimes they cut the boils in order to let the infected fluids out.

The official Church took the plague as an opportunity to repeat and reinforce its recommendations that people should confess their sins and lead a pious and meek life. In the year 1348 Pope Clement VI took the initiative to offer a general indulgence to all Christians who would repent and abandon their sinful life. In accordance with tradition he also declared the mid century year 1350 to be a Jubilee Year with plenary indulgence for all the pilgrims who visited Rome in that year. On the basis of reports from residents in Rome Matteo Villani estimated the number of pilgrims as more than one million in the Lenten period up to Easter 1350. It is not clear whether the pilgrims undertook their pilgrimage because they were scared and hoped to avoid the plague, went to Rome in order to thank God, or tried to shorten their period in Purgatory, but under all circumstances a large part of the population took refuge in a religious solution in hope of salvation.

Even though some were sceptical about the explanation that the plague was caused by God in order to punish the many sins of people in Christianity this interpretation was widespread. In many towns masses and processions were organized in order to appease and mitigate God's anger. The holy cross, the host, or wooden sculptures of saints and relics were carried through the towns in order to show God that people repented and thus worthy to receive His forgiveness and mercy.

The saints were believed to have the function of mediating between God and men. When someone prayed to a saint the latter was able to intercede for the supplicant and ask God for forgiveness. A range of saints might have this function in relation to the plague: Saint Sebastian, Saint Christopher, Saint Valentine and Saint Adrian. Later Saint Roch became the most important saint to worship in order to obtain protection against the plague. Saint Roch got this reputation for miraculously saving several plague victims during his lifetime. He was infected himself by a later minor outbreak of plague (or possibly by another violent disease) but he survived and did not die until 1327. His status increased at the Council in Constance in 1414 when a picture of him was carried through the town in order to save the clerks present at the Council, apparently with success.

One of Saint Brigit's revelations dealt with penance against the plague. It was taken down by the bishop Alphonse who followed Brigit on her travels to Rome:

> This writes Alphonse. The holy Brigit from Sweden, prostate into prayer for the people, received at this time, when the deadly disease first appeared, from the Virgin Mary a special revelation of a means of penance, so that God's anger could be appeased and the time the ravaging of the plague be shortened. Therefore I write briefly the means of penance that ought to be used.
>
> *About means of penance that ought to be used in the churches, by the bishop or his chapter.* First the bishop or his chapter or a vicar should order that every parson with cure of souls in an assembly, once a month during a whole year sing the Holy Trinity's mass and that through his sermon he point out to his parishioners that everybody the same day confess and repent his sins and that the parson and the people that day if possible fast and pray eagerly and piously so that their sins may be forgiven and God's anger be appeased.
>
> *About means of penance that ought to be used in the cathedral, through the bishop and the chapter.* Likewise in the same way the bishop or his vicar and the chapter once every month must keep a solemn procession in his episcopal churches with relics and celebrate the mass of the Holy Trinity. And this day they must invite some poor people to a meal and humbly wash their feet while praying God for mercy.
>
> *About means of penance for citizens of lower position who are not rich.* To obtain mercy from God so that he appeases his anger with the deadly disease that from above has struck the people on account of their sins, citizens of lower positions every one have confessed and repented his sins, fast one day and after read Pater Noster three times and hail Mary and go that day to attend the mass of the Holy Trinity, if they can. And every one must instruct his servants to confess their sins and give up clothes and ornaments that offend God."[31]

On the personal level the threat that death might show up suddenly and unexpectedly was horrible. In such circumstances there was too little time for the priest to come and administer the last rites, and this sacrament was

---

31. Åberg 1963, pp. 32-33.

important because the dying person's confession of his or her sins before death was indispensable in order to be prepared for God's judgment.

A special religious reaction came from groups of flagellants who scourged themselves on their backs with whips or ropes with knots as they walked half naked in processions through various regions in Europe while they clamoured and lamented. The movement spread quickly from Southern Europe to the North. From England a contemporary account gives an impression of the processions:

> In the year 1349 at Michaelmas Day more than 600 arrived in London from Seeland and Holland from where they had walked through Flanders. In London they showed themselves to the crowd twice a day, sometimes at St. Pauls and sometimes at other places. From the hips to the heels they were wrapped in linen. The rest of the body was naked but on their heads they carried a hat adorned with a red cross at the forehead and in the neck. Everybody carried in his right hand a whip. On all of them there was a knot and in the mid of them was often placed a sharp needle.
> They moved forward in a line, one behind the other, and they lashed their naked and bleeding bodies for every step. Some of them sung in the language of their homeland and others answered, exactly like a litany. Three times they threw themselves on the ground during such a procession, everybody at the same time, and stretched out their arms, so that the formed a cross. All the time they continued to sing. The last one in the row stepped over those who was lying in front of him and gave everyone a whip. It continued this way until everybody in this way had given and received his whips. After that they dressed themselves in their ordinary clothes and went home to the places where they lived. But even then they carried the hat with crosses and the whips in their hands.[32]

After some time the flagellants' movement developed into a popular international religious and political movement, but totally anarchistic and without any coordination. They claimed divine protection for their mission, sometimes in the shape of a heavenly letter they said they had received in a miraculous way directly from God.[33] The flagellants first of

---

32. Ibid., pp. 34-35.
33. Herlihy 1997, pp. 67-68.

all criticised the corrupt way of life most priests led, and this challenge to the legitimacy of the official Church soon caused a reaction. The pope banned the movement in October 1349 and in many places the town authorities pursued the flagellants and executed them by hanging or otherwise, so the movement was repressed and disappeared as quickly as it emerged.

The chronicler Matteo Villani from Florence wrote that the expectation had been that the survivors who had preserved their lives while their neighbours were exterminated would behave better, more humbly and more virtuously, avoid iniquities and sins and overflow with love and charity towards one another. But the opposite happened:

> As they wallowed in idleness, their dissolution led them into the sin of gluttony, into banquets, taverns, delicate foods and gambling. They rushed headlong into lust.[34]

There is no doubt about Villani's religious and moral condemnation of this reaction. If his statement is reliable and no common place complaint it is remarkable in so far as it suggests that the religious reaction to the catastrophic events must have been either short-lived or restricted to narrower circles in society. People seemed to concern themselves with their material needs rather than the salvation of their souls in the wake of the plague. Ziegler points to the growth in crime rates, blasphemy and sacrilege became commonplace, sexual morality was dissolved and people cared exclusively about money.

On the other hand he draws attention to the founding of chantry chapels all over England during the period following the plague. Many gifts were given to clerical institutions and masses in deeds of gift and testaments. In the year 1350 requiems were established by family members for 18 deceased people at Ribe cathedral in Denmark and that was more than had been the case for the whole preceding decade.[35]

Ziegler concludes: "Paradoxically, the decades that followed the plague saw not only a decline in the prestige and spiritual authority of the Church but also a growth of religious fervour."[36] The different reactions

---

34. Ibid., p. 65.
35. Åberg 1963, p. 72. I also draw the attention to Lars Bisgaard's article in this anthology.
36. Ziegler 1969, pp. 267-72.

were neither surprising nor paradoxical but on the contrary a logical consequence of the different mentalities in various groups, layers and classes of society.

People who lived in town that was attacked by the Black Death felt that they were first of all *victims*. They felt that they suffered from the effects of powerful forces beyond their reach, whether they were conceived of as God's punishment, the result of cosmic constellations or natural catastrophes like earth quakes or could be ascribed to evil air or demons. People needed not only explanations for the causes of the disease but even more practical measures that could be taken in order to prevent contagion with the plague, not only on the official town or state level but also on a personal level.

The plague tracts from the years of the Black Death and the decades after gave much practical advice to what could be done. John of Burgundy's treatise from 1365 may be regarded as a typical example. Here the remote and the near signs of the plague were listed and means of prevention as well as cure were promoted.[37] His tract was copied several times in the following decades. The majority of the counsels were totally inefficient, except for the measures to isolate plague sufferers or flee the infected places, but the amount of tracts and advices shows that there was a need in the population to be able to do something. It is hard to say whether people believed in the practiced measures that were proposed but at least they felt that it could not harm under any circumstances.

Boccaccio gave one of the most elaborate descriptions of the immediate reactions in Florence. Some people thought the best way of preventing plague was to live isolated in their own houses and behave moderately, far from all abundance of good dishes and costly wines. Others did the opposite. They drank and satisfied all their desires and lusts, while they laughed and mocked everything that happened. A third group had chosen a solution between the two opposites, and they carried flowers, scented herbs or strong spices because they thought that could reinforce the brain and prevent the disease from attacking them. None of these measures had any discernible effect.

In a Swedish manuscript from the early 16th century similar counsels were given in accordance with the international plague tracts and books that dealt with the plague from 1348 onwards:

---

37. Horrox 1994, pp. 184-93.

> For pestilence plague. When pestilence reigns one must live soberly and eat and drink with moderation and one must stay away from fornication. For those who act thus will soon be infected. One ought also protect oneself against evil smell from dead animals and the like and for sour and rotten water from gutters or middens.[38]

It was often believed that the plague could be driven out of the body with the sweat, so means to make the sick person sweat were often used, as a Danish medical advice in a manuscript from the middle of the 15th century stated. The reference to the authorities of the pope as well as the emperor serves to make the advice more reliable:

> This advice the pope sent to the emperor that a person who gets boils either in the armpit or elsewhere then he should take theriac and mustard-seed and leaves of elder and stamp that together and make a compress and place it on the boil and drink cold water with it to help him. Likewise if he cannot get these herbs then take rue and vinegar and lie there upon. If one fears for such a boil then take sage, leaves of rue, leaves of elder, and ginger the same portion of each and stamp together and drink with white wine viij days fasting, then he will not get that boil.[39]

Theriac was the most common universally recommended remedy against plague and other contagious diseases. It was an ointment that consisted of snake meat and many other ingredients. In a Danish manuscript from the 16th century another cure using oil was recommended: "For pestilence one puts iij or iiij drops into wine and smells thereto and smears the wound therewith, that should help".[40]

Bishop Canute's Book summarizes the various counsels in a recommendation that covers religious, medical, and commonplace ideas. First of all a man must confess his sins. It is a good idea to move away from the infected place and to avoid rotten substances and stench. People should also abstain from sexual intercourse. It is important to stay away from

---

38. G.E. Kleming: *Läke- och Örteböcker från Sveriges Medeltid*, (Stockholm, 1883-86), p. 374; Tillhagen 1967 (n 15), pp. 219-20.
39. P. Hauberg: *En middelalderlig dansk Lægebog*, (Copenhagen, 1927), p. 52.
40. *Kulturhistorisk Leksikon for Nordisk Middelalder* (KLNM), vol. XIII, København 1968, column 241.

public bath houses and crowded places. If one can avoid interference with other people it is recommendable in order not to become infected from the breath of sick people. Contagious air shall be kept out of the house and if it gets into the house it can be cleansed by means of herbs that are burned like incense: laurel, juniper, and marjoram – or even better wormwood, mugwort, aloe tree and similar herbs. It is also a good idea to sprinkle vinegar and scatter roses and vine leaves. The author reports that when he went around in Montpellier in order to cure the infected people, he was carrying a sponge or a piece of bread, dipped in vinegar, with him to hold before his mouth and nose.

Also counsels concerning the food and drink were given by bishop Canute. In the morning people ought to eat food which was boiled and in the evening roasted. He recommends various spices, some for the rich and others for the poor. And finally he adds a remarkable psychological counsel:

> An important means to preserve the health of the body is a joyful mind. Therefore man aught to take care not to fear death. When you live happily, without fear and concern about the plague disease or any other danger, then you may hope to live for a long time.[41]

If one has caught the plague the best thing to do will be to drink theriac in order to drive the poison out of the body. And he adds another means:

> You take kidney vetch, thyme, plantain and a little wheat flower and rub it together until it has become fluid. Then you mix the fluid with woman's milk and offer that to the sick to drink."[42]

According to the popular belief plague was caused by evil demons. Michele de Piazza relates an episode from Messina where people believed that demons manifested themselves in the likeliness of dogs that caused harm to the inhabitants of the town. The archbishop had summoned people to a great procession when a black dog suddenly appeared, carrying a naked sword in its paws:

---

41. *Biskop Knuds Bog om Pesten*, p. 40.
42. Ibid., p. 44.

> It rushed raging into the church, and broke and smashed all the silver vessels, lamps and candlesticks at the altars. At this sight everyone, half dead with terror, prostrated themselves. When, after some hesitation, they got up again the saw the dog leaving the church, but no one dared to follow it or to go near it.[43]

Powerful magic was required if the demons were to be chased away, bound, thrown away, locked up, nailed, expelled or killed. No spells from the exact time of the plague have been preserved in Scandinavia but a runic inscription on a stick from Ribe in Denmark from about 1300 may give an idea. The spell was aimed at "cold fever" (malaria) but might as well have been used against plague and other violent diseases and epidemics:

> Earth I ask to help
> and the high heaven
> sun and holy Mary
> and the God-king himself
> that he lend me healing hand
> and curing tongue
> to cure the shivering cold fever
> when cure is demanded:
> of back and of breast
> of body and of limb
> of eyes and of ears
> of all where illness can enter.
> Black is a stone called,
> it stands in the sea;
> on it the nine demons must lie
> they neither shall sleep in peace
> nor wake in heat
> before you are cured
> of this sickness-demon
> whom I have carved runes over
> words to recite
>
>   Amen   let it happen.[44]

---

43. Horrox 1994, p. 38.
44. Erik Moltke, 'Runepindene fra Ribe', *Nationalmuseets Arbejdsmark*, (1960), pp. 122-36. Leif Søndergaard, 'Magiske tegn, figurer og formler i senmiddelalderlige

It is significant that the spell mixes Christian and non-Christian magic. In the later Middle Ages people were pragmatic and it would doubtless increase the power of the spell if it included runes that were often supposed to involve a magic effect, as well as the most powerful Christian names of Christ and Mary. The magician said the spell and when he had acquired sufficient strength he confronted the disease, before he exorcised the demons from the infected body. He transferred the demons from the sick person to a rock in the sea in order to bind them there. This sort of transferral magic and binding magic was common during the Middle Ages. The runic stick may have been thrown as part of the ritual. At the end the magic power which had been accumulated during the recitation was released by means of an "Amen" and "let it happen".

A Christian spell was quoted by Gabriele de Mussi in his chronicle:

> O Saint Sebastian, watch over me and protect me, in morning as well as in evening. Every minute of every hour, while I am still able to think clearly. And, martyr, weaken the force of this wretched disease, called epidemic, which is threatening me. Protect and save me and all my friends from this plague. We trust in God and Virgin Mary and you, Holy Martyr. You, citizen in Milan, can, if you will, stop this disease with the power of God. (...) O, martyr Sebastian! Be with us to all times, and let us through you power stay at good health, protected against the plague.[45]

Harrison terms this a prayer, even though he admits it apotropeic purpose. In my opinion it is rather a spell than a prayer with approximately the same aim as the Ribe spell, namely to protect or eventually exorcise the evil force from the person who recites the spell or for whom it is recited. Spells with non-Christian, Christian or mixed content were used through the Middle Ages and onwards until the 19th century.[46]

Another way of neutralizing the disease-demon could be to bury alive a person who was possessed. We do not have evidence from the time of the Black Death, but during the plague in 1603 a Danish woman buried one

---

kalkmalerier', *Billeder i middelalderen. Kalkmalerier og altertavler*, Lars Bisgaard, Tore Nyberg og Leif Søndergaard (eds.), (Odense, 1999), pp. 176-77.
45. Harrison 2002, p. 262.
46. Søndergaard 1999, pp. 171-74, 197-203.

of her children whom she believed was ill with the plague and possessed by a demon. There also exists evidence from Stockholm in the later Middle Ages that women were buried alive for stealing and other crimes so it seems likely that the procedure might also have been used against the Black Death. The argument for burying the sick person alive was the following: if they died before the burial the demon got the opportunity to escape whereas the demon had no reason to leave the sick person as long as he or she was alive, so burial alive would suffocate not only the sick person but at the same time the evil demon so that it was prevented from infecting others.[47]

It often happened that people looked for a scapegoat in order to give a quick and popular explanation for the plague. Various groups at the margin of society might be blamed for the misfortunes: strangers, travellers, seamen, beggars, cripples, deformed persons, lepers and errant children, but first and foremost Jews.

All over Europe the Jews were prosecuted for poisoning the wells or otherwise being guilty of causing plague, first in France and later in many places in various parts of Germany. According to the chronicle from Lübeck Jews who were forcibly converted to Christianity poisoned people but they were discovered, put into prison and finally burnt. They confessed before death that Jews in big cities had plotted in order to destroy Christianity.[48]

On the Swedish island of Gotland nine persons were executed for poisoning a large part of the population. One of them, who played the organ, admitted that he had poisoned the wells in Stockholm, Västerås and Arboga and other places all over Sweden. In Visby on Gotland he had prepared some powder to poison the whole island. He was forced to admit that he had many fellow conspirators all over the world and in all classes of society. He maintained that they had a secret Greek or Hebrew sign in common, and he finished with the statement that everything was due to the Jews. This confession was probably given under torture and therefore more significant for the expectations, wishes and prejudices of the judicial system than for the accused person who under torture would tell them anything they wanted him to say.[49]

---

47. Tillhagen 1967, pp. 220-25.
48. Harrison 2002, pp. 237-60.
49. Åberg 1963, pp. 77-78.

The flagellants often took the initiative to prosecute the Jews fiercely but they ended up being themselves executed for the same alleged crimes as they had accused the Jews of. In some parts of Europe the princes or the town authorities tried to protect the Jews. The Jews often held important positions in society, not only in the financial sector but also more generally. At other places people just waited in distress and hopelessness for the plague to arrive without blaming anyone.

In Kilkenny in Ireland the grey friar John Clyn described the arrival of the plague and during Lent in 1349 his own monastery was attacked, and he tells that he sits among the dead waiting for death to visit him. He states his awareness of what will come in this way:

> And lest the writing should perish with the writer and the work fail with the labourer, I leave parchment to continue this work, if perchance any man survives and any of the race of Adam escape this pestilence and carry on the work which I have begun.[50]

A few lines later the text suddenly stops ...
    As does this one.

---

50. Ziegler 1969, p. 195.